MIDLIFE ALPHA

How to Transform Your Body for Optimal Health, Strength and Vitality In Your 40s and 50s

The muscle-centric science of fat loss and good health for men in midlife

ANTHONY HEALY

ISBN: 978-1-7392729-0-6 (Hardback)
ISBN: 978-1-7392729-1-3 (Paperback)
ISBN: 978-1-7392729-2-0 (E-book)

Printed in the United States of America.

Interior design by FormattedBooks

DEDICATION

For my most beloved children, Justin and Katie.

CONTENTS

Preface.......vii

PART ONE
THE CHALLENGES

Chapter 1 I coulda been a contender.......3
Chapter 2 The Real Midlife Crisis.......10
Chapter 3 Dad Bod: Who moved my Testosterone?.......17
Chapter 4 It's the diet, stupid.......28
Chapter 5 Where's the beef?.......39

PART TWO
THE SCIENCE OF BUILDING MUSCLE

Chapter 6 The Grecian Ideal.......53
Chapter 7 Skeletal Muscle: Under the Bonnet.......64
Chapter 8 The Mechanics of Muscle Building.......73
Chapter 9 Frequency: The Secret Sauce.......87
Chapter 10 Principles of Program Design: Putting it All Together..98
Chapter 11 Anyone for Cardio?.......118

PART THREE
NUTRITION

Chapter 12 If it fits my what...?.......131
Chapter 13 Then God Created Protein.......142
Chapter 14 Fat: The good, the bad, and the very ugly.......152

Chapter 15 Carbohydrates & Middle age: Frenemies? ... 162
Chapter 16 Micronutrients ... 173
Chapter 17 Nutrient Timing: Another look ... 183
Chapter 18 Supplements ... 191

PART FOUR
MINDSET

Chapter 19 All in the mind? ... 207
Chapter 20 Hacking the Power of Habit ... 220
Chapter 21 The Big Vision ... 227

Afterword ... 235
Resources ... 237
References ... 247

PREFACE

When I first set out on my journey to transform my physique, I imitated the nutrition and training protocols of famous bodybuilders who graced the covers of magazines like *Muscle & Fitness.* I voraciously read anything and everything Arnie Schwarzenegger had ever written.

When I inevitably hit a roadblock and progress stalled, I found myself at a loss. Then it dawned on me. These legends had built their magnificent physiques while young and with the assistance of performance enhancing drugs. I was 43, overweight, and had no desire to jeopardise the health I was trying to create by taking steroids.

This damascene moment was followed by my stumbling upon an article written by Dr Layne Norton entitled, "Anabolic eating for your age". In it, the author introduced the ideas that would become the subject of my research and recurring themes for this book. For the first time, I learned there were fundamental metabolic differences between age groups which affect our ability to lose fat and build muscle, and which should govern how we eat and train.

These age-related differences present challenges such as declining testosterone levels and anabolic resistance. But Dr Norton's article also offered hope that with the right kind of training and nutritional interventions, it is never too late to build the physique of your dreams. This was all I needed. I joined the 5am club and embarked upon four years of research into how best to overcome these challenges, poring through medical journals, expert reviews and weighty tomes to write this book before work.

With nearly a decade of coaching as a Personal Trainer behind me, my work, along with an ever-present passion for my own training, serves as a mobile laboratory for the practical application of the ideas espoused in this book. But the book too has had its own journey, with several iterations.

When I began my own midlife transformation, I was nearly 60 pounds (four stone) overweight. I was fed up with feeling lethargic and looking like a has-been. My principal focus was therefore the science of physique transformation. Fast forward ten years, some gut issues from a stressful divorce in tow, the global health crisis wrought by Covid-19, and the focus pivoted to understand all the constituent elements of health and longevity.

Longevity, as you can imagine, is a big space with even bigger players, and there are some exciting developments in the field of personalised, precision medicine; cutting edge technologies which track the impact of gene expression, the environment and individual lifestyle. But if arresting the decline caused by the sands of time is the goal, nothing accelerates aging more than being overweight, playing havoc as it does with our hormones, immune system and metabolism.

According to the World Health Organisation, there are 1.9 billion adults overweight, with 650 million of these individuals considered obese. Accordingly, the global spread of obesity has been labelled a pandemic. The ill-health from metabolic syndrome which follows in its wake, with high triglycerides, high blood pressure and inability to control blood sugar is linked with all-cause mortality, coronary heart disease and stroke.

Efforts to address obesity have failed so miserably, that societal acceptance now seems to be the order of the day. However, the focus of these efforts has been almost exclusively on weight loss, through a combination of diet and cardiovascular exercise. Yet this approach, even if temporarily successful, often brings about a substantial loss of skeletal muscle. This in turn causes metabolism to slow and a pre-disposition to weight regain.

A muscle-centric approach on the other hand, focuses on transforming body composition, through building muscle and losing fat, not chasing a number on the bathroom scales. But while the importance of muscle to metabolism has long been recognised—at least in the fitness industry—the role it plays in the creation of optimal health has not.

This book, I hope, goes someway to changing that.

PART ONE
THE CHALLENGES

"It is a shame for a man to grow old without seeing the beauty and strength of which his body is capable."

Socrates

CHAPTER 1

I COULDA BEEN A CONTENDER

"I wanted to live deep and suck out all the marrow of life, to live so sturdily and Spartan-like as to put to rout all that was not life..."

Henry David Thoreau

The scene will be etched on my memory forever. Young, lithe-limbed, full-figured in branded lycra, she had caught my eye. But as I moved from one workstation to another it finally dawned on me. I had caught hers too. *Could it really be that this twenty-something was checking me out?* As she fixed her gaze, I did a double take. Just to confirm there wasn't someone else.

Nope. It was me.

And, with that realisation, a long-forgotten sensation; testosterone coursing through my veins and that 'fresh-from-the-hunt', all-conquering kind of self-belief.

I was back.

A year before, things had been very different. Marriage, children, a flagging career, midlife paunch and what looked suspiciously like moobs were accompanied by a gnawing, pervasive feeling that my life was somehow not my own. Before I knew it, I had turned 40. Perched on a bar stool at the 40th birthday party I didn't want to have, talking to someone I didn't want to know, the question begged:

"*Where the hell did my life go?*"

Then things got worse.

My flagging career definitively flagged. The early promise shown in international sales and marketing, in far-flung destinations such as Azerbaijan and Sudan—where I had once schmoozed in diplomatic circles with *the great and the good*—was followed by a series of "entrepreneurial" ventures. Long drawn-out affairs, where "making it" was always just around the corner.

A series of events however, brought things to a head. With confidence at an all-time low, I had made myself entirely dispensable in a company I had helped launch. Following that I lunged at any opportunity like the proverbial hamster on its wheel, running faster and faster but going nowhere.

But misery, as they say, loves company. So, it will come as no surprise to learn that around this time my wife was made redundant. Two kids. No income. No foreseeable future. And, more importantly still, no gas left in the tank. My habitual ability to bounce back, rustle up a rabbit or two, had deserted me. I felt numb, paralysed. The chips were down. The house had won.

Then my mother died.

Watching someone you love, die, will leave an indelible mark on anyone. But there, at the foot of my mother's bed, something other than grief also stirred. I became ominously aware that *my* life was also passing me by. I realised that, in a blink of an eye, another decade might pass without change. If things continued in this vein, I would fritter the days away, reminiscing over a life unlived; a parody of Marlon Brando in 'On the Waterfront': *"I coulda had class, Charlie. I coulda been a contender. I coulda been somebody..."*

Something had to give. Something had to change.

But, in fact, it was I who needed to change.

As my mother drew her last breath I decided, then and there, that I would become the man she always thought I *could* be. There was no master plan. What I did feel however, was an overwhelming sense of urgency and the call to take immediate action.

The very next morning, I got up early and went for a run. A long, painful, heart-pumping-out-of-my chest, kind of run. Although I was forced to stop countless times, and thought of giving up the *whole* way, I didn't. Something spurred me on. An unknown force, a hitherto-forgotten, determination.

That evening, after supper, I opened the garage and rummaged around for some dumbbells. I cleared some space and did some press ups. Three, if I recall. Followed by some bicep curls. It was like a scene from American Beauty. Before I knew it, I was Lester Burnham, chest pressing from a rusty bench. It felt magnificent.

Except...except…I didn't want to look like Kevin Spacey.

I wanted to look like Brad Pitt in Fight Club, abs popping, ripped to shreds. I wanted to look like Daniel Craig in Casino Royale; packing serious muscle, striding out of the sea while an exotic brunette on a white horse stopped dead in her tracks to admire me.

In that garage I came to understand that, whilst my whole life might be in ruins, this was one thing I could control. I could train every day. I could lose weight, build the body I always wanted and, hopefully, gain some of the self-respect I had lost.

Ground zero for me was 97 kilos (213 lbs). A size 39 in 'Dad' jeans. Not a good look at 5ft 7, I can assure you. A year and half later, I had lost 60 pounds and won a trophy in a physique competition (Miami Pro), placing third in the Over-35's fitness model category. When I stepped on stage, at 44 years old, tensing and smiling simultaneously there was a whole lot less of me.

But I was twice the man.

My only regret? That I didn't start earlier.

But back then I didn't know what I know now.

I obviously hoped I would look and feel better. Perhaps recover some self-confidence. But I had no idea my newly acquired muscularity would, like armour, provide resilience in the face of life's adversities. I would have never believed a physical transformation could herald the start of a whole new and engaging career as a Personal Trainer. Nor that passion for my craft would lead to a post-grad diploma in Sports Nutrition and the road paved to study for a Master of Science.

I knew I would become stronger and fitter. But I had no inkling my whole life would take on a greater sense of purpose, direction, and contribution to others. Nor that my mental health would soar and I might, once again, tackle life with hope and optimism.

Of course, the research which associates exercise with positive mental health outcomes is well documented (1,2). But there is also a close link between muscular strength and other aspects of mental health for men, such as self-esteem and self-concept (3,4). Men identify easily with the association muscularity has with virility and health. Being fat is viewed as weakness and a lack of willpower, while a well-hewn, muscular body is inextricably linked with feelings of confidence and power in social situations (5).

Traditionally, women are perceived as being more concerned with their physical appearance, but a growing body of research shows otherwise.

One national survey conducted by the University of the West of England (6) revealed that four in five men regularly engage in conversation about their bodies and that most are unhappy with their muscularity. Many men didn't think their arms (62.8%), or chests (62.9%) were muscular enough.

Whilst a modern-day obsession for the body beautiful, and the pressure men feel today to acquire one, might make for an interesting think-piece, evolutionary psychologists have long suggested that sexual attractiveness is based on physical cues of reproductive potential. In men, this defining physical trait of reproductive potential is upper body strength.

Upper body strength, represented by waist chest ratio (WCR), is consistently cited as a key determinant of male attractiveness by women (7). Women prefer men whose torso has an inverted triangle shape—a narrow waist, broad chest and shoulders—the V-Taper shape consistent with physical strength.

In one study, with women from a diverse set of cultures assessing photos, estimates of physical strength determined over 70% of men's bodily attractiveness (8). Contrary to modern, more fluid ideas of what constitutes male beauty, the strongest looking men were consistently deemed the most attractive, across all samples.

The V-Taper shape is the embodiment of the Grecian ideal of the male body; the sculpted perfection of proportion and symmetry we find in classical art, found in some of the best-known Greek sculptures of classical antiquity. That well-known aphorism, "Mens sana in corpore sana", a healthy mind in a healthy body, also found deep roots in Ancient Greece, whose citizens understood the connection between physical health and mental wellbeing.

But the Greeks recognised that wellness is not miraculously imbibed by a health spa and scented candles but forged by iron and physical exertion. And in this self-determined, physical quest to better oneself, we may also acquire the perennial but seemingly lost virtues of discipline, consistency and patience.

In more recent times, our collective wellness has been severely tested by the global outbreak of Coronavirus. For some however, it provided the catalyst to take their health and fitness seriously. Although I was strong and fit, hearing of middle-aged men die from Covid-19 due to "underlying health causes" also gave me pause for thought.

My marriage had recently ended, and the inevitable emotional fallout had rendered my gut a nervous mess. I had not made any concerted effort to alleviate the gastrointestinal distress with dietary measures, and perhaps as a result, nutrient delivery was compromised (9). At the same time, the short-lived comforts of sugar laden foods had stopped being an occasional treat, but a night-time ritual. I certainly couldn't boast—as I once could—of supporting my immune system with a diet made up primarily of nutrient-rich foods.

So Covid-19 was also a personal wake-up call. I decided to delve beyond the science of physique transformation and understand the many touchpoints of muscle-centric health. With Covid mortality rates for middle-aged men running high across many countries (10), the book, and my profession as a Personal Trainer, had taken on a powerful sense of mission.

While there is no single answer as to why men are more vulnerable to Covid-19, the associations with metabolic conditions such as obesity, diabetes, insulin resistance and hypertension, conditions which affect men globally (11), are clear (12, 13). And skeletal muscle plays a much under-appreciated, but central role in metabolic health. It is not happenstance that muscle mass and strength are predictors of hospital length of stay for patients with Covid-19 (14).

Regardless, the future does not bode well for fat, unhealthy, middle-aged men. But as a demographic, our fate is hardly a cause for public concern. Least of all now, in the post-Harvey Weinstein era, when even the word "masculinity" carries toxic connotations. Yet for me, the kind of boorish machismo that Weinstein epitomised is a parody of masculinity, held together by the very thin thread of a power suit. We are better than that.

Perhaps you also tread the corridors of power but have come undone by a health scare or unexpected life crisis. Or maybe you believe you have missed your shot at the title and feel downtrodden by life's disappointments. Either way, this book is a reminder of our infinite potential for a "comeback" story.

Above all, it is a rallying call to take charge, re-engineer your health and transform your body into a Ferrari Testarossa of physiques. And if you are lucky enough to possess such a car, have the body and physical vitality to match. Now is not the moment to give up, ponder early retirement and don a pair of comfy slippers. Rather, it is time to put the pedal to the metal, ever mindful that *today* is the youngest you will ever be.

CHAPTER 2

THE REAL MIDLIFE CRISIS

"You are born alone. You die alone. The rest are rules to make you forget."

Don Draper, Mad Men

The road to optimal health, strength and fitness for men over 40, is strewn with obstacles particular to our age and sex. How we overcome the physiological challenges make up the raison d'etre of this book. But what of psychological or even sociological barriers? After all, a midlife crisis just doesn't appear out of a clear blue sky.

There was a time, in the not-too-distant past, when a midlife crisis was a simple affair, a rite of passage. Confronted with a growing sense of his own mortality, a man would grapple with his existential angst and buy a sports car, or have an affair, sometimes both. Then, when he *"came back to his senses"* he would settle down to a life of domestic docility, looking forward to retirement and pruning the roses with Dorothy.

In Aboriginal culture, the male leaves home in adolescence to live in the wilderness for up to six months. This journey, a physical and spiritual transition to manhood, is called "Walkabout." Our fathers had the luxury of taking a midlife version of "Walkabout", confident that other important variables would hold the line.

The man in the Norman Rockwell painting "Giving Thanks" had, for example, lifetime employment. He may have worked at IBM, but technology wasn't disrupting industries almost overnight, the way it does now. In stark contrast, the children of these baby boomers, the midlife male of today, has anything but lifetime employment. His job is under siege from young upstarts, armed with nothing more than an iPhone and Instagram.

In the same way, wives in the 1950s and 60s weren't going anywhere. Women then were tied to the family home and hearth—financially, socially, and emotionally. These women, our mothers, felt they had no choice but to turn a blind eye while "he" fooled around. Not so anymore. Now it is *she* who is thinking of leaving him.

But if, as Bob Dylan sang, 'The Times, They Are a' Changin' and society looks very different to what it did back then, how is the midlife male adapting to his new habitat?

Not so well, it seems.

Turns out if you are a middle-aged man, chances are you are not a happy chappy. A recent study revealed that while the middle-aged in general report the lowest levels of wellbeing, men, on average, are even less satisfied than women (1). More worrying still, the Office of National Statistics reveals that men aged 40-44 years, have the highest growing rate of suicide (2) and men are three times more likely to take their own life than women.

If the patriarchy is the ruling system, it's not working for he/him either.

A seminal report by the Samaritan's, "Men, Suicide and Society" (3) suggests identity is at the heart of this malaise and tragic loss of life, with men over 40 belonging to the so-called "sandwich generation". The authors explain: *"Men currently in their mid-years are caught between their traditional silent, strong and austere fathers who went to work and provided for their families, and the more progressive, open and individualistic generation of their sons."*

The loss of clarity around identity and purpose has seen middle-aged men unable to reconcile themselves to the socio-economic upheavals which have changed the face of the modern family and workplace. Moreover, some men don't even want to. They still want to believe in Don Draper and the world he inhabited.

But while a midlife crisis is individual, a very real, generic crisis has developed around male identity in the wake of #metoo. Masculinity itself is on trial. The scale of abuse revealed should rightly give men pause for thought. And understandably, editorial and opinion leaders, on-line forums and even organised movements are awash with discussions about what it means to be male today.

A similar discussion arose in the post-feminist era, giving rise to a men's liberation movement. Running naked in the woods and beating drums became de rigueur, while "male bonding" entered the common lexicon. My intuition tells me that chanting naked in the woods and primal screams might not necessarily cross over today. However, I do believe that any resolution of a male identity crisis must also consider male physiology, its unique drivers and how it affects his psychology.

Man's evolutionary physical adaptations, in comparison to women, with our thicker traps, broader shoulders, and greater muscle mass, were made in response to hunting, warfare, physical and sexual competition with other males (4). Instructively, in the male, these parts of the upper body still hold the highest percentage of androgen receptors, making them more responsive to testosterone surges (5).

Sabre tooth tigers no longer lie in waiting ready to pounce from behind our walk-in wardrobes. But our physiology remains hard wired. In many ancient cultures, such as the Red Indian and Aborigine, this uniquely male energy was forged into a hunter-warrior spirit and code of conduct. Not so in the west. Today, we are unsure about teaching the values of competitive sport...but happy to trade insults as keyboard warriors.

But as a result of spending most of our days snacking in front of a screen, the physiological identity of your average American male has changed dramatically in the last 50 years. In 1960, he weighed 166 pounds. By 2002, that had crept up to 191 pounds. Today he weighs in at a largely muscle-less 198 pounds. The weight increases are greatest amongst middle aged men: 25 pounds or 15% heavier by 2002, the end of the study period (6).

The British don't lag far behind. In the UK during the 1960s, only 1% of men were classed as obese. Today, it is a staggering 25% of the male population. Furthermore, the rate of those classified as obese in middle age has risen by 16% in the last two decades. Little wonder Public Health England felt obliged in 2016 to launch a health awareness campaign "One You", aimed specifically at adults between the ages of 40-60 (7).

Their research revealed that 77% of middle-aged men are overweight or obese, drink excessively or take little exercise. And by *little* exercise, we mean 6.3 million middle-aged Brits don't achieve ten minutes of continuous brisk walking over the course of a month! Many more middle-aged men are being diagnosed with diabetes, the rate amongst 40–60-year-olds doubling in the past 20 years.

It is well documented that the overweight and obese are at an increased risk of diabetes, hypertension, insulin resistance, sleep apnoea, cardiovascular disease, and stroke. What is less well known is the association between rising levels of obesity and falling testosterone levels. Using data from one of the largest studies of its kind, *The Massachusetts Male Aging Study* composed of men aged 45-79 years, Travison and colleagues (8) reported that testosterone levels have dropped by 17% in the last two decades.

Such alarming figures coincide with higher rates of testicular cancer, lower sperm counts and *cryptorchidism*—the absence of one or both testes. Ouch. Big Pharma aggressively markets to an aging male population, creating a growing awareness of the impact that Testosterone Deficiency Syndrome (TDS) has on libido, mood, energy, and comorbidities such as obesity, depression and erectile dysfunction.

A diminished libido is of course, often attributed to low levels of testosterone. But low testosterone levels have also been associated with impaired quality of life due to cognitive impairment (9), a poorer sense of psychological well-being (10) and anxiety in otherwise healthy older men (11).

Our understanding of mental health is growing, and high-profile celebrity-endorsed campaigns such as Mental Health Awareness Week are engaged in ambitious agendas to end the stigma and discrimination faced by people with mental health problems. Indeed, one in six adults has a common mental disorder such as depression, anxiety or obsessive-compulsive disorder.

But practitioners worry how many more men remain undiagnosed, as common mental disorders like depression, are notoriously hard to assess. For one thing, men are far more likely to mask their problems with drink or other stimulants. Men are, in fact, nearly three times more likely than women to become both alcohol dependent and to report frequent drug use. On average, it has been found that men aged 45-64 drink 37 units a week and that nearly 800,000 men are consuming more than 50 units (the equivalent of 21 pints) per week.

Tellingly, in findings from the alcohol industry funded charity, Drinkaware, many middle-aged men simply don't believe their health is at risk. According to this organisation, *"more than half (53%) of middle-aged men drinking above the low-risk guidelines, do not believe they will incur increased health problems if they continue drinking at their current level"* (12).

The other reason why male mental health disorders are underreported is that men, as Cosmopolitan readers know only too well, do not "communicate." Not to our partners, not to our mates, not to our employers. Indeed, although men experience more mental health issues than women due to their job, the data shows they are far less likely to seek help and take time off work (13).

High suicide rates in young men always receive public attention—the tragedy of lost youth—while high-profile suicides in middle age, like that of Steve Bing or Chester Barrington from Linkin Park, take us by surprise. But perhaps they shouldn't.

Divorce is a significant stressor of mental health, and while divorce rates drop across many demographics and age spectrums, they are now on the up between the ages of 44-60. Sadly, suicide attempts were three times higher in divorced men and two times higher among separated men as compared to those that are married or with long term partners.

Financial difficulties are another. Losing your job in middle age is different to when you are young, and the panorama of your life still spreads before you long and wide. In your 40s, it feels like the sunset is fading fast. Little wonder, research by sociologists at McGill University in Montreal (14) found men who are made redundant in middle-age are 83 per cent more likely to die earlier. The loss of socio-economic status and the burden of failure are sometimes too much to bear.

Following unprecedented levels of borrowing to fund the global "lockdown", the spectre of inflation, economic stagnation and personal tragedy looms large and oppressive.

In short, the physical and psychological profile of the average 40 to 50 something male today is not altogether flattering. There is a very strong possibility that he is obese, a functioning alcoholic or stimulant-dependent, depressed and divorced. If he is married, there is a strong chance he isn't getting any. None of us have any real mates and suicide is, apparently, a viable solution.

Our troubles and travails certainly don't seem to be a topic of interest at the water cooler either. Some will believe we have brought this on ourselves. The sins of the fathers have finally visited the sons.

They may have a point. In which case, it is incumbent on us, and us alone to prevail. Rather than lamenting the passing of the good ol' days and the loss of a privileged place we once held in society we need to dig deep and lead. Who knows, with discipline, courage and some moral fibre we may even earn that place back.

We can start by taking action to transform our health, mental and otherwise—both of which, are intimately linked to our male physiology. The Spartan warriors of Ancient Greece used to say, "he who sweats more in training, bleeds less in war." So, move and lift something heavy. And while physiological health will not inoculate you from the trials and tribulations of midlife, rest assured the lack of it will surely compound them.

CHAPTER 3

DAD BOD: WHO MOVED MY TESTOSTERONE?

"Rage, rage against the dying of the light."

Dylan Thomas

On March 30th, 2015, Mackenzie Pearson, a sophomore student at Clemson University, wrote a blog post claiming, "girls are all about that *dad bod.*" The dad bod, she went onto explain, 'is a nice balance between a beer gut and working out. It says, 'I go to the gym occasionally, but I also drink heavily on the weekends and enjoy eating eight slices of pizza at a time.'

The post went viral, and mainstream media took up the story with gusto. The phenomenon, which mostly consisted of middle-aged men celebrating their moobs, beer bellies and love handles with smug selfies, was the launchpad for Instagram sites such as "*That Dad Bod Tho.*" Paul Rudd and Adam Sandler were the obvious poster boys, but the movement reached its nadir when legendary NBA star Kobe Bryant posted, then quickly deleted, his one-year, post-retirement, "Dad Bod" on Instagram with the self-deprecatory hashtag #mambathick.

The more serious of weeklies and men's magazines lent gravitas to Pearson's ideas, setting them against a wider anthropological backdrop. One scientist, Prof Richard Bribiescas, went so far as to claim "chubbier" men were more attractive to the opposite sex. He explained becoming fat *"not only causes men to shop for more comfortable pants but also facilitates...a hormonal milieu that would more effectively promote and support paternal investment."*

Fat. Safe. Less likely to wander off.

A complete absence of virility, but more likely to hang around and share the school run.

However, the tradeoff is significant. The changes from being overweight to the hormonal milieu the Professor refers to, are a body blow to men's health. They also strike at the very core of our physiological identity.

Moreover, is this really what women find attractive?

Fans of Aidan Turner, the actor who became an overnight success playing Poldark, probably beg to differ. Wielding nothing more than a scythe and six pack, *that* Poldark scene trended for nearly 24 hours on Twitter and was later voted the 'Best TV Moment of 2015' by 44,000 Radio Times readers!

Not an ounce of chub on him.

In fairness to Mackenzie Pearson, the "Dad Bod" she was alluding to didn't belong to middle aged men at all. She was actually referring to the frat boys on campus she and her friends found attractive: "He's probably that guy who played football in high school and came to college and didn't play football. Maybe he had a few too many slices of pizza and just ended up with a little bit of *squish on top of his muscle...*"

But then she drops a clanger, rationalising that dating a boy with a Dad Bod, has an upside: "*we know what we are getting into, when he's got the same exact body type at the age of 22 that he's going to have at 45.*'"

Newsflash. *That* guy who stopped playing football in high school, drank and ate too many slices of pizza through college...continued drinking beer and eating too many slices of pizza, right throughout his twenties and thirties. He continued to play little or next to no sport.

Instead, he sat down in an office chair one day. And stayed there.

By the time *that* guy is 45, the deleterious effects of bad nutrition and lack of exercise have compounded. He certainly doesn't have the body he once had at 22! Instead, he finds himself forming an orderly cue for metabolic syndrome, obesity, high blood pressure and increased risk of heart attack. At the age of 45, he is *all* squish. Layers of the stuff.

Mackenzie, however, did inadvertently stumble on the very real story of many a middle-aged man. That guy was *me*. And he is probably *you*, too.

So how did we end up here?

The problem is, by the time you hit 40, everything has changed. Everything.

The aging process is, as we know, unkind. But fundamental shifts begin to quietly take place in our mid to late thirties, affecting everything from hormones, to blood circulation, muscle loss, mood, sleep and libido. With time these changes stack up, altering how we respond to exercise and how we metabolise energy from nutrition, making fat gain easier and building muscle harder.

These changes are largely unknown to the general public, and certainly overlooked by a youth-obsessed fitness industry. Attempts to lose weight or build muscle on cookie-cutter programs which don't take them into consideration will flounder. Yet unaddressed, these age-related changes will impact your health significantly. Ignored, "Dad Bod" is a car crash waiting to happen.

Changing Hormonal Profile

These metabolic shifts are largely driven by growing imbalances in our aging hormonal profile.

Hormones play a critical role in our body's chemistry, carrying messages between cells and organs. They are secreted directly from endocrine glands, such as the pituitary or adrenal glands, into the bloodstream. When balanced, these hormones help our body to thrive. Controlled by endocrinal systems, they work holistically on a 24-hour time cycle (*circadian rhythms*) to create a state of equilibrium, which biologists refer to as homeostasis.

To maintain this desired state of constancy, hormones ebb and flow; when one increases, another decreases. For example, during exercise, cortisol, the stress hormone, rises while at the same time insulin secretion is suppressed mobilizing the breakdown of fat for fuel and a greater uptake of glucose into muscle rather than storage (1).

This complex interplay of endocrine changes and hormonal systems can, for anyone, be temporarily thrown out of whack by poor nutrition, stress, or a few days without sleep. But as we age, the endocrine function itself declines as the hormone receptors become less sensitive with age (2).

Testosterone: Elixir of Life

Testosterone, the primary male sex hormone, decreases with age. At some point after we hit our mid-thirties, it begins to lower every year, by about 1-2% (3). The decline in *total* testosterone is accompanied by an even greater fall in *free* and bioavailable testosterone, which decreases by as much as 2-3% per year (4).

Significantly, it is these levels of bioavailable and free testosterone, not total testosterone, which most affects bone mineral density (5), muscle mass and strength (6).

Throughout the ages alchemists have sought the Philosopher's stone, the means to formulate an elixir of life; a potion to restore vigour and youth. The rejuvenating properties of testosterone, have long been revered throughout history. Indeed, the Greek physician Pliny, recommended the ingestion of animal testicles to promote athletic performance and sexual drive over two thousand years ago.

To be fair to Pliny, testosterone has some fairly magical properties, vital for male well-being and health. A natural, anabolic steroid, testosterone is responsible for the development of primary and secondary male sex characteristics. But testosterone also plays a critical role in male behaviour, mood, identity and perceived quality of life (7). And healthy testosterone levels are also positively associated with metabolism (8), cardiovascular health (9), bone mineral density (10), cognitive function (11), mood (12), erectile function and libido (13).

> **Anabolic** the set of growth promoting metabolic pathways which build, constructing larger molecules from small units. Testosterone, (both natural and synthetic) is an anabolic steroid.

It is also associated with increased lean muscle mass (14). The positive anabolic actions of testosterone on muscle mass are attributed to its capacity to promote muscle protein synthesis (15), while inhibiting muscle breakdown (16). Similarly, testosterone stimulates the release of growth hormone, which works alongside Insulin-like growth Factor (IGF-1) (17) to create the right anabolic hormonal milieu for building muscle.

HEALTHY 'T' LEVELS?

A simple blood test can measure your Testosterone levels.

Testosterone levels are most often expressed as nanomoles per litre (nmol/L) or nanograms per deciliter of blood (ng/dL).

A mole is a large number of molecules (6 followed by 23 zeros). A nanomole is one-billionth of a mole. A nanogram is one billionth of a gram. A deciliter is one-tenth of a litre.

Normal, healthy testosterone levels fall somewhere between 10.4 nmol/L (300 ng/dL)—34.6 nmol/L—(1000 ng/DL). Under 6.9 nmol/L (200 ng/dL) is considered low.

Nevertheless, it is possible to have normal T levels and still experience symptoms of low testosterone – e.g. diminished sex drive, depressed mood, poor sleep. This is due to the difference between levels of *total* testosterone and *free* testosterone.

Free testosterone is a biologically active fraction of circulating testosterone which travels unbound by plasma proteins. It is free to diffuse from blood vessels into the cells and tissues of the body to exert androgen activity.

However, only 2% of circulating testosterone is free. Approximately two-thirds of total testosterone is tightly bound to the glycoprotein, sex-hormone-binding-globulin (SHBG). Synthesised by the liver, SHBG levels regulate the amount of testosterone our bodies can use. With age they rise, binding more testosterone and limiting the activity of the free, non-protein-bound concentrations.

So if you do get your T-levels tested, be sure to check for free testosterone as well as total testosterone levels.

The Andropause

Although testosterone levels decrease with age, the decline is gradual at 1-2% a year. If there is such a thing as the male menopause or "andropause" it is not the equivalent of the vertiginous female menopause.

Yet nearly 40% of men over 45 have low, unhealthy levels of testosterone (18). Other than the aging process, what might account for this? A prominent study published in the Journal of Clinical Endocrinology and Metabolism (2007) suggests there are other factors. Analyzing data from "The Massachusetts Male Aging Study", a survey of men 40 to 70 years old, it reported that men's Testosterone levels have all but dropped off a cliff, declining by 17% since the 1980's (19).

The study concluded that the age-matched decline is likely due to modern, sedentary lifestyles, obesity and the presence of endocrine disrupting chemicals (EDCs) in the environment which are producing these falling testosterone levels and semen quality (20, 21).

Cortisol v Testosterone

Men over 40 are no strangers to protracted periods of stress. Marriage, divorce, troublesome teenagers, sick or aging parents, health and financial concerns are just some of its potential triggers: the inevitable rites of passage for the middle aged.

But as a physiological response, cortisol, known as the "stress" hormone, secreted from the adrenal cortex, literally prepares the body for a "fight or flight." To this end, cortisol mobilizes the breakdown of fat but also protein from muscle to provide energy for action, while stabilizing blood glucose levels.

> **Catabolic** the set of metabolic pathways which break complex molecules down into smaller molecules. Cortisol is a *catabolic* hormone and muscle wasting.

Unfortunately, there is an inverse relationship between cortisol and testosterone (22). As one rises, the other falls. From an evolutionary perspective this makes perfect sense. Reproduction is hardly a priority while the sabre-tooth tiger lies in wait, ready to ambush. Cortisol and testosterone also beat a different drum to circadian rhythms. Testosterone rises through the night, while cortisol rises rapidly on awakening, and decreases over the course of the day.

Alongside stress, the catabolic nature of long distance endurance sport (23) elevates cortisol and lowers testosterone levels, as does food and sleep-deprivation (24).

Obesity & Testosterone

Correlation, quipped the 19th century British statistician Karl Pearson, does not imply causation. But it is surely no coincidence that the average weight for men has increased dramatically in the past 20-30 years (25). More worryingly still, the heaviest cohort was between the ages of 40 and 49, weighing on average, 201.7 pounds. That's a full 21 % heavier than he was in the 1960's.

As lower levels of testosterone may also be a *consequence* of obesity, a direct causal effect cannot be drawn. Nevertheless a *bi-directional* relationship is said to exist between testosterone and obesity with every pound of weight loss revealing proportional increases in testosterone (26). Indeed, epidemiological data suggests obesity is the single most powerful predictor of low testosterone (27).

Reductions in circulating testosterone levels are consistently associated with lower levels of lean muscle and fat free mass (28, 29). Low baseline testosterone concentrations are also directly associated with impaired glucose control and insulin resistance. As such, testosterone is considered a key hormone in the pathology of obesity, metabolic syndrome, and Type 2 Diabetes (30).

Obesity and testosterone: a bi-directional relationship (26)

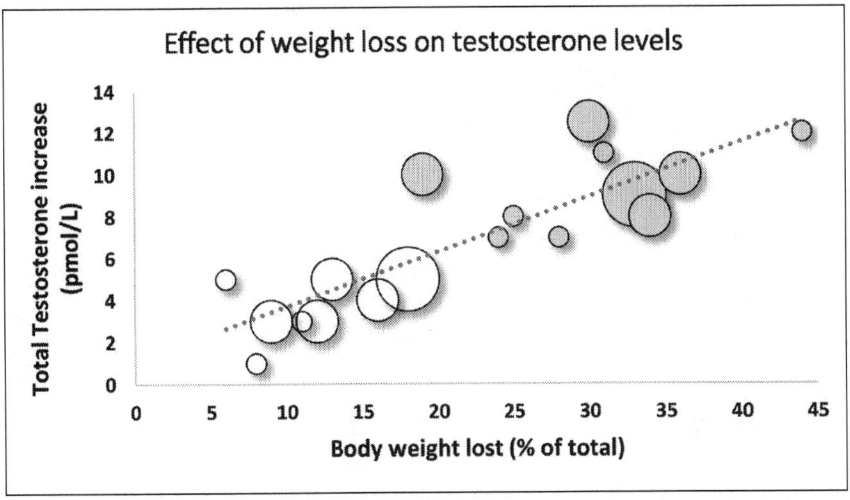

Adapted from Mathis Grossmann, Alvin M. Matsumoto; A Perspective on Middle-Aged and Older Men with Functional Hypogonadism: Focus on Holistic Management, The Journal of Clinical Endocrinology & Metabolism.

Are those man boobs?

The virilizing effects of testosterone on fat metabolism and glucose control are tissue-specific, producing different effects on muscle and regional fat storage sites such as chest and the abdominal area (33).

Indeed, as men grow fatter, especially around the abdominal area, testosterone doesn't just disappear but is converted to oestrogen, the primary female reproductive hormone. And not your garden variety of oestrogen either, but estradiol, an "uber" female hormone, responsible for the development of female tissue such as the breasts, uterus, and vagina.

The conversion of testosterone to oestrogen is known as "aromatization" (34). This on account of aromatase, the rate-limiting enzyme responsible for the local production of estradiol. Estradiol is found to be most active in the fat cells and adipose tissue around the waistline. In fact, abdominal fat actually acts as a secretory gland emitting excessive levels of estradiol into the bloodstream. Having a flat stomach then, if not a full set of washboard abs, is a first line of defense for testosterone levels.

It is for this reason that *aromatase* inhibitors are often prescribed for male breast reduction. The term *"man boobs"* couldn't in fact, be more descriptive. The medical term, gynecomastia, also hints at the stark reality of this process of hormonal imbalance: the fatter you grow, the more woman-like you become.

It probably comes as no surprise that in 2019 male breast reduction was the 2nd most popular surgery for men in the United States (35). Before Covid struck and put a halt to surgeries, breast reduction for men was the fastest-growing cosmetic procedure in the United Kingdom (36).

Grandfathers, on both sides of the pond, are turning in their graves!

Get lean. Stay mean.

The good news is that it is possible to arrest this middle aged decline into Dad Bod and the cascade of hormonal dysfunction it unleashes.

Restoring and maintaining healthy levels of testosterone is a vital piece of the puzzle for re-engineering men's health over 40. Getting lean with a muscle-centric approach to fat loss will do much of the heavy lifting, as it is integral to our genetic blueprint for health. But sleep, nutrition, and supplementation can play important roles and are discussed at length in this book.

One thing is for sure. In these post-Covid-19 days, "Dad Bod" is not the way to go. Similarly, physiological health is not a dispensable luxury for the midlife male.

It is a battle cry.

TEN SCIENCE-BACKED WAYS TO BOOST 'T' LEVELS NATURALLY:

1. Get lean! (26).
2. Engage in a resistance training program, which acutely elevates testosterone levels. (37)
3. Perform HIIT (high intensity interval training) which increases free testosterone levels (38).
4. Eat a protein rich diet. This can help lower sex-hormone-binding-globulin (SHBG) levels and free up more bioavailable, unbound testosterone (39).
5. Eat cruciferous vegetables such as broccoli, cauliflower and kale. They help metabolise surplus estrogen and lower SHBG (40).
6. Avoid low-fat diets (41).
7. Consume carbohydrates around the workout period to reduce cortisol (42)
8. Limit alcohol intake (43).
9. Aim for 6-8 hours of quality sleep (44).
10. Consider supplementation with Vitamin D (45), Zinc (46), Magnesium (47) and possibly fish oil (48).

CHAPTER 4

IT'S THE DIET, STUPID

"Tell me what you eat, and I will tell you who you are."

Jean Anthelme Brillat-Savarin

Bill Clinton's campaign manager, James Carville, famously kept his staff on message by coining the phrase, *"It's the economy, stupid."*

When it comes to fat loss and building muscle, the message is similarly unequivocal. Training is only one variable of the equation. The other is nutrition. Without the right diet, transformative results will continue to elude you.

Yet when it comes to diets, confusion abounds. So, which one?

Paleo, South Beach, Atkins, Ketogenic, Intermittent Fasting. These are just some of the diets to have taken hold of the public's imagination during my lifetime, *all* offering a novel dietary approach and the "secret" to losing weight. Irrespective of whether the diet was low or high carb, involved fasting or eating fruit before 12pm (guilty), all these diets grew in global popularity and gained an almost evangelical following.

So many of us struggle with losing weight, lurching from one diet to another. Perhaps, like me, you have tried them all. So, when one finally works, it is understandable that people become overly enthusiastic, attributing the diet with magic-like qualities. In addition, there is a social aspect. "Friends" are quickly made online. You join a tribe and bask in the glow of shared success, while the "non-believers" around you flounder. It's a powerful club.

This is the foundation for the kind of impassioned debate and dietary zealotry we tend to see online. For example, for members of the Ketogenic club, anyone losing weight on a plant-based, "high-carb" diet would likely be ignored as a freakish outlier. Such is the power of confirmation bias. Yet it is possible to lose weight on many diets, all with *very* different and sometimes contradictory nutritional guidance, each one purporting to be superior to the other.

Adherence

However, in the end, there are only two reasons why a diet works.

The first pertains to adherence—the individual's ability to stick to a diet. All of us are so very different. And whether it is the diet's underlying philosophy or the attractive front cover of a book, some diets will strike a chord and inspire you to act. Yet, in the final analysis, it is your ability to be consistent and stay the course that produces results.

Ease of compliance with the diet's "rules" is a critical factor. If the celebrity, or guru du jour lost weight while eating breakfast, but you cannot stomach food first thing in the morning, their diet is not for you. The willpower required to consistently go against the grain is not sustainable. The day our would-be dieter learns he can follow his natural inclinations, skip breakfast and still lose weight, is the day real progress begins.

Ease of compliance, however, is both personal and entirely relative.

Take "clean eating". For a foodie, the idea of eliminating an entire food group, whether it is carbs, dairy or meat might be tantamount to sacrilege. Yet, led by the movement's high priestesses, legions of social media followers are inspired to buy organic foods, ditch wheat and gluten (despite not suffering from any known intolerance), dip everything in coconut oil and serve kale with every meal.

The reference to high priestesses is, of course, tongue in cheek. Nevertheless, there is something about diets which take on aspects of religion. This explains the fervour of its followers, often called upon to make heroic acts of self-denial. It is also implicit in its language. Unprocessed foods are not just nutrient-rich or low glycaemic, but clean, virtuous. Processed, nutrient-poor, fat and sugar laden foods are dirty, sinful. By extension, when eating this way, one assumes the virtue or vice of the food, experiencing guilt and redemption in equal measure.

Orthorexia is defined as an obsession with healthy eating. "Ortho" means right or correct and "rexia" means desire. The desire to be correct. Although not currently recognised as a clinical diagnosis, clinicians are becoming more aware of its symptoms as many consumers self-diagnose, deciding to restrict their diet unnecessarily to the detriment of their health.

When Jordan Younger, a photogenic, raw-food blogger, wrote her memoir, "Breaking Vegan" in which she revealed she suffered from orthorexia nervosa, there was a growing clamour for the disorder to be officially recognised. The backlash Jordan suffered from the vegan community for her volte-face was remarkable for the vehemence and scale of social media abuse directed at her. The "ethical" vegan community, it seems, takes no prisoners.

The conclusions drawn by the founder of a successful raw-vegan juice company are particularly instructive: *"Basically what Jordan is saying is that the diet is too hard for her. Having a clean diet is an extraordinary thing. Having a crappy diet is mediocre. And if you have to white-knuckle it to get to extraordinary, that's your choice."*

You might be forgiven for thinking his passionate response is commercially driven, rather than ideological zeal. Certainly, the two are by no means mutually exclusive. But it is important to consider how commerce and industry, not science, can drive dietary choices. For example, the supermarket aisles are chock full of gluten-free products realising year on year market share growth—while only 1% of the population has coeliac disease.

An Inconvenient Truth: Calories In, Calories Out. (CICO)

Some people find it is easier to adhere to a diet which eliminates certain foods or limits entire food groups. The binary nature of the diet lends itself to decisiveness. There is no need for a prolonged debate every time you sit down to eat. And the rules quickly become engrained habits.

This is entirely legitimate. Anything that can help with dietary adherence is useful. But there is no need to resort to complicated hypotheses to understand why the diet works. Proponents of low carb diets, for example, often cite the role of insulin in obesity, expounded in the carbohydrate-insulin model of obesity (1). The truth is far simpler. Limiting an entire food group, such as carbohydrates, will ensure a whole lot less food is being eaten!

The inconvenient truth is that any diet can work so long as a calorie deficit is created. A calorie deficit is simply the energy deficit created when fewer calories are consumed than the body expends. The body then makes up for the deficit by burning energy from stored fat. Which is why Professor Haub, a professor at Kansas State University, was able to lose 27 pounds on the Twinkies, Doritos, and Oreos diet (2).

Unfortunately, the essential simplicity of calories in calories out (CICO) (3) doesn't lend itself to selling fad diets to those in quest of a magic bullet. Nevertheless, people intuitively understand the laws of energy balance. Take Christmas, for example. Anyone who gains weight over the holiday season *knows* it is on account of overeating and barely moving from the sofa. And yet, it seems that when it comes to tackling weight loss, people will try anything other than snacking less, being mindful of portion sizes and taking more frequent walks.

This notwithstanding, the principle of energy balance and CICO is behind nearly every controlled, long term weight loss study conducted in the last 100 years (4-6). Studies show, time and again, that meaningful weight loss requires energy expenditure to exceed energy intake. It is an inconvenient truth, for sure: it implies personal responsibility for putting on the weight. Nonetheless, the data is overwhelming.

THE TWINKIE, DORITOS & OREOS DIET (2)

In 2010, Mark Haub, a professor of nutrition at Kansas State University, set out to prove that when it comes to weight loss, achieving a calorie deficit over time is the only gig in town.

On a diet of 1800 calories, largely comprised of "junk" food, such as Twinkies, Doritos and Oreos he lost 27 pounds in two months. He lowered his body mass index (BMI) from nearly 29, to just under 25.

More surprisingly still, his health markers also improved. LDL cholesterol dropped by 20 percent. His "good" or protective cholesterol, HDL, increased by 20 percent. His triglycerides levels dropped by a staggering 39 percent!

Excessive body fat is associated with inflammation and hormonal imbalances, which negatively affect cholesterol and other blood lipids. Being overweight may lead to metabolic syndrome and a cluster of conditions such as high blood pressure, diabetes and obesity. Losing weight, through calorie restriction, even in this rather extreme manner, almost seems to justify the means.

Metabolism: A Moveable Feast

However, the science of sustained weight loss management is more nuanced than the mantra of "eat less, move more." For one thing, eating behaviours are a complex interplay of physiological, psychological, social, and genetic factors (7).

The other is the moveable feast that is metabolism.

Metabolism is a commonly enough used word, but less commonly understood. People often cite a slow metabolism to rationalise diet failures or, less generously, a fast metabolism to explain another's success. People tend to equate metabolism with how quickly their body expends energy derived from food. But this is only part of the picture.

ENERGY METABOLISM

Energy metabolism has various constituent parts. The most significant is your **Basal Metabolic Rate** (BMR).

BMR is the energy associated with the daily maintenance of bodily functions, such as cell growth, the regulation of body temperature, blood circulation, and a myriad

number of biochemical reactions occurring at any one time. In fact, before you have even moved a muscle your BMR can account for up to 70% total daily energy expenditure (TDEE) (8).

Two other important elements of energy metabolism are the **thermic effect of food (TEF)** and the **thermic effect of activity** (TEA).

The thermic effect of food is the energy required to digest, absorb, and store nutrients from your food intake. It accounts for up to 10% of your total daily energy expenditure, although this can change according to food choices. The thermic effect of activity (TEA), the amount of energy burned in all physical activity, similarly varies widely in individuals, ranging from 15% in sedentary individuals, to considerably much higher in highly trained athletes (9).

The final, often overlooked, element of energy metabolism is ***Non-Exercise Activity Thermogenesis*** (NEAT). This can include fidgeting, chewing or even maintaining one's posture upright!

With its moving parts, metabolism is constantly adjusting to the energy demands of our bodies and the environment. Dieting, for example, may sometimes result in metabolic adaptations aimed at preserving energy and increasing hormonal cues to eat more (10, 11). Survival is the body's priority, and it is unlikely to lose any sleep over your beach body goals.

Weight loss, irrespective of the diet, improves health markers. Even modest weight loss (5-10%) can prevent the progression of Type 2 diabetes, register improvements in blood pressure, HDL cholesterol, and reduce the risk of cardiovascular disease (12).

Ultimately, our physiological health and longevity is inextricably linked to being lean. Men tend to accumulate more visceral fat around the abdomen, itself a strong predictor of mortality (13). Therefore, a flat stomach, if not a full set of washboard abs, is not only aesthetically pleasing but a badge of health.

But while weight loss alone—even that prized from the Twinkies and Doritos diet—will always improve health markers, this is not to say that food choices don't matter. They do. Even Professor Haub was notably careful to have a protein shake, eat vegetables and take a multivitamin pill, alongside all that "junk" food.

Satiety

For one thing, eating foods that encourage satiation (the feeling of fullness or satisfaction) and satiety (feeling less hungry between meals) makes a calorie-restricted diet easier to follow. A breakfast of rolled oats, a complex carbohydrate which breaks down energy steadily, is not the same as a croissant with butter and jam which, although delicious, is nutrient poor and calorie rich.

Unsurprisingly, single-ingredient foods which are high in protein, dietary fibre and water rank higher on the satiety index (14) than the more processed foods we find hard to resist, which often contain large amounts of fat and sugar. These highly palatable, calorific foods lack fibre and micronutrients such as essential vitamins and minerals.

There are nearly 30 vitamins and minerals that the body cannot produce in sufficient amounts. Without them, disease is inevitable. So, while one can conceivably lose weight on a diet of pizza, diet coke and Krispy Kreme donuts (the best!), the bleeding gums from scurvy will play havoc with your dental health.

Are all calories made equal?

Calories are simply a unit of measurement for energy. Therefore, in terms of energy intake, 200 calories of chicken breast is the same as 200 calories of white rice. However, once ingested they are metabolised quite differently by the body.

The energy required to absorb and digest food and dissipated as heat—the thermic effect of food—varies quite widely between macronutrients. The thermic effect of protein, for example, is nearly five times that of fat and carbohydrates. Protein burns between 25-30% of its calories (15), while carbohydrates have a TEF of 6-8% and fats, 2-3%.

Predictably, studies have shown that the thermic effect of highly processed foods is substantially less than its wholefood counterparts (16). And a diet high in protein has a much greater impact on thermogenesis when compared to other diets (17, 18). This may explain why high protein diets may lead to greater fat loss than other diets, when calories are equated (19, 20, 21).

The studies, however, do not disprove CICO and the laws of energy balance. Rather they confirm it. The confirmation lies with the greater energy expended by the body to digest protein. The success of high protein diets belongs in part, to the calories "out" element of the CICO equation. Nevertheless, it is a factor to consider when optimising food choices for weight loss.

Macronutrients

Protein, fats and carbohydrates are referred to as macronutrients. Macronutrients are the energy and nutrients we derive from food, but which we require in large amounts. With respect to the energy input of macronutrients, protein and carbohydrates each provide 4 calories per gram, while fats provide 9 calories per gram.

Popular diets have always tended to demonise one macronutrient or the other. Today the arch enemy is sugar and carbohydrates. This hostile war applies not only to highly refined sugars but absurdly to fruits also, due to their sugar content. But, for anyone growing up in the 1970's, the macronutrient villain of the day was dietary fat. Instead of grass-fed butter, the food industry targeted housewives promoting the benefits of Flora margarine. Instead of coconut oil, everything was doused in sunflower oil—the "heart-healthy" choice of the day.

The history of dieting is seemingly characterised by one myth replacing another.

Carbohydrates are a readily accessible source of energy, very easily digested, processed and converted into sugar (glucose). Carbohydrates help replenish glycogen (carbs stored and used by the working muscle) which becomes depleted during training (22). They are also spare protein which is better used for building and maintaining muscle.

Nevertheless, as we age, a more moderate, strategic approach to carbohydrates is sensible. In the post-prandial state (after eating), skeletal muscle accounts for approximately 75% of glucose uptake from the blood (23). Therefore, the age-related muscle loss (sarcopenia) we experience in middle age (24) has a direct impact on carbohydrate metabolism, blood glucose control and insulin resistance (25). Secondly, carbohydrates do not provide the same anabolic growth stimulus for muscle building as they do for the young (26).

Thanks to Instagram warriors and the popularity of Keto, fat has made something of a fashionable comeback. This is not altogether a bad thing. Like protein, but unlike carbohydrates, certain fatty acids (Omega 3, Omega 6) are considered "essential"—the body requires them but cannot synthesise them without dietary consumption.

Fats are also vital for hormonal health and to optimise testosterone levels (27). Nevertheless, the emphasis should be on the cardio-protective, polyunsaturated omega-3s like salmon and monounsaturated fats like olive oil and avocado (28).

Omnivorous

Personally, I espouse an omnivorous diet derived from all macronutrients optimising the health benefits to be gleaned from both plants and animals; lean and organ meats, fish and eggs for protein, creatine, iron, zinc and the B vitamins, choline and selenium, some red meat—for the iron more easily absorbed by the body. In addition, I eat plenty of fruit and vegetables and yes carbohydrates—especially around the workout period.

Later, in the chapters dedicated to nutrition, we discuss the relative importance of each macronutrient, providing age-appropriate recommendations for their daily intake. These distinctions are important because while the fundamentals of weight loss are always the same (CICO), the pursuit of a calorie deficit is not our only target. This is not a weight loss club. Our objective is a radical transformation of your physique, body composition and health.

And this requires a muscle-centric approach to nutrition, prioritising the building and preservation of muscle, while losing fat. Similarly, there are tweaks we can make to overcome the age-related challenges of fat loss and building muscle. Little-known differences, but which together compound to make *all* the difference to your success in this endeavour.

CHAPTER 5

WHERE'S THE BEEF?

"There is nothing stronger than a man who has rebuilt himself..."

Spartan Warrior

In the 1980s, Wendy's, an American chain of hamburger restaurants—a *David* to the Goliaths of the hamburger industry, McDonald's and Burger King—ran an enormously successful advertising campaign. Should it have run today, it would have gone viral. The campaign's strategy was to focus on the oversized bread bun used by their competitors, drawing attention to Wendy's larger beef patty.

In the ad, three older ladies, examine a disproportionately large bread bun, unveiling the measly hamburger with its cheese and pickle and comment to each other: *"It certainly is a big bun. It's a very big bun. It's a big fluffy bun..."* only to repeatedly ask, each time more indignantly, *"Where's the beef?"* The tagline, quickly became a national catchphrase repeated in television shows, films, magazines, and evening chat shows.

A similar charge could be leveled today at the average, squishy, tone-less, middle-aged man: *"Where's the beef, bro?"*

In 2019, The NHS Health Survey found that three-quarters of British adults, aged 45-74, are either obese or overweight (1). With one in four adults getting less than 30 minutes of exercise per week perhaps this is only to be expected. But equally, of those middle-aged men who *do* exercise regularly, many practise almost exclusively cardiovascular exercise, like running or cycling.

Every weekend you can spot them a mile off. Walking into cafés for a pre- or post-ride expresso, the click-clack of cleats announcing their arrival in a haze of form-hugging, fluorescent lycra. The MAMIL, "Middle Aged Man in Lycra", needs no introduction. For those who catch the bug it's easy to see why. Physical action, camaraderie, the chance to face down a challenge. The sense of achievement from having done so.

This notwithstanding, many a middle-aged man took up cycling with a view to losing weight. And whilst cycling is undoubtedly an excellent form of cardiovascular exercise, it is not, judging from all the bulge peering over the Lycra, a panacea for weight loss.

Similarly, any significant weight loss will likely involve the loss of muscle (2). When performed at longer distances, endurance exercise stimulates the release of cortisol, a catabolic hormone which mobilises the breakdown of fat for fuel, but also muscle protein breakdown (MPB) to meet its energy requirements (3). Anecdotally, one need only look at the striking differences in musculature between a sprinter and a marathon runner to get the picture.

Sarcopenia

Whether you are a cycling enthusiast or not, muscle strength peaks in the average male by the age of 30. Worse, at some point in our mid 30's, if not addressed by resistance training, we begin to *lose* both strength and muscle mass, by approximately 3-8% per decade (4). By the time we hit our 60's (5), the rate of decline is fairly precipitous.

This involuntary, age-related loss (atrophy) of skeletal muscle mass and strength is in medical parlance referred to as "sarcopenia" (6,7). The term is derived from the Greek, "sarco-" meaning flesh and "penia" meaning poverty. Yet most men are blissfully unaware of sarcopenia.

A lack of general cardiovascular fitness is more easily identified as a cause for concern. One only has to get out of breath walking up a flight of stairs, before deciding it's time to take action. In contrast, we only ever really require about 30% of our strength to perform everyday tasks. So, unless challenged by your 12-year-old to do push-ups in the park, you will likely not notice this decline in muscle mass and strength.

Yet a study in 2019, demonstrated that the higher our capacity for push-ups, the lower the incidence of cardiovascular events (8). Strength matters to health, and the consequences of sarcopenia are real, serious, and in the long-term, potentially fatal. Characterised by the loss of muscle, strength and function it is a predictor of all-cause mortality (9) and closely associated with frailty, fractures and falls (10).

The Holy Trinity

The mechanisms of sarcopenia are complex and as yet not fully understood. Inflammation, oxidative stress and vascular endothelial dysfunction (see breakout boxes), are just some of the contributing factors we observe. Age-related hormonal imbalances however, and the downregulation of anabolic signaling pathways which mediate muscle hypertrophy play a critical role.

OXIDATIVE STRESS & SARCOPENIA

Oxidative stress results from our antioxidant defenses becoming compromised by Reactive Oxygen Species (ROS). These oxygen-containing free radicals are a normal bi-product of energy production. However, when created in excess they cause an imbalance between our oxidant and antioxidant levels.

Free Radicals are highly reactive molecules which can donate an electron or accept an electron from other molecule. They therefore behave as oxidizing or reducing agents.

With age, all tissues, including skeletal muscle, demonstrate an accumulation of oxidative stress at (57) leading to damage and even apoptosis (cell death).

The main targets of oxidative stress are proteins, lipids, and DNA/RNA, resulting in an increased sensitivity to muscle protein breakdown and hindering of muscle protein synthesis (58). In turn, oxidative stress leads to chronic low-grade inflammation which compromises the immune system, contributing further to aging and muscle loss (59).

ENDOTHELIAL DYSFUNCTION & SARCOPENIA

"*You are as old as your arteries*," so the saying goes. But age-related inflammation leads to arterial stiffness and vascular, endothelial dysfunction.

The endothelium, made up of endothelial cells, is the delicate lining of the entire circulatory system, and serves as a barrier between blood vessels and tissue. A healthy endothelium controls the flow of substances, such as the build-up of cholesterol on the artery wall.

Endothelial dysfunction, on the other hand, impairs the functioning of this lining and is characterised by a decrease in blood flow (60), which in turn contributes to poor nutrient delivery, anabolic resistance and muscle loss.

The mechanisms of endothelial dysfunction relate to a reduction in the production and bioavailability of nitric oxide (61). Nitric oxide is a signalling molecule associated with cardiovascular health and a prominent role as a vasodilator, helping to relax and widen blood vessels and improve blood flow (62).

Nitric oxide supplements are popular among gym-goers. At a basic level, wider blood vessels increase the delivery of nutrients and oxygen to working muscles during exercise. They also facilitate the "pump", whereby muscles engorged with blood and intracellular fluid produce cell swelling and initiate protein synthesis (63).

Testosterone, Insulin-like growth factor 1 (IGF-1) and growth hormone form the holy trinity of anabolic, muscle-building hormones. Testosterone, the primary anabolic hormone (11), exerts its anabolic, muscle building effects by stimulating amino acid uptake and protein synthesis. But it also inhibits muscle protein breakdown, blunting the catabolic influence of cortisol, the stress hormone (12).

> **Anabolic** the set of growth-promoting metabolic pathways which build larger molecules from smaller ones. Muscle Protein Synthesis is an anabolic process.

Growth hormone, long considered a "fountain of youth," plays a pivotal role in improving body composition, mobilizing the breakdown of fat and promoting the uptake of amino acids to stimulate protein synthesis (13). It works synergistically with testosterone to stimulate Insulin-like growth factor 1 (IGF-1) (14).

IGF-1 similarly triggers the release of fat (fatty acids) for energy production and enhances insulin sensitivity (15). There are however, several variants of IGF-1. One variant in particular, Mechano Growth Factor (MGF), is expressed locally in skeletal muscle and is especially responsive to resistance training (16).

Together, these hormones communicate with an intricate network of cell signaling pathways, to create an anabolic environment favorable for building muscle. Essential to muscle hypertrophy, is their activation of the mTOR/Akt signaling pathway. mTOR (mammalian target of rapamycin), is an enzyme known as the master regulator, and it has the most important task of initiating protein synthesis (17).

Unfortunately, with advancing years, this finely-honed system of communication becomes distorted as our hormonal production downregulates. Testosterone, as we know, begins to steadily fall after we hit 30 by about 1% a year (18), and low levels of testosterone affect nearly 40% of men over the age of 45 (19).

But growth hormone and IGF-1 follow suit in a condition referred to as "somatopause" (20). The progressive and simultaneous decline of growth hormone and IGF-1 levels contributes to an overall deterioration in the quality of skeletal muscle, with the accumulation of intramuscular fat (21).

Finally, as if to add insult to injury, older adults are less sensitive to the anabolic effects of insulin which, in the young, mediates an increased muscle blood flow and improves nutrient delivery (22).

Anabolic Resistance

The net result of these hormonal imbalances and downregulation of anabolic signaling pathways, is a breakdown of the muscle building "machinery", referred to as anabolic resistance.

The engine and driving force behind the "machinery" of muscle building, is muscle protein synthesis (MPS). An anabolic process, muscle is hewn from the building blocks of protein known as amino acids. These organic compounds are continuously being created and broken down, in a dynamic process referred to as protein turnover.

However, in order to achieve muscle hypertrophy (growth) muscle protein synthesis (MPS) must exceed muscle protein breakdown (MPB) and a positive net protein balance achieved (23).

> **Muscle Growth:**
> Muscle Protein Synthesis > Muscle Protein Breakdown = Positive Net Protein Balance

In young, healthy individuals, muscle protein synthesis (MPS) is easily triggered by the twin anabolic stimuli of training and nutrition—most notably, the ingestion of dietary protein (24,25). The normal response to these stimuli is an upsurge of anabolic, growth-promoting hormones like testosterone, growth hormone and insulin-like growth factor 1 (IGF1), activating the signaling pathways which initiate protein synthesis.

However, with age we develop a blunted response to these stimuli, known as *anabolic resistance* (26). This desensitization suppresses the stimulatory effects of training on MPS (27) and produces a diminished response of MPS to dietary protein (28). For good measure, an age-related reduction (~10%) in the digestion and absorption of protein (29) contributes further to a sluggish response to dietary protein.

Over time, anabolic resistance leads to muscle loss (atrophy), a result of the prolonged imbalance between muscle protein synthesis and muscle protein breakdown. As we also experience more muscle protein breakdown with age (30), the positive net protein balance necessary for muscle growth requires specific, targeted nutritional interventions once we reach our 40s. (See Chapter 13, "Then God created Protein").

THE GENE EXPRESSION OF (AGING) MUSCLE

One fascinating area of research on anabolic resistance at a cellular level, is that being conducted by Dr Roger Fielding, from the **Human Research Center on Aging** at Tufts University, into the gene expression of muscle following exercise.

Employing techniques that permit the measurement of changes to gene expression, it has been shown that following a bout of resistance training, for young men the expression of over 150 genes was modified, while in older men, it was only 42 genes (64).

Resistance exercise can be a powerful anabolic stimulus that modifies the expression of genes associated with muscle growth and function (65). The reduction in number of genes modified by exercise as we age, impairs this response and reduces the adaptability of aging muscle.

Muscle: Organ of Health

For those still in their early 40s, you might be forgiven for wondering how sarcopenia impacts your life? After all, vulnerability to fractures and falls seem some way off.

Sure, you would like to lose the midlife paunch. But wouldn't going for a run and eating more salads do the trick? Besides, who realistically can look like the front cover model of Men's Health magazine at this age? Yet the significance of muscle mass (and its loss) is not limited to functional movement or beach body aesthetics. Skeletal muscle plays a critical but much underappreciated role in metabolism, health and the prevention of disease (31,32).

As the largest organ in the human body, representing 40% of total body weight, skeletal muscle is the body's principal reservoir for storing protein (amino acids). It serves as a critical line of defense when we are sick or bed-bound in hospital, maintaining protein synthesis for essential tissues and organs. In fact, muscle mass is even a predictor of length of stay in hospital, including those with Covid-19 (33).

The immune system also requires robust protein synthesis for the healing of wounds and recovery from traumatic injury. Recovery from severe burns, for example, is lowest in those individuals with reduced lean body mass (34). Skeletal muscle plays an important regulatory role in the immune system (35) and sarcopenia is linked with its deterioration (36).

The release of anti-inflammatory myokines (amino acids) by skeletal muscle *during* exercise is the perfect foil for the build-up of chronic inflammation from being overweight and leading a sedentary lifestyle (37). It also serves as a timely reminder that bodies were designed to move, and that herein lies our genetic blueprint for health.

> **Myokines** proteins secreted by the muscle during contractions, help regulate metabolism, the immune system and have anti-inflammatory effects.

In terms of weight loss, skeletal muscle is critical to metabolism—the series of reactions which convert the available fuel sources (fatty acids and glucose) we derive from foods into energy (38,39). Muscle accounts for 70-80% of glucose uptake from the blood after a meal (40), encouraging the healthy regulation of blood sugar levels. In contrast sarcopenia is associated with insulin resistance and the disruption of energy balance (41).

Metabolism, contrary to popular opinion, does not always slowdown in middle age (42) Nevertheless, skeletal muscle, which represents 40% of our total body mass is an important determinant of metabolic rate (43). Basal Metabolic Rate (BMR), which equates to the minimum calories we need to function, forms the largest part of our daily energy expenditure. Therefore, the loss of any muscle is significant to metabolism and "may be wholly responsible for age-related decreases in basal metabolic rate" (44).

In this context, the almost exclusive focus by the government, media and society at large on weight loss alone, without improving muscle mass is wholly misguided (45). Muscle loss alters our body composition, and poor fat-to-muscle ratios, particularly around the abdominal area, are primary drivers of metabolic syndrome (46).

Metabolic syndrome is a cluster of risk factors for type-2 diabetes and cardiovascular disease, including elevated blood sugar levels, high triglycerides, reduced HDL (good cholesterol) obesity and high blood pressure (47). The prevalence of metabolic syndrome amongst middle-aged men (48) should provide sufficient motivation to get anyone into the gym!

Old dog. New tricks.

So far, so depressing.

And certainly, losing weight and building muscle in midlife presents some very real challenges, not least those spearheaded by anabolic resistance. But both your immediate health, and the quality of life you may enjoy in the future, depend on how you tackle these challenges *now*.

Recent attempts to change may have felt like an uphill battle. Something akin to playing rugby against the All Blacks, away, and with the sun in your eyes. In this book we show you how to level the playing field, flicking the anabolic switch back on, through optimized nutrition, training and lifestyle protocols.

Of course, a muscle-centric approach means doing things differently.

A little more beef. A bit less cake.

PART TWO

THE SCIENCE OF BUILDING MUSCLE

"There is no such thing as tough. There is trained and untrained. Now which are you?"

Denzel Washington—John W. Creasy, Man on Fire

CHAPTER 6

THE GRECIAN IDEAL

"Man is both the marble and the sculptor. In order to uncover his true visage, he must shatter his own substance with heavy blows of his hammer."

Alex Carrel, Man, the Unknown

As we have discovered, getting lean and building muscle in midlife is not without its physiological challenges. However, one common psychological barrier is the negative perception held of those that take building muscle most seriously, namely bodybuilders.

The general public's image of bodybuilders is that of simian-like, muscle-bound men with disproportionately thick necks and bad postures, who are seemingly unable to walk properly, look good in a suit, or share an elevator. Athleticism, grace and intelligence are not qualities that spring to mind.

The unfavourable image stems I believe, from the steroid taking and modern day professional class, which at times bears more resemblance to a freak show than a sport. In contrast, building muscle without recourse to performance enhancing drugs, is a quest to fulfil one's own genetic potential. It is dependent on size, weight and bone structure. The look achieved is proportionate, attainable and more akin to the front cover of Men's Health magazine, than anything you might see on a professional bodybuilding stage.

Steve Reeves: A Natural Icon.

Growing up, I loved all the classic movies from iconic studios such as MGM. Big production, epic 'sword and sandal' films like Spartacus, with the inimitable Kirk Douglas, biblically based stories like Ben Hur or Samson and Delilah, and historical dramas such as my favourite, El Cid; a medieval tale of chivalry and nobility featuring the impossibly beautiful Sofia Loren. My youthful ideas of masculinity were moulded by the square-jawed heroism of Charlton Heston, Kirk Douglas and Victor Mature.

Unsurprisingly then, having decided to transform my physique, the vision I aspired to crystallised on reading Steve Reeves' *"Building the Classic Physique—The Natural Way."*

Steve Reeves was best known for his barrel-chested portrayal of Hercules and by the 1960's he ranked as the number-one box-office draw in twenty-five countries around the world. At the peak of his career he was the highest paid actor in Europe. He was, nevertheless, not a firm favourite with the film critics. Howard Thompson, of the New York Times, wrote of Steve's portrayal of Hercules, *"the only thing even remotely akin to acting is Mr. Reeves' expression of fixed intelligence."*

STEVE REEVES, LABORS OF HERCULES, 1958

But, as a bodybuilder, Steve Reeves was exceptional. He won the Mr. America title in 1947, following it by becoming Mr. World. He was crowned Mr. Universe twice, in 1948 and 1950. Competitive bodybuilding had started to become popular in the US in the 1950s and 1960s when personalities like Steve, Jack Lalanne and Reg Parks came to the fore. The 1970s heralded what is now seen as the "golden era" of bodybuilding when the likes of Arnold Schwarzenegger, Frank Zane, Lou Ferrigno, Franco Columbu and Serge Nubret captured the imagination of the bodybuilding world.

But it wasn't until Arnie's charismatic performance in the docudrama *Pumping Iron*, that the sport stepped out of its cult-like dungeon-gyms and entered into mainstream consciousness. The film, which became a box office success, helped inspire the growth of the fitness industry in the 1980s, the global expansion of commercial gyms, and the evolution of scientific interest in health, fitness and muscle building.

I am in complete awe of everything Arnold has achieved. Just as I am of Franco Columbu's strength, the aesthetics of Frank Zane, the intensity of Dorian Yates and Phil Heath's winning mindset. But it was Steve Reeves and the philosophical underpinnings of his whole approach to bodybuilding and nutrition—a health-centred approach—and a commitment to build and sculpt his body with symmetry, balance, proportion, detail and aesthetics, which made the sport come alive for me.

Steve Reeves was always something of an outlier. Athletes, sportsmen, bodybuilders, professional and recreational, have been using anabolic-androgenic steroids (AAS) since the 1940's. Bucking the trend, Steve was always a natural drug-free bodybuilder. On the issue of anabolic steroids, Steve was unequivocal: *"I don't believe in bodybuilders using steroids. If a man doesn't have enough male hormones in his system to create a muscular body, he should take up ping pong..."*

Steroids, you might be surprised to learn, are organic compounds produced naturally in the human body. They form an essential structural component of our cells. They are also hormones and signaling molecules (such as testosterone and oestrogen) which help regulate the immune system, metabolism, inflammation and the development of sexual characteristics.

The synthetic drugs—man-made, anabolic-androgenic steroids—simply imitate and magnify the effects which naturally produced testosterone has on the human body. They interact with androgen receptors in muscle cells, activating and enhancing the muscle protein synthesis required to increase muscle mass and bone synthesis. Importantly, they also inhibit muscle protein breakdown (catabolism).

As a Personal Trainer, I am often asked if a "bro" is on steroids. Short of knowing someone's height, measurements and body composition stats it is difficult to know with any degree of certainty. But there are a few tell-tale signs. Firstly, there are the spotty backs. Men on steroids are prone to breaking out in acne as well as male-pattern baldness. Secondly, the neck, shoulders, and traps, which have the highest concentration of androgen receptors, respond very quickly to anabolic steroid drugs (1).

So, when your bro suddenly develops full, rounded, "capped" shoulders overnight, it might not be his #dedication, or love of duck's eggs...but more likely, the special juice.

Anabolic Steroids

Personally, I find the idea of taking synthetic, anabolic steroids an anathema. I strive to build a body that fulfills its natural potential. I love the sense of achievement that comes with it and seeing the progress made from having put in the hard graft. On steroids, I would feel like I was cheating. I am also in the business of health and fitness and while some of the short-term effects like acne are reversible, there are other long-term ones which are not.

Supraphysiological doses of anabolic-androgenic steroids (AAS) may produce a range of adverse cardiovascular effects. Cardiac impairment in long-term users may be more severe than once thought, sufficient enough to increase the risk of heart failure (2). Hypertension and dyslipidemia (high LDL cholesterol, low HDL cholesterol) likely remit when use stops but atherosclerosis and cardiomyopathy may be irreversible (3,4). Steroid compounds can increase blood viscosity which makes the heart work harder and more likely to clot. The size of your heart may also increase (5).

> **Supraphysiological:** pertaining to amounts greater than naturally found in the body.

Besides the potential physiological side-effects, there are also psychological issues to consider as anabolic steroids are associated with a variety of psychiatric effects (6). Users may become dependent and some field studies have documented withdrawal symptoms and even depression when coming off a cycle of steroids (7). Steroid use suppresses endogenous (natural) testosterone production and it may take several weeks before it ramps up again (8). Anecdotally, one of the strongest possible deterrents to steroid use is watching the indignity of a man coming off a cycle, deflating like a balloon before your eyes, converting overnight from a strutting peacock to a flapping hen.

There is of course nothing new about man's desire to gain a competitive edge and enhance sporting performance by trying to influence one's biochemistry. Athletes of Ancient Greece gorged on meat for days before a competition and many would even ingest the raw testicles of animals in the hope that the animal might somehow transfer some of its power and virility.

At the highest competitive levels, the temptation from coaches and athletes alike to bend the rules is overwhelming. The rewards for winning are compelling drivers for steroid use in competitive sport. Bigger, stronger, faster. This is undoubtedly the winning financial formula for modern day sports entertainment. And it applies as much to tennis, rugby, cycling, and American Football as it does to bodybuilding.

Enthusiasts of bodybuilding history, however, point to 1992 as a watershed moment. This was when Dorian Yates won the Mr. Olympia, weighing in at over 250 Lbs. At 5' 10, he combined enormous muscle mass with very low levels of body fat and granite hard conditioning. Dorian ushered in the modern era of "mass monsters." But as judges began to reward the accretion of mass and minimal body fat over classical proportions, so the use of steroids became ever more sophisticated and ever more excessive.

Today, professional bodybuilders are using much higher doses of anabolic steroids than in Arnie's era, for longer cycles and alongside human growth hormone (GH), insulin and IGF-1. The simultaneous use of growth hormone and insulin has been widely blamed for the development of what has now become a feature of modern-day bodybuilding—a distended gut, where some competitors, when relaxed, appear several months pregnant! In the absence of peer reviewed studies, the evidence that GH and Insulin are solely responsible for this phenomenon is circumstantial. But regardless, it is incredibly ugly.

By today's professional standards Steve Reeves, the Hercules of his day, would be considered small. Needless to say Steve was not a fan of modern-day bodybuilding: "*today's bodybuilders are carrying too much muscle for their frames....when your arms are bigger than your head, something is wrong*"(9). In contrast, Steve focused on building a body of perfect proportion and symmetry, sculpting body parts to accentuate his V-Taper with wide, athletic shoulders, narrow waist, a chiseled chest, biceps with peaks like mountains, and all mounted on two oak-like legs with diamonds for calves.

The Grecian Ideal

This was the Grecian ideal of the male form, the sculpted perfection we find in classical art. And it is what Steve worked intensely hard to achieve.

While prehistoric representations of the human form were more concerned with fertility, by the time of the Ancient Greeks the depiction of the human body in art became an ideal to be attained, a striving for perfection. The Doryphoros of Polykleitos, the standing warrior with muscular, athletic proportions, and the Discobolus, all symmetry, balance and contained athletic energy, are some of the best-known Greek sculptures of classical antiquity.

Eugen Sandow, a German strongman and the "father of bodybuilding", would measure these statues in museums and from studying their proportions, which reveal the small waist, wide shoulders and defined midsection, developed the "Grecian Ideal" as the vision one should aspire to for building the perfect male physique. Turns out, there is actually a mathematical formula for such perfection and it has its underpinnings in an irrational number known as the "Golden Ratio."

The "Golden Ratio", symbolised by the Greek letter *phi,* is numerically delineated as 1.618. It reveals itself when the ratio of a whole entity to its larger quantity is equal to the ratio of the larger quantity to the smaller one.

Whilst no one knows with any certainty who first unveiled the mysteries of Golden Ratio, it has fascinated artists, scientists, mathematicians, and philosophers throughout the ages. Euclid of Alexandria (300 BC) the "founder of geometry", defined it as the "extreme and mean" ratio, while for Pythagoras it illuminated mathematical patterns of harmony. Plato wrote of its universality and Phidias relied on it to sculpt the statues we find today in the Parthenon.

This special number has been discovered throughout history; in great art, sculpture and architecture, photography, the geometry of crystals, and even in the patterns we find in nature, such as the spiral arrangement of leaves.

But perhaps it is nowhere more beautifully expressed than in the human form, where the closer it approximates the 'divine proportions' of the Golden Ratio, the more beautiful it becomes to the naked eye. A beautiful face will form, for example, a golden rectangle with the eyes at its midpoint. The mouth and nose a proportional distance between the eyes and the chin. Little wonder that the human anatomy held such interest for that most celebrated artist of all time, Leonardo da Vinci.

He filled many a notebook with his anatomical studies. Not, as you might imagine, to simply improve his craft and ability to depict the human form, but as a reflection of his belief that "man is a model of the world", a key to unravelling the workings of the Universe. In his Vitruvian man, Leonardo drew inspiration from *De Architectura* by the ancient Roman architect, Marcus Vitruvius, who correlates the geometry of beautiful architecture with the symmetry of a "well-shaped man."

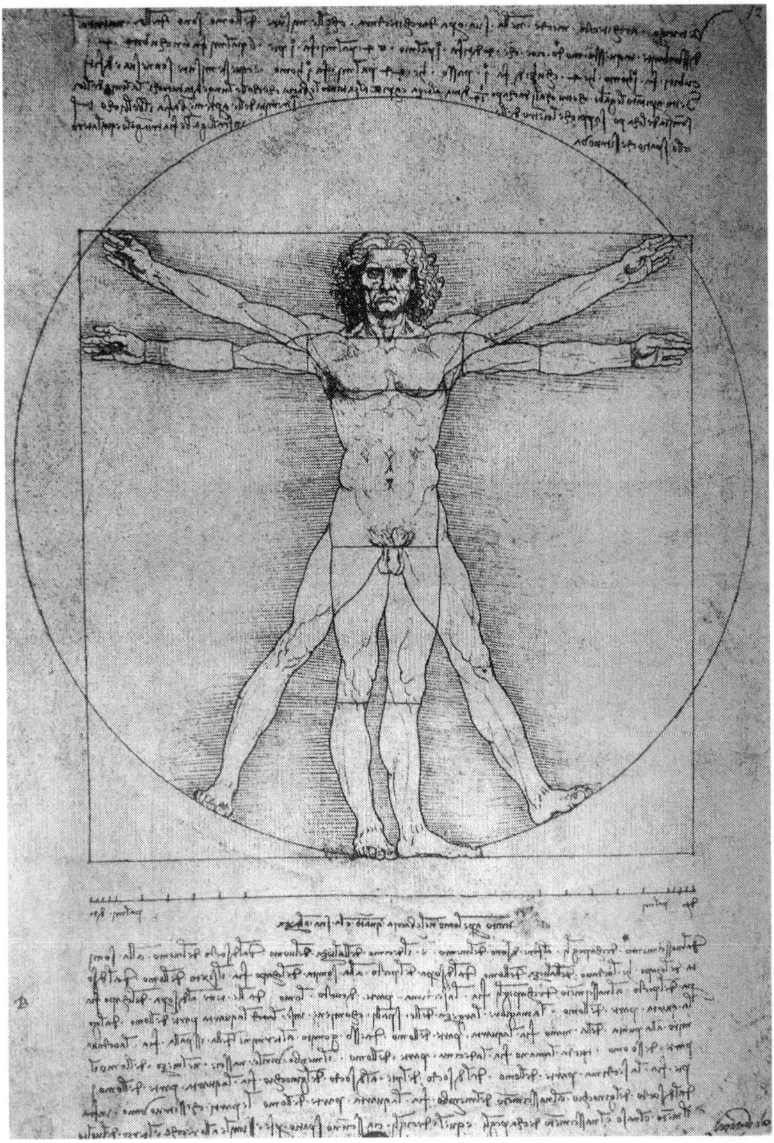

Vitruvian Man, Leonardo da Vinci

In the notes which accompany the drawing, sometimes referred to as "The Canon of Proportions", Leonardo provides detailed measurements, which he attributes to Vitruvius, of the ideal proportions of the human body where each separate part becomes a unique fraction of the whole.

THE CANON OF PROPORTIONS: MEASUREMENTS FOR VITRUVIAN MAN

- **From above the chest to the top of the head is one-sixth of the height of a man**
- **From above the chest to the hairline is one-seventh of the height of a man**
- **The maximum width of the shoulders is a quarter of the height of a man**
- **From the chest to the top of the head is a quarter of the height of a man**

In his book, "Building the Classic Physique: The Natural Way" Steve Reeves picks up where Leonardo left off, outlining his own mathematical formula for achieving the ideal physique. This is calculated by measuring a series of body parts which serve as benchmarks for other parts and help us ascertain all-important bone to muscle ratios.

Some of these measurements such as the wrist or the knee, are unchanging. Others like the waist, less so. The size of your wrist, however, will determine how large your arms should be, that of your knee will dictate the optimum size for your thighs.

STEVE REEVE'S MUSCLE TO BONE RATIOS:

Arm size = 252% of wrist size
Calf size = 192% of ankle size
Neck Size = 79% of head size
Chest Size = 148% of hips size
Waist size = 86% of hips size
Thigh size = 175% of knee size

Reeves also hypothesized that there are ideal height to weight ratios, and that adding mass beyond these limits distort the lines of one's natural symmetry. The ratios are as follows:

HEIGHT TO WEIGHT RATIOS:

5'5"	160 Lbs.
5'6"	165 Lbs.
5'7"	170 Lbs.
5'8"	175 Lbs.
5'9"	180 Lbs.
5'10"	190 Lbs.
5'11"	195 Lbs.
6'0"	200 Lbs.

Aspiring to the "Grecian Ideal" vision of building a classic physique may inspire you as it continues to do so for me. It may also seem an awfully long way away if you are a beginner. Nevertheless, Steve Reeves has set the benchmark and his measurements are a valuable tool to monitor and track progress. In the end however, the real beauty of physique transformation is the canvas it provides to progress, striving to outdo last year's version of yourself.

Building a well-proportioned physique requires craftsmanship, attention to detail, and patience. Michelangelo famously wrote of his sculpture, *David*, that masterpiece of renaissance Florence, *"I saw the angel in the marble, and carved him till I set him free."* It took over two years for Michelangelo to sculpt *David*. Sculpting your ideal physique will take considerably longer.

Perhaps inevitably this quest for perfection remains frustrated. But there is such beauty, value and self-discovery in the journey.

CHAPTER 7

SKELETAL MUSCLE: UNDER THE BONNET

"It doesn't matter whether you are a lion or a gazelle: when the sun comes up, you'd better be running."

Dan Montano

The human body is a miraculous feat of engineering and design. Nowhere is this better illustrated than when in action. This is when skeletal muscle comes in to its own. In fact, even the simplest of movements requires a highly orchestrated series of events, often involving many muscles at one time.

Skeletal muscle is the most abundant tissue in the human body. Attached to the bone via tendons, there are over 600 muscles in the human body. It constitutes 40% of our total body mass (1) and is a major determinant of basal metabolic rate (BMR) (2). A primary site for glucose uptake and storage (3) it is also a reservoir of amino acids for protein synthesis and where required (e.g., during illness), energy production (4). As such, in addition to its primary functions of keeping us breathing, upright and moving, muscle plays a critical role in the maintenance of metabolic health.

Skeletal muscle is one of the body's most malleable and dynamic of tissues. It possesses an extraordinary capacity for adaptation (5), able to change its structural and functional properties to match the work required of it and the demands of the environment.

For example, stuck in a jungle with minimal food to eat, the reality TV star's muscle begins to break down, providing protein as an energy substrate for movement (6). An important survival mechanism, this helps spare glucose for vital organs and the brain. At the same time, muscle glycogen is re-synthesised preferentially via gluconeogenesis (7). In this way, our celebrity may find enough intramuscular energy to make a 20-yard dash if chased by a real-life tiger.

Now that would make for good TV…

> **Gluconeogenesis** refers to the synthesis of new glucose from non-carbohydrate precursors such as amino acids and glycerol, providing glucose when dietary intake is insufficient.

Life In the Old Dog Yet

Aging has been defined as the progressive deterioration of the organism over time (8). It is marked by inflammation and the loss of regenerative potential. As the 19th century German naturalist August Weismann wrote, *"Death takes place because a worn-out tissue cannot forever renew itself, and because the capacity for increase by means of cell division is not everlasting, but finite"* (9).

Not so with muscle. Due to its plasticity, it retains an impressive ability to adapt throughout our lives. Composed of post-mitotic tissue, it does not undergo major cell replacement. Instead, its repair and regeneration come from a dynamic shift towards protein synthesis (anabolism) over protein degradation (catabolism). And while aging and inactivity impair the balance, resistance training and adequate protein intake can swing the pendulum back towards growth and synthesis (10).

> **Post Mitotic Tissue** the constituent make-up of cells that are not capable of undergoing mitosis or cell division.

Muscle Hypertrophy (growth)

Having established that the cells of human skeletal muscle do not themselves divide and regenerate to increase the number of muscle fibres, (hyperplasia) how does muscle grow? (hypertrophy)

A closer look at a cellular level, reveals the muscle fibre is packed with small rod-like units, called myofibrils (Fig 1). The engine room of the muscle fibre, myofibrils are responsible for the muscle's ability to contract. The force of a muscular contraction is generated by the binding of myofibrillar proteins, most notably actin and myosin.

FIG 1. THE MUSCLE FIBRE

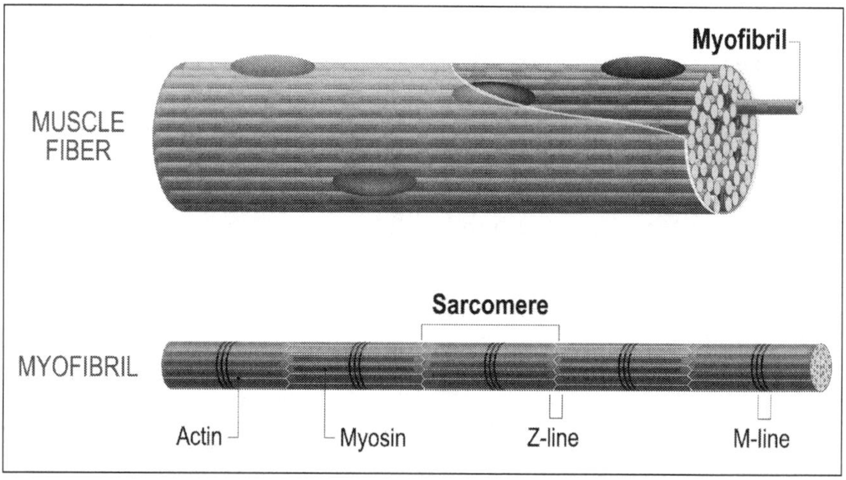

Mechanical tension exerted on muscle by powerful or extended contractions, causes it to adapt and grow, laying down additional myofibrillar proteins. The result is an increase in the size and cross-sectional area of the *individual* muscle fibre (11). This growth is referred to as myofibrillar hypertrophy.

The addition of myofibrillar proteins laid down in parallel is one mechanism for muscle growth. But it is often accompanied by an increase in other non-contractile elements such as glycogen and intracellular fluid along with significantly, satellite cell content (12). Satellite cells are not muscle's homage to Star Trek, but stem cells located on the outer surface of the fibre—hence the name.

These stem cells confer a mitotic, cell regenerative capacity to muscle because when it is damaged, they divide and fuse with existing muscle fibres donating their nuclei to repair the damaged fibres. Although not a pre-requisite for growth, satellite cells play an important role in muscle hypertrophy (13). Unsurprisingly, an age-related reduction in the satellite cell content of muscle is thought to contribute to sarcopenia, the loss of muscle with age (14).

> **Myofibrillar hypertrophy** increases the number of myofibrils within the muscle fibre, by laying down additional myofibrillar proteins. The result is an increase in size and cross-sectional area of the *individual* muscle fibre.

May The Force Be with You

Skeletal muscle's moment in the sun is, quite naturally, the voluntary contraction. All movement as we know, is accomplished by the interaction of muscle with the skeletal system. *But how does muscle regulate force?* How do we gently, but firmly, hold a new-born baby and with those same hands crush an empty can of coke?

The answer lies with the intricate set of communication pathways between muscle and nervous system known as the neuromuscular system. The voluntary contraction of muscle begins with the nervous system generating a signal, an electrical impulse, known as an action potential which then travels to the muscle via nerve cells called motor neurons.

> **Neuromuscular System** includes all the muscles in the body and the nerves serving them. It is the biomechanical apparatus through which the CNS executes postural actions.

A single motor neuron is "assigned" a fixed number of muscle fibres with which it can communicate calls to action. Together, they make up a motor unit. But the number of muscle fibres innervated by a single motor neuron depends on the size and function of the muscle.

For example, the hand may have fewer than 100 muscle fibres per unit, whereas a big, power generating muscle like the quadriceps can have up to a 1000 (15). The force exerted by muscle during a contraction, therefore, depends on the number of motor units "recruited" for the action, and the rate at which these signals are discharged (16).

There is also a sequential order to motor unit activation. According to Henneman's size principle (17), it is the smaller, low-threshold motor units with few muscle fibres which are recruited first, followed by the larger, high-threshold motor units. In this energy-conserving, functional context, larger forces are therefore only harnessed when necessary.

A good thing for the babe in arms. Bad news for the empty coke can.

Muscle Contracted: Two Heads. Same Coin.

Contrary to what you might expect, in contraction, muscles can only pull. They do not push. Consequently, they work in pairs to move a joint through its full range of motion.

For example, the biceps curl raises the forearm by contracting and pulling the biceps towards its point of origin, at the shoulder joint. When lowering the weight back down, the opposite (antagonist) muscle, the triceps, also contracts, pulling the biceps towards the elbow.

Therefore, this simple action of the biceps curl involves different contractions. The first, known as a **concentric** contraction, generates force by shortening the biceps muscle, closing the angle of the joint and causing the arm to bend at the elbow. (Fig 2) Simultaneously, the triceps muscle lengthens.

FIG 2. CONCENTRIC CONTRACTION (BICEPS CURL)

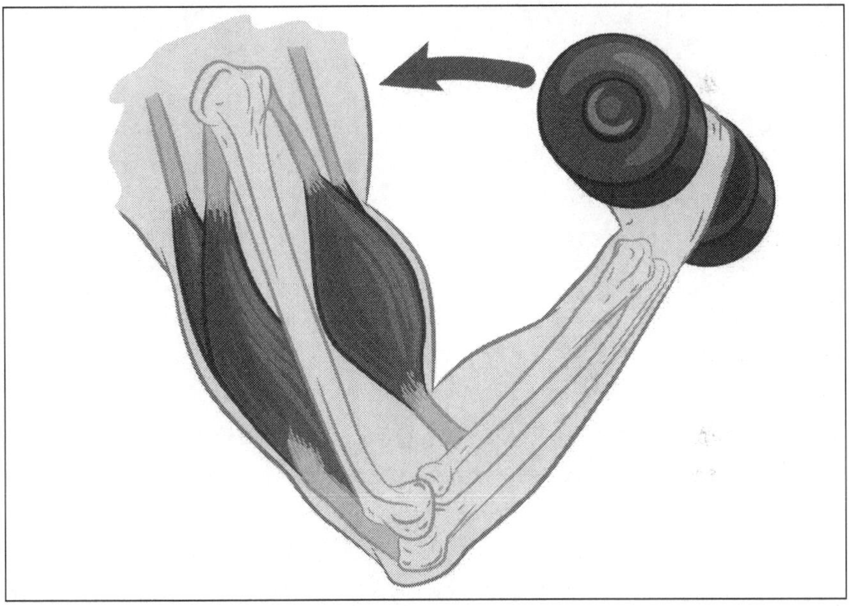

The second action, referred to as the **eccentric** contraction, lengthens the biceps whilst simultaneously shortening the triceps. (Fig 3.) Under tension, the muscle elongates, acting as a break to control the load by decelerating the joint at the end of the movement.

FIG 3 ECCENTRIC CONTRACTION (BICEPS CURL)

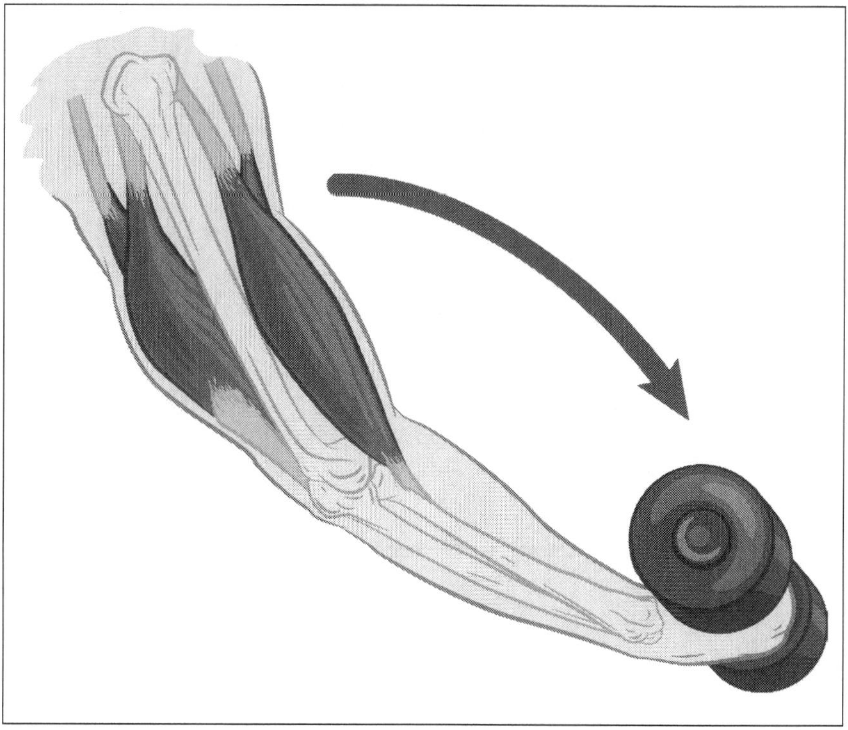

We are stronger by some 25-30% on this eccentric phase, with the same absolute force being generated with less motor unit activity during lengthening contractions (18).

These different types of muscle contractions have different effects on muscle growth and in different regions of the muscle. Through their stretch-mediated actions, eccentric contractions tend to produce greater growth in the length and fascicle of the muscle. Concentric actions, on the other hand, which shorten the muscle and stimulate growth in fibre diameter, bulge out in the middle region of the muscle.

Born or made?

In his bestseller, "Outliers: The Story of Success", Malcom Gladwell quantified the idea that practice makes perfect—10,000 hours to be precise—advancing the claim that concerted effort, not genius or innate talent is the key to excellence in any endeavour. The notion is, of course, incredibly seductive—as it means we all stand a chance!

Nevertheless, at least as far as superior athletic performance is concerned, what every individual takes from an hour of deliberate practice is very much regulated by genetics. For example, one gene, the ACTN3, which makes a protein called alpha-actinin, is almost exclusively found in fast-twitch muscle fibres.

Fast-twitch muscle fibres allow for the explosive acceleration of sprinters like Usain Bolt, but not the sustained aerobic exertion require by a long-distance runner like Mo Farah. Capable of rapid, powerful contractions, fast-twitch fibres rely on anaerobic, glycolytic pathways. They also run out of gas more quickly than slow-twitch fibres.

Slow twitch, Type I muscle fibres have, as the name implies, slower but more sustainable contraction rates. They display a strong oxidative capacity, high mitochondrial content and are resistant to fatigue. Unsurprisingly, these slow twitch fibres are found to be proportionally higher in elite endurance athletes, like Mo (19).

Apart from obvious outliers, such as the calves, the muscles of the human body are an evenly distributed, mixed bag of fast and slow twitch muscles. Weight training stimulates muscle hypertrophy in both types. Nevertheless, it is the Type II, fast-twitch muscles which respond most easily, with greater rates of muscle protein synthesis (20) producing as much as 50% more growth (21, 22).

The Quality of muscle

Predictably, with age these fast twitch-fibres breakdown faster and there is a transition towards having more slow-twitch fibres (23). Indeed sarcopenia, the age-related loss of skeletal muscle mass and strength is marked by changes to the composition and quality of muscle itself. This is then reflected in poorer muscle function, with slower, less powerful contractions (24).

A consequence of inactivity and sedentary lifestyles, the development of fat tissue in skeletal muscle helps foster this transition towards slow-twitch fibres (25). The deterioration of muscle quality from ectopic fat infiltration is known as myosteatosis. It occurs both beneath the muscle and between muscle groups, and at a cellular level (26). The accumulation of ectopic fat is pro-inflammatory, impairs organ function, disrupts metabolic processes and is associated with insulin resistance (27).

> **Ectopic Fat** is the storage of triglycerides in tissues and organs that normally contain only small amounts of fat, such as the heart, liver and skeletal muscle.

Muscle health: A blueprint for longevity

The aging process is associated with the gradual, physiological impairment of the body's organs and their systems. But due to its marvellous malleability and contractile nature, skeletal muscle has a remarkable capacity to regenerate. And at any age.

Consequently, resistance training increases the satellite cell content of muscle (28) and its percentage of fast-twitch fibres (29), reduces ectopic fat (30) and improves its oxidative capacity (31). It is this unique ability to restore the quality, composition and metabolic function of muscle (32) that makes resistance training an essential tenet of our blueprint for re-engineering men's health in middle age.

Time to get liftin', folks.

CHAPTER 8

THE MECHANICS OF MUSCLE BUILDING

"I hated every minute of training, but I said, 'Don't quit. Suffer now and live the rest of your life as a champion."

Muhammad Ali

Muscle growth (hypertrophy) is dependent on three interconnected events.

1. Hypertrophy Stimulus (Mechanical Tension/Metabolic Stress/Muscle Damage).
2. Mechanotransduction (Molecular Signalling Events/Hormonal Responses).
3. Muscle Protein Synthesis (Positive Net Protein Balance).

Two of these events, mechanotransduction and muscle protein synthesis, are well documented and for the most part easily understood. The first, however, which involves the stimulus to hypertrophy initiated by resistance training, is a matter of some debate. And source of no little confusion for those wishing to learn how to train optimally for muscle growth.

Mechanical tension, metabolic stress and muscle damage are three, distinct physiological stimuli, all triggered by resistance training (1). But, while no one doubts their existence, their *independent* contributions to muscle growth are difficult to measure. They also frequently appear in tandem, so drawing an exclusive relationship between one training method and the hypertrophy stimulus it provokes, is challenging.

Down at the coalface, best practice in weight training remains a mixture of gym folklore (*"it worked for Ronnie")* and 'bro-science', (*"it jacks up growth hormone by 1000%")*. So, in this chapter we take a deep dive to shed some light on the science of muscle growth and provide some actionable takeaways.

Chasing The Pump

In an iconic scene from the 1970's movie, "Pumping Iron," Arnold Schwarzenegger, compares the "pump" of working out to sex, a rush of endorphins where muscles engorged with blood swell up: "*The most satisfying feeling you can get in the gym is the pump. Let's say you train your biceps; blood is rushing into your muscles and that's what we call the pump. Your muscles get a really tight feeling like your skin is going to explode any minute*" (2).

Ahem.

"Chasing the pump," became the colloquial description for training like Arnold with comparatively moderate weights and a high volume of reps and sets. Although bearing the hallmarks of 'bro-science', the pump is a real, physiological phenomenon (3).

Resistance training is often anaerobic and uses glycolysis to create energy from glucose. The body responds to a lack of oxygen with the build-up of metabolites, such as lactic acid. The accumulation of these biproducts draws more fluid into the cell, causing the muscle fibre to swell. This, along with the pooling of blood to the working muscle, creates the sensation of the "pump" (4).

The metabolic stress of the pump causes fatigue (5) and an involuntary slowing down of reps towards the end of the set. The muscle responds to this stress with a hormonal surge (e.g., growth hormone, IGF-1), and the anabolic, intracellular signalling which initiates muscle protein synthesis (6,7).

> **Glycolysis** an anaerobic process that breaks down glucose to produce ATP (energy). Glycolysis cannot be sustained for long periods (more than 1 minute) of activity.

All well and good. The pump is real.

But training with moderate loads and high reps to elicit metabolic stress also seems to contradict the first edict of gym folklore to, "*Go heavy or go home.*" "Ditch the biceps curls and do heavy compound exercises," they said. "Focus on putting more weight on the bar and getting stronger," they entreated.

So, off you go to train like a powerlifter in quest of PB's (Personal Bests) on the three 'big' barbell lifts. Sure enough, you get strong. But not muscular. And then some built guy at the gym, who uses machines and cables throws you a curve ball. A nugget of unsolicited advice such as I received as a newbie: lift light weights with loads of reps and get that defined, ripped look.

Confusing, to say the least.

New Science

Aside from myths that perennially escape 'busting', some of the confusion stems from the seemingly contradictory research published in scientific journals. However, the science of muscle hypertrophy is a relatively new endeavour. And, like all science, it evolves with every fresh discovery. Whilst consensus exists in certain key areas, what was gospel ten years ago is being challenged today.

For example, one hypothesis thought to explain growth from the metabolic stress of 'chasing the pump', is sarcoplasmic hypertrophy. The sarcoplasm is a solution which surrounds the muscle fibre and is made up of non-contractile elements such as water, stored ATP (energy), glycogen and creatine (Fig 1). Sarcoplasmic hypertrophy is when this intra-cellular fluid, critical for the anaerobic energy we use when lifting weights, increases.

> **Sarcoplasm** the cytoplasm of the muscle cell. A solution that fills the cell, composed of water, ATP, glycogen and creatine, along with enzymes critical for energy metabolism.

FIG 1. SARCOPLASM

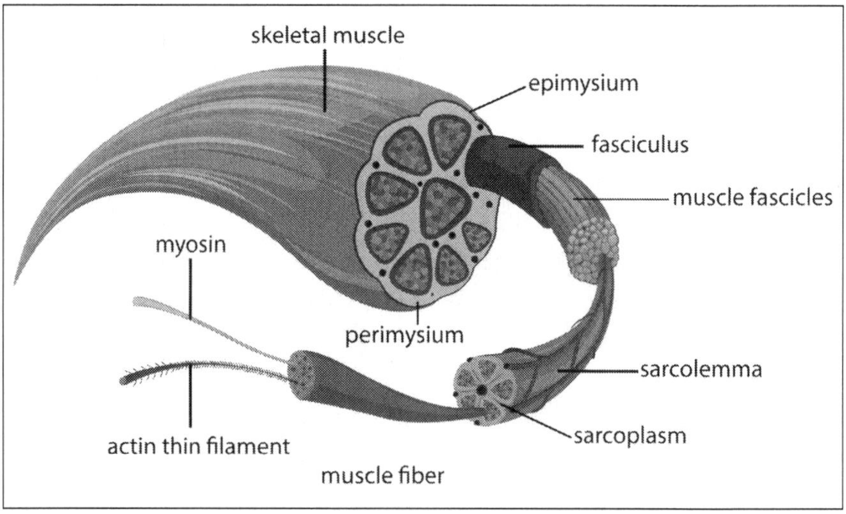

The first study providing good evidence of sarcoplasmic hypertrophy in humans was published nearly 40 years ago (8). A more recent study, in 2019, confirmed that the growth seen in response to 6 weeks of high-volume resistance training was "largely attributed to sarcoplasmic hypertrophy" (9).

Nevertheless, sarcoplasmic hypertrophy has been in and out of favour with the scientific community for nearly all the 40 years spanning its research. Initially, at least, it was enthusiastically received as a convenient explanation for the differences in muscularity and body composition between powerlifters and bodybuilders.

Bodybuilders, who train differently to powerlifters typically showcase more muscular, aesthetic physiques. And their different style of training is thought to be associated with sarcoplasmic hypertrophy (10).

Bodybuilders v Powerlifters

The primary objective for powerlifters is to increase maximal strength. Therefore, they train almost exclusively with heavy loads and take lengthy rest periods between sets. They strive to improve their 1 Rep Max (1RM) on big compound lifts like the deadlift, squat and bench press. They practice singles and doubles, but rarely complete sets of more than 5 reps.

> **Compound Lifts** are exercises which work multiple muscle groups simultaneously. For example, the squat, which works the quadriceps, glutes, and calves.

Bodybuilders on the other hand, train in a variety of rep ranges (6-8, 10-12, 15+), sometimes with heavy loads but frequently with light to moderate ones. Exercise selection is also more varied, with isolation exercises (e.g., the biceps curl) accompanying compound lifts. All manner of advanced techniques including rest-pause, drop sets and blood restriction are also employed to grow more muscle.

Sarcoplasmic hypertrophy offers a plausible explanation for the aesthetic differences between powerlifters and bodybuilders. But it is not the only one. Strength adaptations, contrary to popular opinion, are not always accompanied by similar increases in muscle growth. There is a significant skill component to strength training and this skill acquisition embeds patterns of movement in our neurology, which contributes greatly to strength gains (11).

The most yoked guy in the gym is rarely the strongest...

Mechanical Tension: Alpha and Omega

Sarcoplasmic hypertrophy may help explain growth from training which causes metabolic stress. But this style of training (moderate loads/ higher reps) may also produce mechanical tension. Mechanical tension is widely accepted as the primary stimulus for muscle growth 12,13).

Mechanical tension is produced by the force generated from within muscle fibres during contraction (14). When the tension exerted is enough to stimulate growth, the muscle lays down additional myofibrillar proteins, adding sarcomeres in parallel. The resulting increase in size and cross-sectional area of these pre-existing, *individual* muscle fibres is known as myofibrillar hypertrophy (15).

> **Sarcomere** the force-producing units of muscle which are built and added in parallel, increasing muscle cross-sectional area.

Most importantly, mechanical tension is governed by the force-velocity relationship. This fundamental principle of neuromuscular physiology states that *as force increases, velocity must decrease.* This has important implications for how we grow muscle.

The force capacity of a muscle is directly related to the number of cross bridges formed by the myofilaments, actin and myosin, which overlay during contractions. (Fig 2.) However, the formation of cross-bridges is not immediate. At faster velocities the myofilaments detach too quickly. The force produced by, and the mechanical tension exerted on the working muscle is therefore greater during slow (involuntary) contractions (16).

FIG 2.

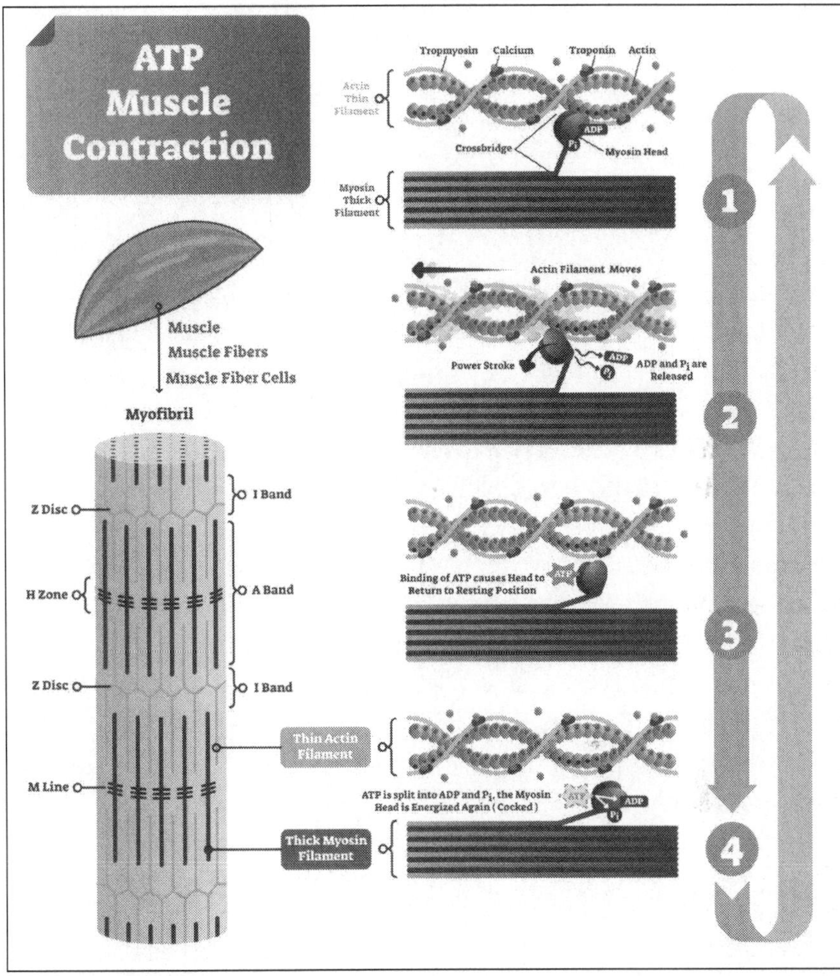

We see this most obviously when lifting heavy weights. The heavier the load, the greater the external resistance and the slower our bar speeds and muscle contractions become. Similarly, when muscles are forced to contract slowly due to heavy loads, high threshold motor units are also recruited. These motor units control the large, strong groups of muscle fibres which are more responsive to growth.

> **Myofibrillar hypertrophy** increases the number of myofibrils within the muscle fibre causing it to grow by laying down additional myofibrillar proteins. The result is an increase in size and cross-sectional area of the *individual* muscle fibre.

When Failure is Winning

As a result, mechanical tension has become synonymous with lifting heavy loads. Yet mechanical tension is also present when lifting light loads in higher rep ranges, *when* they are taken to failure. Training to failure is the end point when our neuromuscular system can no longer produce the force necessary to overcome a specific workload. In other words, there isn't another rep left in the tank.

This is significant. Because when we train towards "failure" with lighter loads and higher rep ranges, muscle fatigue will set in during the last four to five reps and there is a gradual reduction in contraction speeds. The force-velocity relationship therefore mandates that those last few, more taxing reps exert greater mechanical tension. Despite the lighter loads, the (involuntary) slower contractions ensure the formation of more cross-bridges.

> **Training To Failure** Repeating an exercise to the point of momentary muscular failure. At this point, the neuromuscular system can no longer produce adequate force to overcome the workload.

Similarly, in accordance with Henneman's size principle, the low threshold motor units (which control small numbers of less responsive fibres) recruited for the less taxing reps at the beginning of the set, handover to the big guns and high threshold motor units as momentary failure approaches.

The Gospel according to *Instagram*...

The internet is awash with gurus preaching the virtues of one repetition scheme or another. Perhaps they made gains and positive body composition transformations by switching from moderate loads with 10-12 reps, to heavier loads in the 5+ rep range. Or vice-versa.

Either way, they figure *you* need to know about it...

And it's certainly hard not to be swayed by their impressive physiques and Instagram-friendly evangelism. What they have in common, however, is dogmatism and belief that they have discovered the holy grail of loading schemes and rep ranges. Yet the science unequivocally demonstrates that *when performed to momentary failure*, equivalent results for muscle hypertrophy are obtainable with light, moderate and heavy loads (17, 18, 19).

A hard pill to swallow for their fan boys.

However, training to failure on *every* set is not always necessary (20) nor even advisable for the purposes of recovery (21). Indeed, when volume is equated, stopping just short with one to two reps in reserve (RIR) produces comparable results without inducing the same levels of muscular fatigue (22).

The problem is that both beginners and intermediate lifters tend to underestimate what they can lift and therefore underpredict what constitutes failure (23). Falling one rep short of failure is very different from four reps shy and that kind of maths undoubtedly produces inferior results.

The mechanosensors on the membrane of each muscle cell (24), responsible for detecting mechanical tension, are sensitive to both load *and* duration. Which explains why training singles, or even doubles, with high loads (>80% 1RM) may increase strength but not muscle growth (25). Individual muscle fibres need to sense sufficient time under tension to initiate mechanotransduction and the muscle building machinery.

> **Mechanotransduction** The mechanism by which mechanical forces acting through skeletal muscle cells generate intracellular signalling to elicit specific responses.

Blood and guts

Muscle hypertrophy therefore requires training with at least 5+ reps per set. This proviso adhered to, what ultimately will determine your progress, however, is intensity of effort. So, go all in!! Try to hit momentary failure occasionally, and near failure regularly, setting benchmarks for what you are truly capable of. And then get better. Certainly, maximal efforts involve some discomfort. But without it, what reason are you giving for the muscle to adapt and grow?

And when progress is stalling and the *gainz* aren't showing up, rather than fixating on the minutiae of program design or whether your intra workout drink has enough Beta Alanine, try channelling Dorian Yates first and some "blood and guts" approach to your training.

No pain, no gain?

If you perform eccentric training which forcibly lengthens the muscle or are unaccustomed to exercise, muscle soreness and localised damage to the muscle tissue may result. And muscle damage, alongside metabolic stress and mechanical tension has been hypothesised as a pathway for muscle growth (26, 27).

> **Eccentric Training** is the repetition of eccentric, or negative contractions, which lengthen the muscle under load. The action of lowering the bar to the chest during a chest press is an example.

DOMS (Delayed Onset of Muscle Soreness) a characteristic of muscle damage, is often worn as a badge of honour. If you can walk 24 hours after "leg day", you probably didn't train hard enough. But while the exhortation to train hard behind the "*no pain, no gain*" mantra is laudable, the presence of DOMS is not always a reliable indicator. In fact, over time the body adapts due to the "repeated bout effect" (28).

> **Muscle Damage** from unaccustomed exercise or eccentric actions and sometimes accompanied by delayed onset muscle soreness (DOMS), is best indicated by loss of muscle strength and range of motion.

The body responds to muscle damage in the same way it does to an infection or injury—by inciting an inflammatory response (29). This response is critical for ultimately repairing the damage.

It initiates the removal of cellular debris, the production of cytokines and the recruitment of satellite (stem) cells to the site of muscle damage. Satellite cells can then divide, fuse with existing muscle fibres and donate their nuclei to repair the damage and regenerate the muscle (30). The heightened satellite cell activity undoubtedly helps repair damaged muscle tissue.

However, whether it also contributes to the building of *new* muscle is difficult to discern. Eccentric training, for example, causes muscle damage and is certainly an effective method for building muscle (31). But the growth may also occur due to the greater mechanical tension which occurs from forcibly lengthening the muscle (32). As we know, muscle hypertrophy results from the muscle fibre increasing in length, not just its diameter.

Signalling Pathways & mTOR

But whether muscle damage or indeed metabolic stress are hypertrophy stimuli or simply coincidental to mechanical tension is of secondary importance. What matters is that the stimulus from training be sufficiently robust to trigger mechanotransduction, intracellular signalling and a cascade of hormonal responses which promote anabolism and muscle protein synthesis (33).

> **Mechanotransduction** The mechanism by which mechanical forces acting through skeletal muscle cells generate intracellular signalling to elicit specific responses.

The signalling pathway known as mTOR (Mammalian target of rapamycin) is the key enzyme involved in muscle protein synthesis. While other signalling pathways and genes play a role in the regulation of muscle size, their contribution to muscle hypertrophy from resistance-training is less understood (34).

mTOR is a nutrient sensor, responsive to amino acid (protein) availability but it can also sense mechanical forces from resistance training (35). It is often referred to as the "master regulator" and plays a critical role in many cellular processes, metabolism and muscle hypertrophy (36, 37, 38).

Aside from nutrient availability and energy status, mTOR is sensitive to hormonal surges from growth hormone and Insulin-like Growth factor-1 (IGF-1). IGF-1 especially is a potent upstream trigger of mTOR signalling; an anabolic hormone which responds acutely to training and mechanical loading (39,40).

The Big Kahuna: Muscle Protein Synthesis

The final cog in this muscle making machinery is muscle protein synthesis (MPS).

An *anabolic* process, called into action by mTOR and hormonal responses, it constructs proteins from the smaller building blocks of amino acids. Conversely, muscle protein breakdown (MPB) is a *catabolic* process involving the degradation of proteins via the digestive process.

Protein synthesis and protein breakdown are the very essence of metabolism. Dynamic processes, they are simultaneously active throughout the day. Their constant turnover breaks down the old, damaged proteins to synthesise new ones. And, in this way, it maintains your muscle mass.

In young people, skeletal muscle protein daily turnover rate remains constant and between 1-2% of muscle proteins are synthesised and broken down daily. Unfortunately, the aging process creates an imbalance between protein synthesis and degradation leading to slower turnover rates of muscle protein (41).

Muscle Hypertrophy:
Positive Net Protein Balance = Muscle Protein Synthesis > Muscle Protein Breakdown

For muscle to grow, there must be a positive Net Protein Balance Protein (NPB), whereby total muscle protein synthesis exceeds total muscle protein breakdown.

Muscle protein synthesis and protein breakdown rates are responsive to stimuli such as fasting, feeding, and training. For example, fasting encourages muscle protein breakdown. Nutrition (feeding) and training, on the other hand, are two of the most anabolic, potent drivers of Muscle Protein Synthesis (MPS) (42, 43).

Of the two stimuli, training and nutrition, training is the most responsive. In fact, resistance training can increase muscle protein turnover for up to 48 hours (44). To a lesser extent training simultaneously triggers muscle protein breakdown (45) and it is not until the next protein feeding that a net positive balance is reached (46).

Moral of the story? Don't forget your protein shake!

KEY TAKEAWAYS

- ✓ Mechanical Tension is the most significant driver and primary stimulus of muscle growth.
- ✓ The force produced by, and the mechanical tension exerted on the working muscle is greatest during slow (involuntary) contractions.
- ✓ When performed to momentary failure, equivalent results for muscle hypertrophy are obtainable with light, moderate or heavy loads.
- ✓ Muscle hypertrophy requires at least 5+ reps per set, as the mechanosensors which perceive mechanical tension are sensitive to both load and duration.
- ✓ MTOR, the "master regulator" is responsive to protein availability and mechanical forces. It is the key enzyme involved in muscle protein synthesis.
- ✓ For muscle to grow, there must be a positive Net Protein Balance Protein (NPB), whereby total muscle protein synthesis (MPS) exceeds total muscle protein breakdown (MPB).

CHAPTER 9

FREQUENCY: THE SECRET SAUCE

"I learned something from all those sets and reps when I didn't think I could lift another ounce of weight. What I learned is that we are always stronger than we know."

Arnold Schwarzenegger

Arnold Schwarzenegger proved himself a charismatic figurehead for the body beautiful movement that paraded the beaches of Southern California. Meanwhile, his mentor Joe Weider, responsible for bringing Arnie over from Austria, grew a flourishing fitness empire of magazines, supplements, competitions and equipment. Together perhaps more than anyone they popularised weight training. Alongside Jane Fonda and the explosion of aerobic fitness classes they helped fashion the look and feel of the modern-day commercial gym.

Southern California: where it all began.

Integral to Joe Weider's marketing was the promotion of the "Weider Training System", a set of principles and scientific-sounding techniques, (e.g., the "flushing" method) behind his methodology for building the "physiques of champions." The full-body workouts of Steve Reeves were replaced with a new focus on individual muscle groups, which became known as the 'body-part split.'

A bodybuilding 'split' is simply how to structure a weekly workout routine. It is both a plan and road map to organise training and recovery. There are many types of splits, but a typical five-day body-part split might look something like this:

Monday:	Chest and Triceps
Tuesday:	Back and Biceps
Wednesday:	Shoulders
Thursday:	Rest Day
Friday:	Legs
Saturday:	Arms
Sunday:	Rest Day

Immortalised forever in Schwarzenegger's Encyclopaedia of Bodybuilding and featured monthly in Weider magazines such as Muscle & Fitness and Flex, the body-part split was heavily endorsed by champions who would occasionally reveal 'game-changing' tweaks and variations.

Weider's methodologies were immensely popular if not altogether ubiquitous. *But is the body-part split an optimal way to structure the training week?* And are there other factors we should consider when designing a split for the middle-aged, such as anabolic resistance or the ability to recover?

> **Anabolic Resistance** The age-related, diminished response from skeletal muscle to the anabolic stimuli of nutrition and training.

Volume: Too much of a good thing?

In recent years, the body-part split has fallen out of favour and is sometimes derogatively referred to as the 'bro-split'. In part, this fall from grace was due to the excessive volume practiced by its advocates, which was deemed necessary to make gains. The stars that graced the front covers of Weider's magazines, regularly trained 24-30+ sets per muscle group in one session.

And to the reader this approach made sense. If you can only train chest once a week, best make it count. But as a result, it left mere mortals spinning their wheels, chasing the perfection of the gods, forever in awe but unable to replicate these marathon-like training sessions. The mortals were also of course, blissfully unaware that *these* gods recovered with the help of performance-enhancing drugs.

Yet volume does matter. Expressed as the total product of sets and repetitions, it is considered a key driver for stimulating muscle growth (1, 2). The evidence that a high volume of training and multi-set protocols stimulates muscle hypertrophy is also compelling. For example, a meta-analysis of 15 studies showed there is a clear dose-dependent relationship between weekly volume and increases in muscle hypertrophy (3). Another, covering eight studies, revealed multi-set protocols are associated with 40% more muscle hypertrophy gains than single sets (4).

That being said, more is not always better. There exists an upper threshold of volume beyond which additional work will amount to wasted sets. Quality also matters. It stands to reason that after 20 sets of chest exercises, form and execution will inevitably decline as does the ability to reach somewhere close to failure. And the further away we train from failure, the less effective our training for hypertrophy.

Brad Schoenfeld illustrates this law of diminishing returns in his "Science and development of Muscle Hypertrophy", with an inverted curve. (Fig 2) The curve shows how progress increases with volume, peaks, and then tails off. It also reveals a point where further work may impair gains, due to overtraining (5).

FIG 2 DOSE RESPONSE EFFECT OF VOLUME ON HYPERTROPHY (5)

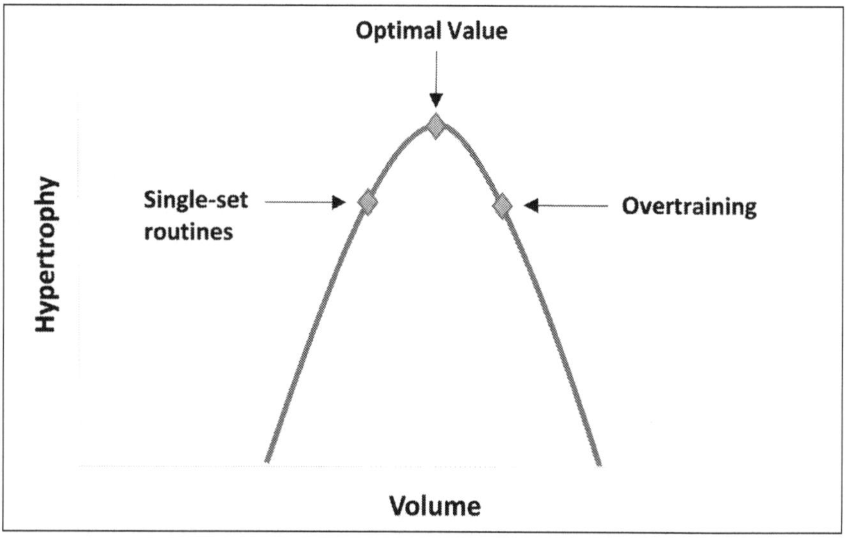

Adapted from the Science and Development of Muscle Hypertrophy, Dr Brad Schoenfeld

Exactly how much volume is optimal differs, sometimes widely, according to the individual. It depends on genetics, training status, age and even the body-part trained. As you might expect, the upper threshold for an advanced lifter is considerably higher than that of a beginner.

Similarly, the threshold will be less with age due to a diminished capacity for recovery (6). Nevertheless, the consensus of the literature points to a *minimum* threshold of weekly volume of 10+ sets per body part (7).

Accumulating Volume (a minimum threshold)

Per session:
3-5 Sets per exercise
40-70 repetitions

Per week:
10+ sets per body part

Go heavy or go home?

Unsurprisingly, there is also an inverse relationship between how heavy one can lift, and the volume of reps and sets performed. A higher volume of training will involve some sacrifice of load. Hence powerlifters, performing heavy singles or doubles and resting 4-5 minutes between lifts, find it difficult to build the kind of training volumes a bodybuilder can.

Intensity of load, not to be confused with intensity of effort is, like volume, a training variable which we can manipulate to optimally structure our training program. It is measured as a percentage of Repetition Maximum (RM). This is the maximal weight an individual can lift one time, on any given exercise.

> **Intensity** The amount of load lifted, expressed as a percentage of Repetition Maximum (RM).

For example, if an individual's 1 Rep Max on the Overhead Press is 100 Lb (45.5Kg), then performing five reps at 70 Lb (31.8Kg), the *intensity* of load will be 70% of his one Rep Max. Heavy loads, or a high *intensity* of load is considered equal to, or greater than 80-85% of 1RM.

The characterisation of intensity as heavy, moderate, and light loads can be further broken down into Training Load Zones with repetition ranges. A heavy intensity of load, typically with loads of 85% of 1RM, is lifted for 1-5 repetitions. More moderate loads are performed at 70% of 1RM, in a medium range of 6-12 Reps. Finally, light intensity loads of 65% of 1RM are performed in the 15+ rep range.

Intensity of Training: Load Zones

1. Heavy intensity: ≥ 85% of 1RM, lifted for 1-5 repetitions.
2. Medium intensity: ≥70% of 1RM, medium range of 6-12 Reps
3. Light intensity: ≤ 65% of 1RM, typically performed in the 15+ rep range

While all these training zones may produce similar gains in muscle hypertrophy, it is important to reiterate that, when training with light loads, reaching near or absolute failure is critical. Without this effort, it is difficult to create sufficient mechanical tension to trigger anabolic processes and muscle protein synthesis (8,9).

High intensities of load on the other hand, produce high levels of mechanical tension. Similarly, moderately heavy to heavy load training produces greater cross-sectional area growth in Type II muscle fibres. Hypertrophy of Type I, endurance muscle fibres with more mitochondria and a high capacity for fat oxidation, is greater when training with light loads (10).

Nevertheless, prescribing the correct load for an individual will also depend on training status (11). Untrained individuals for example, need not concern themselves with heavy loads in the initial phases, but rather focus on skill acquisition and improved motor learning (12). With time and as the lifter progresses, greater loads may be added.

Frequency

Frequency of training is the number of workouts performed in a period, for example, a week. It may also refer to the number of times a specific muscle group is trained. But when compared to volume and intensity, frequency of training is the poor relation of training variables, often overlooked in the scientific literature (13).

It has been suggested that the relative paucity of studies examining frequency, is related to the widespread belief that volume is the key variable for muscle hypertrophy. A recent (2019) systematic review and meta-analysis of 25 studies by Messrs Schoenfeld, Grgic and Krieger seemed to confirm this, showing that *when volume is the same*, training with more frequency confers no special advantage, nor superior gains (14).

However, for the drug-free, middle-aged lifter, frequency of training may well be a game-changer. A *secret sauce*, which unlike the 'special juice,' is free. Nor will it bring you out in acne or cause a cardiovascular event.

The Sweet Spot

For the overzealous reader it might be wise to state from the outset that training with more frequency *and* more volume is not an option! The body needs time to recover, repair and build and without this time, overtraining becomes a very real prospect.

> **Overtraining:** A maladapted response to excessive exercise without adequate rest, resulting in perturbations of the body (neurologic, endocrinologic, immunologic) and mood changes.

Whilst a minimum volume of 10 sets per muscle group per week is a good rule of thumb, optimal thresholds of volume are individual and will depend on training status. Nevertheless, if we structure a split to train individual muscle groups more frequently, we can find that sweet spot whereby we hit optimal amounts of volume but spread more evenly over the course of the week.

Indeed, there is wide consensus that training a muscle group at least twice a week is preferable to the traditional body-part split to maximise muscle growth (15). A training frequency of x2 sessions per muscle group accommodates a variety of training splits, including full body workouts. My personal favourite, though perhaps more suited to the intermediate or advanced lifter, is the push, pull, legs split:

Monday	Tuesday	Wednesday	Thursday	Friday	Saturday	Sunday
PUSH	PULL	LEGS	PUSH	PULL	LEGS	REST
Chest	Back	Quads	Chest	Back	Quads	
Delts	Biceps	Hamstrings	Delts	Biceps	Hamstrings	
Triceps	Traps	Calves	Triceps	Traps	Calves	

A full body or alternatively an upper body, lower body split, might be more readily suited to the requirements of a beginner:

Monday	Tuesday	Wednesday	Thursday	Friday	Saturday	Sunday
Full Body	REST	Full Body	REST	REST	Full Body	REST

Benefits

The principal benefit of high frequency training is as a tool for hitting volume targets, while still being able to perform quality sets. It stands to reason that the quality of smashing out 16-20 sets on leg day, is likely considerably poorer than 8-12 sets of leg exercises executed twice a week with greater form, range of movement and intensity—both that of load and effort.

Incorporating more weekly frequency with shorter sessions will also facilitate quicker recovery, due to less muscle soreness and less cumulative fatigue (16). Sustained physical exercise of any kind leads to fatigue and a reduced capacity for performance. But there are two types of exercise-induced fatigue.

Peripheral fatigue involves the mechanical and cellular processes of the muscular system. It is localised to the muscle. Central nervous system (CNS) fatigue on the other hand, results in a reduced capacity of the central nervous system to activate muscle. Produced by the inflammatory response, it affects the whole body and may last for days. Recovery from CNS fatigue is important as it decreases our ability to recruit the high threshold motor units, which control the muscle fibres most responsive to growth.

Somewhat counterintuitively, workouts involving light loads to failure cause more CNS fatigue than heavier load workouts (17,18). Similarly, workouts of long duration with high volume. Nevertheless, without the aid to recovery that performance enhancing drugs provide (19) recovery becomes slower with age regardless of the type of fatigue induced by training.

Even elite master's athletes, who may not experience greater peripheral fatigue than their younger counterparts, are slower to recover from CNS fatigue most notably because of muscle damage (20).

You're no spring chicken!

Smashing oneself into the ground with marathon sessions, getting all the volume in one session, are not viable options for middle age lifters. No more than it is to go out all night and function at work in the way you could in your twenties!

Yet age is not an excuse to train without intensity. We can and should train hard. But we should also train more intelligently. The goal as eight times Mr Olympia Lee Haney used to say is to stimulate the muscle, not annihilate it. So, train hard, train frequently, but for shorter durations.

Get in. Get it done. Get out.

Shorter, more frequent workouts will also help to manage cortisol, the 'stress hormone' better. The acute release of cortisol is necessary for training as it mobilises energy sources from fat (lipolysis) and glycogen (glycogenolysis). But it also stimulates the catabolic breakdown of proteins (21) which will increase the longer we train. Indeed, endurance athletes often exhibit higher cortisol levels than their resistance-trained counterparts (22).

In fact, the ratios between cortisol and testosterone (which have an inverse relationship) is commonly used to measure stress levels in response to exercise. Splitting up high weekly volume into more frequent workouts improves the testosterone-to-cortisol ratio, which in turn facilitates recovery (23).

As a key hormone implicated in the aging process and age-related disease (24), we ought to do all we can to mitigate the catabolic effects of cortisol. In addition to shorter training sessions, resting two to three minutes between sets may result in greater testosterone levels relative to cortisol (25). This in turn, contributes to a more favourable anabolic milieu which helps gain muscle mass and aids recovery.

Anabolic Resistance

As we have learned previously, muscle protein synthesis (MPS) must exceed muscle protein breakdown (MPB) for muscle to grow. With age, this becomes more challenging due to anabolic resistance – the blunted response from muscle to anabolic stimuli (26).

The most potent forces available for stimulating (naturally) the anabolic processes which drive MPS are resistance training and nutrition. Nutrient-stimulated increases in protein synthesis are however, short-lived. Of the two stimuli it is training which has the most potential to ramp up muscle protein synthesis—anywhere from 24-48 hrs (27, 28).

It stands to reason therefore, that with a higher frequency of training we have more opportunities to stimulate muscle protein synthesis. These more frequent elevations of muscle protein synthesis alongside well-timed nutrition, are the secret sauce to overcoming anabolic resistance and building muscle in middle-age.

KEY TAKEAWAYS

- ✓ Volume of training matters for muscle hypertrophy. But there exists an upper threshold of volume—different for everyone—beyond which, additional work will amount to wasted sets.
- ✓ For muscle hypertrophy, the literature points to a *minimum* threshold of weekly volume of 10+ sets per body part. This increases as we become more advanced lifters.
- ✓ Training a muscle group at least twice a week is preferable to the traditional body-part split to maximise muscle growth.
- ✓ The principal benefit of a higher frequency of training is to make hitting your weekly volume targets easier, while performing quality sets.
- ✓ More frequency of weekly training, along with shorter sessions will facilitate quicker recovery, due to less cumulative fatigue.
- ✓ Training is more powerful than nutrition to ramp up muscle protein synthesis—anywhere from 24-48 hrs. So, train frequently!

CHAPTER 10

PRINCIPLES OF PROGRAM DESIGN: PUTTING IT ALL TOGETHER

"Suffer the pain of self-discipline. Or suffer the pain of regret."

Jim Rohn

Greg Doucette, a record-breaking powerlifter and IFBB pro-bodybuilder from Canada, runs a popular YouTube fitness channel. The show is spearheaded by an entertaining and refreshingly honest '*Natty or Not*' series, where he debates the natural or performance drugs-enhanced status of film stars and fitness influencers. He also offers sound, credible advice on nutrition and training. Among other pearls of wisdom, he entreats followers to not get bogged down in the minutiae, but to simply train "*harder than last time.*"

And he's not wrong. In fact, Greg's pithy catch phrase encapsulates the one training principle which ought to inform the design of any good muscle building program, and that is *Progressive Overload.* Progressive overload is the gradual increase of stress placed upon the body, *forcing* it to respond and adapt. One such adaptive response is growth. New muscle tissue forms so that it may be relied upon in the future to meet new demands.

The principle of progressive overload was most notably first put into practice by a Dr Thomas DeLorme, while working with American soldiers injured in World War II. As part of their rehabilitation, he developed a Resistance Training program which included 3 progressively heavier sets of 10 repetitions. He referred to the program as "Progressive Resistance Exercise," and so laid the foundation for the science of resistance training.

Milo of Croton

According to legend, Milo of Croton, a 6th century Greek wrester and early adopter of progressive overload, trained by carrying a calf daily from its birth until it became a full-sized ox.

Since then, however, progressive overload has become largely synonymous with heavier weights and higher intensities of load. But simply increasing the load in a linear fashion *ad infinitum* is not possible. Training plateaus, fatigue and even monotony are all factors which may stall progress (1).

Yet progressive overload is also the addition of extra repetitions with the same weight. Or a final set of dumbbell presses, followed by 3 drop sets with increasingly lighter weights. There are any number of variables and training techniques we can manipulate to ensure progressive overload. The important takeaway is the need for a plan to structure these variables and continually make progress.

Periodisation

One way to structure such a plan and which incorporates the principles of progressive overload, is Periodisation. A broad definition of periodisation, one that alludes to its original purpose, is "*the planned manipulation of training variables to optimise performance at appropriate time points, manage fatigue, and prevent stagnation*" *(2)*.

Periodisation effectively provides a structure for variation, forcing the body to continually adapt to new stress by manipulating other training variables while managing fatigue and recovery (3). The precepts of periodised training can be traced back to Ancient Greece and Olympia, where "tetrads", or four-day Microcycles, alternated vigorous training with workouts of a gentler persuasion (4).

But what modern-day sport understands for a periodised training plan is a legacy of the Soviet Scientist, LP Matveyev, whose theories were published and applied with great success at the 1960 Olympics. Periodisation became a global tool for sport planning following the translation into English in 1981 of "*The Fundamentals of Sports Training*" (5), with its clear hierarchy of training cycles, logical and structured variation.

These stages or training cycles, consist of Macrocycles, or long-term periods, which can be a sports season, six months or a calendar year. Macrocycles are further broken down into smaller Mesocycles, typically a block of training lasting 28 days, and Microcycles, usually consisting of a week.

Linear Periodisation

Linear periodisation is the progressive transition from a high volume of training with relatively light loads, to low volumes with heavier loads. Linear periodisation is based on the inverse relationship between volume and intensity of load. To sustain progress, as one variable goes up, the other must come down.

WEEK	Example Set & REP scheme w/ % 1RM Load
Week 1:	3 sets of 12 Reps w/65%
Week 2:	3 sets of 10 Reps w/70%
Week 3:	3 sets of 8 Reps w/75%
Week 4:	3 sets of 6 Reps w/80%

Reverse Linear Periodisation is as the name suggests the exact opposite. It begins with heavy intensities of load which are then gradually reduced over time as the volume of training increases.

Beginners can greatly benefit from a program of linear periodisation. In the early stages of training, it is the nervous system which plays a lead role in adaptations to training. The development of neural patterns, improved firing rates and motor unit recruitment (6), rather than muscle hypertrophy itself, are responsible for strength gains (7). After roughly 4-8 weeks of consistent training, these early strength gains are accompanied by muscle growth.

With the focus on accumulating some volume in the earlier mesocycles, the beginner builds motor control and motor unit recruitment. Like an apprentice, he learns his craft. As muscle hypertrophy develops, the increased cross-sectional area of muscle allows for greater force production. This new strength can then be put to the test in following phases, where loads are steadily increased while decreasing overall volume.

Does periodisation work?

The early, and almost universal acceptance of periodised programs was in part due to the dazzling array of Olympic successes from the Eastern Bloc. Different forms of periodisation also developed out of perceived limitations and drawbacks. For example, block periodisation was developed for top-level athletes who needed several, multi-peaking platforms for a competitive season (8). Daily Undulating Periodisation (DUP) was developed to provide more variation in the training stimulus than the linear model (9).

But while sporting success and global acceptance from coaches stacks up, *is the widespread belief in periodisation justified?* In fact, a sizeable body of literature does point to periodised programs providing superior results (10). One review of 15 studies concluded periodised training provides superior performance improvements, compared with constant-repetition programs (11).

One glaring weakness of the research, as addressed by John Kiely in, "*Periodization Paradigms in the 21st Century: Evidence-Led or Tradition-Driven?*" (12), is that the comparisons are made with constant-repetition programs that have no in-built variation. There is no research for example, which compares the results of a bodybuilder who trains instinctively and who will randomly incorporate variation.

On balance it would seem periodised programs work because they structure progressive overload, while balancing key and opposing training principles such as specificity with variation. They also help avoid fatigue, overtraining and monotony. In the end, however, periodisation is just a framework for changing training variables over time. Performer-generated feedback, individual trends and the flexibility to review and refine should be incorporated by any good coach into program design, periodised or otherwise.

An Absolute Beginner

When designing a program for the absolute beginner, the goal is to establish first a foundation base of strength, using a selection of exercises which embed fundamental movement patterns. Adding layers of complexity such as changing tempo, varying exercise selection or going to failure are best left until after there is some mastery of the basics (13).

We should aim for a minimum of three sessions per week. This kind of training frequency will allow us over time to build up towards a weekly volume of 10 sets, per muscle group. To facilitate this, it is helpful to include several compound exercises. Compound exercises, such as the deadlift, spread the external force over multiple joints, stimulating more muscles than an isolation exercise. As more muscles are engaged, the beginner may progress more quickly in terms of the loads lifted.

On the other hand, isolation exercises are single-joint movements. They work relatively less muscle mass, which also translates to lighter loads.

For example, the deadlift is considered by many to be the compound exercise *par excellence*, involving nearly every joint and major muscle group. The emphasis is on the prime muscles of the posterior chain—hamstrings, glutes, traps and back—but the movement is assisted by many others.

However, as we progress, the opposite is almost true. We want to create the maximum amount of mechanical tension loading the targeted muscle, and not have this tension spread over different synergist muscles. And this is where isolation exercises, machines and cables come into their own. Building muscle, after all, is not simply powerlifting with more reps!

Movement Patterns

Muscles have primary functions. For example, that of the quadriceps is knee extension. The role of the hamstring is knee flexion.

Understanding these distinctions helps refine exercise selection, especially as we advance.

But it is also beneficial, especially as a beginner, to think in terms of primary movement patterns. By incorporating different exercises which require similar movement patterns, their repetition facilitates learning and skill development.

Hip Hinge Movements

Hip hinge exercises work the posterior chain, including hamstrings, glutes and spinal erectors. Examples of exercises which require a hip hinge are:

1. Romanian Deadlift
2. Deadlift
3. Glute Bridge
4. Hip Thrust.
5. Good Mornings.

Romanian Deadlift

Coaching Cues:

Hips pushed back into full flexion, core engaged, soft bend at the knee. Hamstrings and glutes are the main hip extension muscles worked in this hip-hinge movement.

Barbell Hip Thrust

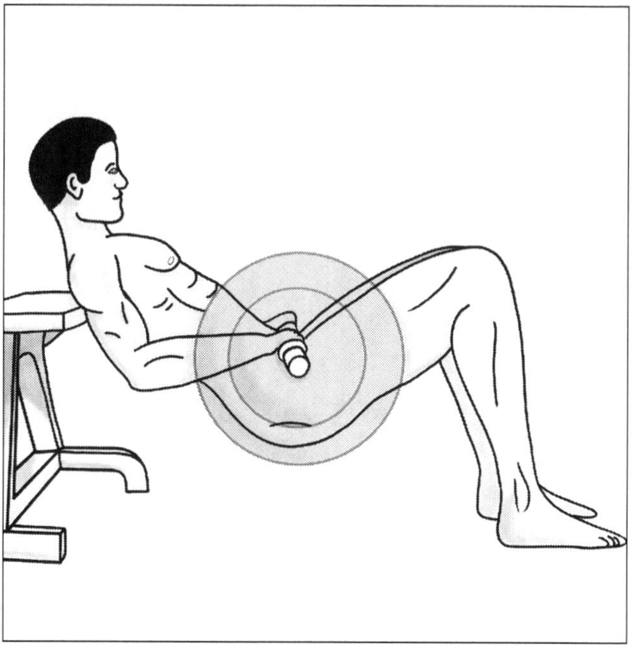

Coaching Cues:

Sit back onto bench, positioned just below shoulder blades. Legs shoulder-width apart, knees flexed and barbell lying in hip crease. Engage core, drive feet through floor to push hips upwards and through the bar, while keeping neck tucked in. Hold at the top for 1-2 seconds, contract glutes, before controlling the descent.

Squat Movements

Squat movements involve the knees and hips and work the quadriceps and glutes predominantly. Examples of exercises which require a squatting movement are:

1. Barbell Squat
2. Goblet Squat
3. Hack Squat
4. Split Squats.

Goblet Squat

Coaching Cues:

Hold dumbbell vertically (like a goblet), feet shoulder width apart. Breathe in deeply, brace core and lower into squat by pushing hips back and bending at the knees simultaneously. Aim for a squat depth where thighs are at least parallel (90°) with the floor.

Split Squat (Dumbbells)

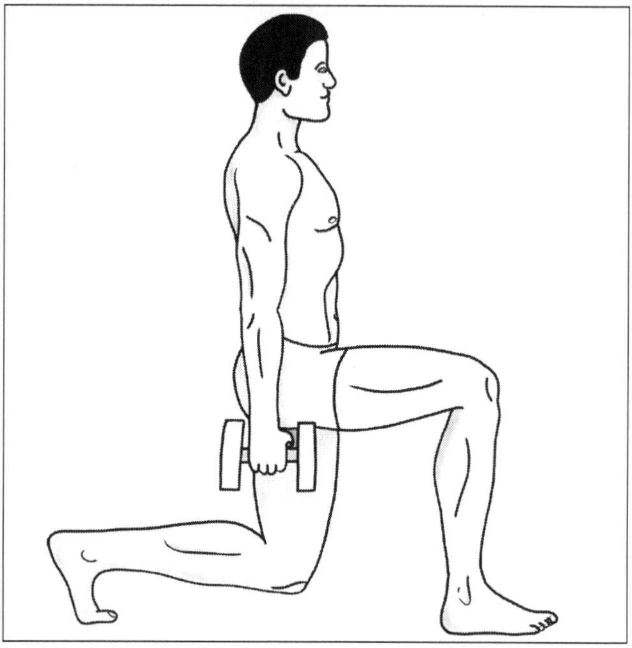

Coaching Cues:

Feet, shoulder-width apart, dumbbells to your side. Position front knee forward, while bending back knee towards the floor. Push through ball of front foot, contracting glutes and quads to drive back upwards to starting position and by extending the front knee.

Pull & Rowing Movements

Pull (horizontal and vertical) and rowing movements work the muscles of the upper back, along with the elbow flexors (biceps). Examples of pull and rowing exercises are:

1. Bent-Over Rows
2. Inverted Row.
3. Chin Ups
4. Lat Pulldown

Single Arm, Bent-Over Row (Horizontal)

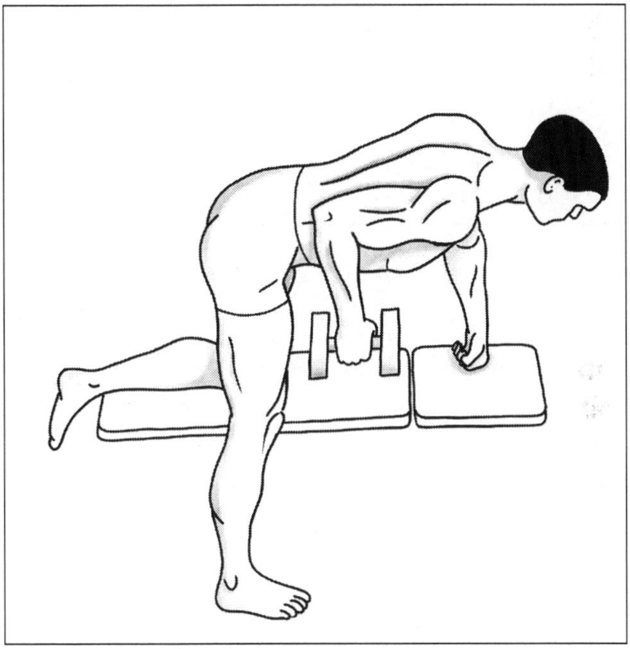

Coaching Cues:

With one leg supported on a bench, position other leg at hip level. Lean forward, keeping spine neutral. Brace core, retract shoulder blades and drive arm back, flexing at the elbow. Lower dumbbell to starting position in a controlled fashion.

Lat Pull Down (Vertical)

Coaching Cues:

Grip bar just outside shoulder-width with overhand grip. Lean back slightly and pull bar down and to the top of your sternum, driving elbows down towards your hips. Keep feet firmly on the floor, making sure that your glutes do not come off the seat at any time during the exercise.

Push & Press Movements

Push and pressing movements, work the muscles of the upper torso, including pectorals, deltoids and triceps. Examples of push and pressing exercises are:

1. Flat Chest Press.
2. Incline Chest Press.
3. Overhead (Military) Shoulder Press
4. Push Up

Flat Chest Press (Dumbbells)

Coaching Cues:

Position dumbbells down towards your chest and out to your sides at an angle. Press feet into floor, contract glutes, engage core and drive weights up and inwards towards the midline. Lower in a controlled fashion till weights are at chest height.

Shoulder Press (Dumbbells)

Coaching Cues:

Stand with feet shoulder-width apart. Brace core. Contract glutes. Press up dumbbells above shoulders, pushing upper arms towards your ears. Keep dumbbells parallel with floor. Lower weights in controlled fashion.

Beginners Program, 1 Week Sample: Lower Body/Upper Body (4-Day Weekly Split)

WEEK 1
DAY 1: Lower BODY

Exercise	Set	Rep	Rest *(mins)*	Notes
Body Squat	3	12	2	Feet shoulder-width apart. Breathe and brace core. Look straight ahead, torso upright. Push hips back and bend knees simultaneously to sit down into the squat. Avoid knees caving inwards. Drive heels into ground, push floor away, and accelerate through the lift to return to starting position.
Romanian Deadlift (Dumbbells)	3	12	3	Drive hips back behind and into hip flexion. Lower weights in a controlled fashion, keeping a soft break at the knees. Torso upright, chin tucked in. Brace core and maintain neutral spine.
Goblet Squat (Dumbbells)	3	12	3	Position dumbbell vertically on chest, bending elbows to hold like a goblet. Breathe in, engage core, then push hips back, bending knees to sit down into the squat. Look straight ahead, torso upright, spine neutral. Thighs should be parallel with the floor before, driving heels into ground to return to starting position

Leg Extension	3	12	2	Squeeze handles of machine to push down into seat, stabilizing pelvis. Keep lower back flush with the pad and extend at knees raising ankle pad with dorsiflexed ankles. Don't throw the weight up but focus on contracting the whole quad. Lower in controlled fashion.
Bodyweight Lunges	3	12	3	Feet, shoulder-width apart. Engage core and drive front knee forward in controlled fashion, while bending back knee towards the floor. Push through ball of front foot, contracting glutes and quads, to drive back upwards to starting position, by extending the front knee.

WEEK 1
DAY 2: Upper BODY

Exercise	Set	Rep	Rest *(mins)*	Notes
Press-Ups	3	10	3	Arms slightly wider than shoulder width and placed directly under shoulders. With soft elbows close to body, descend towards floor until chest and thighs touch the ground. Push back up through chest and triceps to ascend to starting position.
Lat Pulldown (Machine)	3	10	3	Lean slightly back, contract muscles of upper/mid back, and with palms faced down, pull bar down towards your sternum. Think about driving elbows into hips. Keep glutes glued to seat and feet firmly on the ground.

Chest (Dumbbell) Press	3	12	3	Position dumbbells down towards your chest and out to your sides at an angle. Press feet into floor, contract glutes, engage core and drive weights up and inwards towards the midline. Lower in a controlled fashion till weights are at chest height.
Back Row (Barbell)	3	12	3	Stand with mid-foot under the bar. Bend down driving hips back into flexion, keeping lower back neutral. With palms facing down, lift bar toward your chest, to row back pulling elbows behind body.
Triceps Pushdown (Ropes)	3	12	2	Keep chest proud and stabilize upper back. Lock elbows into sides, brace core and drive ropes towards waist. Do not flare elbows. When fully extended, pause to maximally contract triceps.

WEEK 1
DAY 3: Lower BODY

Exercise	Set	Rep	Rest *(mins)*	Notes
Goblet Squat (Dumbbells)	3	12	2	Position dumbbell vertically on chest, bending elbows to hold like a goblet. Feet shoulder-width apart. Breathe and brace core. Look straight ahead, torso upright. Push hips back and bend knees simultaneously to sit down into the squat. Avoid knees caving inwards. Drive heels into ground, push floor away, and accelerate through the lift to return to starting position.

Stiff Legged Deadlift (Dumbbells)	3	12	2	Drive hips back behind and into hip flexion. Lower weights in a controlled fashion, keeping stiff at the knees. Torso upright, chin tucked in. Brace core and maintain neutral spine.
Glute Bridge (Body weight)	3	12	3	Lie on back with knees bent and feet, hip-width apart, arms by your sides. Contract glutes and raise hips toward ceiling. Keep chin tucked in, and squeeze glutes tightly at top of the range. Lower hips down to the floor maintaining tension in glutes.
Leg Extension (Machine)	3	12	2	Squeeze handles of machine to push down into seat, stabilising pelvis. Keep lower back flush with the pad and extend at knees raising ankle pad with dorsiflexed ankles. Don't throw the weight up but focus on contracting the whole quad. Lower in controlled fashion.
Dumbbell Lunges	3	12	3	Feet, shoulder-width apart, a set of dumbbells in each arm. Engage core and drive front knee forward in controlled fashion, while bending back knee towards the floor. Push through ball of front foot, contracting glutes and quads, to drive back upwards to starting position, by extending the front knee.

WEEK 1
DAY 4: Upper BODY

Exercise	Set	Rep	Rest *(mins)*	Notes
Standing Shoulder (dumbbells) Press	3	10	3	Stand with feet shoulder-width apart. Brace core. Contract glutes. Press up dumbbells above shoulders, pushing upper arms towards your ears. Keep dumbbells parallel with floor. Lower weights in controlled fashion.
Lat Pulldown (Machine)	3	10	3	Lean slightly back, contract muscles of upper/mid back, and with palms faced down, pull bar down towards your sternum. Think about driving elbows into hips. Keep glutes glued to seat and feet firmly on the ground.
Chest (Dumbbells) Press	3	12	3	Place dumbbells down and out to your sides at an angle. Press feet into floor, contract glutes, engage core and drive weights up and inwards towards the midline. Lower in a controlled fashion till weights are at chest height.
Barbell Row	3	12	3	Stand with mid-foot under the bar. Bend down driving hips back into flexion, keeping lower back neutral. With palms facing down, lift bar toward your chest to row back, pulling elbows behind body.
Seated Biceps Curls (Dumbbells)	3	12	3	Press against seat pad and stabilise shoulders. With palms facing upward, curl dumbbell towards the shoulder, keeping shoulder still. Bring forearm into contact with upper arm. Finish curl by supinating at the wrist and squeezing little finger. Lower weight in controlled fashion.

CHAPTER 11

ANYONE FOR CARDIO?

"Run Forrest, Run."

Forrest Gump

It is early morning, January 1st, 2022. I am struck by the timeliness of writing this chapter as many people, buoyed up by hope, good resolutions and brand-new trainers will be heading out for a run shortly. Others will be signing up for gym memberships, joining dance and aerobic classes, or taking their first swim of the year. All in the name of losing weight.

And this can only be a good thing. After all, in terms of the global pandemic, all the evidence points to obesity and its related metabolic complications as serious risk factors for Covid 19 (1). In the same way, we know that increasing one's aerobic capacity may protect against pneumonia and acute respiratory distress syndrome (ARDS) (2), two commonly fatal disorders associated with Covid 19.

Cardiovascular exercise, be it running, swimming, cycling or even Zumba, undoubtedly develops cardiorespiratory, neuromotor and musculoskeletal fitness (3). There is also very strong data to support its role in psychological health and wellbeing (4). Nothing clears the head like going for a run in the fresh air!

Cardio and weight loss?

However, while the benefits of aerobic, cardiovascular exercise are compelling (5-6), its contribution to weight loss is more nuanced (7). Cardio undoubtedly burns calories and will, for some individuals, achieve weight loss (8). But weight loss from cardio alone without dieting is almost always much lower than expected (9).

Sometimes this is a consequence of simply overestimating calories burned. Which is easily done as activity trackers are notoriously inaccurate (10). But unwittingly, people also engage in compensatory behaviour, 'rewarding' their efforts for doing cardio by increasing food intake (11). Similarly, they may unconsciously decrease every day non-exercise activity (NEAT) (12), such as taking the stairs.

So, if cardio isn't the panacea for weight loss people think it is, why do it?

The etymology of "cardiovascular" is a combination of the Ancient Greek word *Kardia,* meaning heart, and *vascular* from the Latin 'vas' for vessel, which means 'relating to blood vessels.' And the benefits of regular cardiovascular exercise, for both heart and the blood circulatory system, are abundant.

> **Cardiovascular Exercise** depends on the cardiorespiratory system to supply oxygen and can be sustained continuously for an extended period.

Pertaining to the heart, cardio increases stroke volume, the amount of blood pumped during each contraction of the heart. It also increases cardiac output (13), the amount of blood the heart pumps in one minute. Critically, it helps improve our *resting* heart rate by decreasing it.

Pertaining to the circulatory system, cardiovascular exercise is a potent stimulus for improving arterial stiffness and the vascular dysfunction associated with aging and a sedentary lifestyle. It improves blood circulatory (vascular) flow, creates more blood vessels (angiogenesis) and increases capillary density, improving the transport of oxygen and nutrients to the muscle (14).

A healthy circulatory system also plays a role in building muscle, especially with age, as vascular dysfunction plays a significant role in anabolic resistance (15)—the blunted response to anabolic stimuli such as training and nutrition. However, our interest in cardiovascular exercise goes well beyond the realms of fitness, influencing the function and health of all organs and even the aging process itself (16).

Cardiovascular exercise improves our health at a cellular level, increasing oxygen flow and uptake to the cell's mitochondria. Mitochondria, the 'powerhouses' of the cell, are rod-shaped organelles which convert oxygen and dietary nutrients into energy. Improving cardiovascular fitness increases the number (density) of these mitochondria and the quality of the cell's mitochondrial function (17) which helps it become more efficient at producing energy.

BENEFITS OF CARDIO

- ✓ Increases oxygen flow to muscles and mitochondria.
- ✓ Increases myoglobin, the protein that stores and transports oxygen in muscle cell.
- ✓ Increases amounts of mitochondrial enzymes.
- ✓ Increases overall density of mitochondria in muscle tissue.
- ✓ Improves blood flow, creating more blood vessels to transport *more* oxygen.
- ✓ Increases stroke volume—the amount of blood pumped from the ventricle during each contraction of the heart.
- ✓ Increases cardiac output, or the volume of blood pumped by the heart each minute.
- ✓ Decreases resting heart rate.
- ✓ Aids muscle recovery, eliminating metabolic waste products

Cardio & Muscle?

All well and good, but what has this to do with building muscle?

Well firstly, while powerlifting is almost exclusively anaerobic, resistance training taxes the aerobic energy system more than most people realise. Indeed, training to momentary failure has even been shown to improve cardiovascular fitness (18). Building a more powerful aerobic system from cardiovascular training therefore enables you to go to failure more often, do more reps and recover better between sets and workouts. In short, doing cardio makes you better building muscle!

Yet traditionally, bodybuilders tend to avoid cardio like a strain of the bubonic plague for fear of losing their hard-earned muscle gains. *But is there any truth to these fears?*

The scientific term for combining strength training with cardiovascular exercise is "concurrent" training. And early studies into concurrent training seemed to validate concerns for muscle loss, revealing endurance training as detrimental to strength (19), muscle growth and power (20).

Certainly, strength training and cardiovascular exercise elicit very distinct adaptations—a result of competing physiological responses (21). But, while it is generally accepted that a high volume of endurance-based cardio will have 'interference' effects on muscle hypertrophy (22), when it comes to cardio and muscle loss the volume, type, duration, timing and even sequence (23) are all determinant factors.

A moderate amount of cardio is associated with very little of these blunting effects (24, 25). On the other hand, long distance endurance training may quickly become catabolic, negatively impacting on muscle gains (26). To understand this intuitively, one need only visit the athletics track and observe the differences in body composition between a sprinter and a long-distance runner. Long distance running especially, with its high impact and eccentric loading may cause excessive muscle damage, impinging on the recovery process.

> **Catabolic**—catabolic reactions break down complex molecules such as fat and muscle into simpler ones, releasing chemical energy.

First Things First. (*Cardio or Weights?*)

To minimise interference effects, cardio and weight training are best performed separately and if possible, on different days. If done on the same day, enough time should pass between the two exercise modalities to allow for recovery.

This was highlighted in a study from the French Federation of Rugby Union (27) which demonstrated that interference is largely dependent on the time allocated for recovery. The authors concluded that "coaches should avoid scheduling two contradictory qualities, *with less than 6-hour recovery b*etween them, to obtain full adaptive responses to concurrent training" (28).

While training on separate days or at separate times of the day is optimal, this may not always be practical for the general population. So, if pressed for time, *which should come first, cardio or weights?*

Here the research is unequivocal. Doing cardio first risks systemic fatigue and premature muscle loss. Common sense also dictates that it leads to lower training intensities for weight training, an impoverished training stimulus and the loss of strength gains (29,30). There are also some health-related benefits for doing light cardio after weights, as it can help improve vascular function and decrease arterial stiffness (31).

The Fat Burning Zone

Whilst it should be easy to appreciate the health benefits of doing cardio, most of those who take it up are often motivated by fat loss.

There is, however, an important difference between exercise which is *fat burning* and fat loss itself. Step on to any treadmill or bike and you will likely find yourself transfixed by a colourful chart, delineating different heart rate ranges. Steady state, low intensity cardio, between 55-65% of maximum heart rate (MHR) is clearly labelled the "*fat burning zone.*"

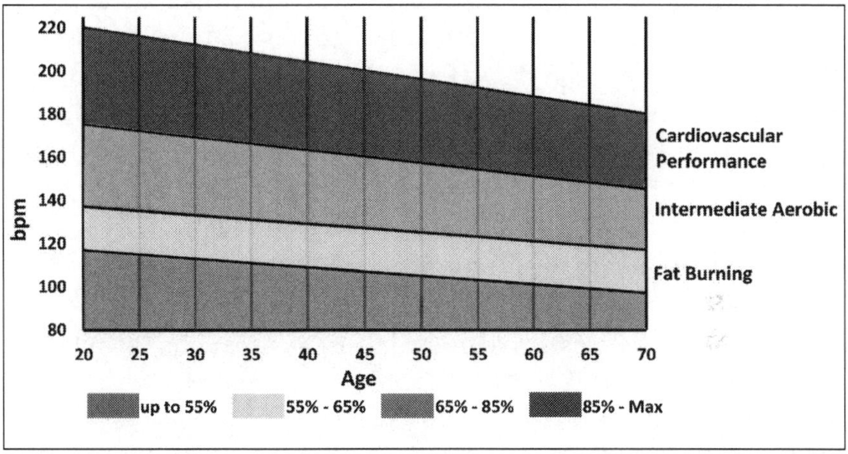

Adapted from Romijn et al; Relationship between fatty acid delivery and fatty acid oxidation during strenuous exercise. 1995. Journal of Applied Physiology.

Given this kind of cardio is not taxing, and you can feasibly watch an entire episode of your favourite box set, this is a popular option. Unfortunately, the "fat-burning zone", while strictly correct, is not a signpost to some mythical land where all fat loss is easy. Instead, it refers to a study by Dr Romijn (32), which demonstrated that cardio at lower intensities (<65 % MHR), burn a higher proportion of its calories from fat, rather than carbohydrates.

However, this "fat burning" zone of greater fat oxidation rates does not necessarily equate to more *total* calories being expended (33)—which is, ultimately, what fat loss is predicated upon (34). Rather, it simply indicates the energy being predominantly used (at lower intensities, fat) to fuel the exercise. Conversely, at higher exercise intensities, a greater percentage of carbohydrates and muscle glycogen is used.

Fasted Cardio

In the same way, fasted cardio also stimulates higher fat burning rates than exercise performed in the fed state (i.e., having eaten) 35). Nevertheless, spending hours on the treadmill in the "fat burning" zone, or doing fasted cardio, believing it superior for fat loss, ignores the dynamic nature of our metabolism which is continually adjusting (36). In fact, the research shows that, while we may use more fat as energy for fasted cardio, or exercise performed at lower intensities, this is compensated for by a greater use of carbohydrates later in the day (37).

High Intensity Interval Training (HITT)

Other variables to consider with cardiovascular training are intensity and duration.

Low intensity, steady state (LISS) cardio such as walking, or taking a leisurely bike ride has the advantage of burning some calories without taxing the nervous system. But endurance-based cardio of more prolonged duration may be catabolic and muscle wasting (26).

High intensity interval training (HITT), on the other hand, which alternates short periods of all-out, gut-busting intensity with periods of rest and recovery may preserve or even build muscle (38). This is likely related to its higher level of muscle fibre recruitment and ability to stress the more responsive, fast twitch Type II fibres (39). The metabolic demands of high intensity sprints, for example, are not dissimilar to resistance training, requiring force outputs from specific muscles.

Hormonal Response to HITT

HITT cardio may also create a more favourable muscle building, anabolic environment, acutely increasing circulating levels of growth hormone, insulin-like growth factor-1 (IGF-1) (40), total and free testosterone (41, 42). One noteworthy study involving master's (older) athletes showed that, by replacing high-volume aerobic training with low volume HITT training, peak power output improved, and levels of free testosterone increased (43).

HITT is also associated with an increase in the secretion of growth hormone (44) and catecholamines (45), which accelerate lipolysis and body fat loss. Catecholamines are a group of hormones secreted by the adrenal glands which include dopamine, norepinephrine and epinephrine (adrenaline).

Epinephrine drives fat loss from both subcutaneous and visceral (abdominal) fat stores. Interestingly, more *β*-adrenergic receptors are found in abdominal fat, compared to subcutaneous fat (46). This suggests HIIT may mobilise the abdominal fat stores we can't seem to shift with steady-state cardio.

> **Lipolysis** a metabolic pathway through which triglycerides are hydrolysed into a glycerol and three fatty acids. Mobilises stored energy during fasting or exercise.

Obesity and excess body fat are as we know related to several metabolic alterations including insulin resistance. High Intensity cardio also improves insulin sensitivity (47, 48) which positively impacts glucose control and on how we partition nutrients, driving them into the muscle for growth and fuel for exercise, rather than as fat storage.

Finally, HITT stimulates the release of hormones involved in appetite control. Studies have shown that a program of high intensity interval training can stimulate the secretion of the PYY hormone (49), which promote feelings of satiety after a meal while suppressing ghrelin, (50) often known as the "hunger hormone."

BENEFITS OF HITT FOR FAT LOSS

- ✓ Elevates metabolic rates post-exercise—possibly for up to 24 hours.
- ✓ Stimulates the secretion of growth hormone, increasing the use of fat for fuel.
- ✓ Improves nutrient partitioning—driving nutrients into the muscle for growth.
- ✓ Elevates catecholamine levels, hormones which stimulate lipolysis and mobilise abdominal fat stores.
- ✓ Increases insulin sensitivity, which improves glucose control and helps regulate metabolism.
- ✓ Stimulates secretion of appetite suppressing hormones, which may help regulate energy balance.

KISS goodbye to LISS?

With so many benefits to be derived from high intensity interval training and the popularity of sweat-soaked HITT classes, low intensity steady state training (LISS) has for many, become the poor relation of cardio. However, I don't recommend you kiss goodbye to LISS just yet.

Although HITT is an effective and time-efficient fat loss tool, it is also physiologically and neurologically demanding. If done too frequently, (e.g., more than 2-3 times a week) and concurrently with weight training, it may interfere with your recovery and muscle building efforts.

Low intensity, steady state cardio (LISS), on the other hand, such as walking uphill on a treadmill or a gentle bike ride for 35-50 minutes burns some calories, is low impact, does not fatigue and, by stimulating blood flow, can help the recovery process from weight training. It can also be done most days and that can have a cumulative, compound effect on weight loss. Not to mention heart health.

So, get those 10,000 steps in!

KEY TAKEAWAYS

- ✓ Do cardio! Walking, cycling, jogging—the exercise modality doesn't really matter. Pick one you enjoy and do it regularly.
- ✓ The goal is to lose fat, but also build and preserve muscle. So, avoid long distance endurance cardio. 35-50 minutes is sufficient.
- ✓ Be mindful that cardiovascular exercise is a tool and not a panacea for weight loss. Do it primarily because of its benefits for heart, respiratory, vascular and mitochondrial health.
- ✓ The "fat burning" zone or "fasted cardio" uses fat primarily as its fuel. What matters to fat loss, however, is how many calories you burn.
- ✓ High Intensity Interval Training (HITT) saves time and may help preserve muscle. Done correctly, it is also very demanding. Limit to 2-3 times per week.
- ✓ Low Intensity Steady State (LISS) cardio takes time but doesn't expend a lot of energy (calories). For that reason, you can do it almost every day (e.g., walking)—and this can have a cumulative effect on weight loss.

PART THREE
NUTRITION

"Man is What He Eats"

Lucretius

CHAPTER 12

IF IT FITS MY WHAT...?

"If we could give every individual the right amount of nourishment and exercise, not too little and not too much, we would have the safest way to health."

Hippocrates

In 2009, Eric Koenreich, a former professional wrestler, better known by his ring name Erick Stevens, unwittingly became the father of an eating movement known as IIFYM (*If It Fits Your Macros)* or flexible dieting. It quickly took off, firstly in bodybuilding circles and later in the evidence-based fitness community, endorsed by its leading lights, such as Alan Aragon and Dr Layne Norton, who affirmed the validity of its nutritional guidance.

> **Macros** abbreviated form of macronutrients: the nutrients we require in large amounts from protein, fats and carbohydrates.

Before IIFYM, when dieting for a competition, bodybuilders would routinely and obsessively (the personal stakes are high) ask coaches what and when they could eat: "*Can I have fruit after a workout?*" "*Is brown rice better than white rice?*" "*Do I have to eat broccoli?*" Exasperated by the minutiae of individual preferences informed by taste, bias and a hodgepodge of knowledge rooted in gym folklore, Erick began answering forum questions with what soon became a catch-all phrase, *"If it fits your Macros."*

The philosophical underpinning of Eric's advice embodied in this phrase is that, for fat loss and building muscle, getting the basics right and practicing them consistently, week in and week out, is what really matters. Certainly, the human body metabolises different foods differently. Sometimes it may even respond differently to the same foods, eaten at different times, for example, during and after exercise.

But taking a snapshot of metabolism at a given point in time and extrapolating *"the fastest way to burn fat,"* or *"the best way to do cardio"*, fails to consider how it may change over the next 24-48 hours. Unfortunately, many an overly restrictive diet or fitness regime has been launched on the back of these time-sensitive studies.

Camels and gnats?

So how do we avoid swallowing the camel, while straining out the gnat? How do we structure a sustainable diet, one that allows us to consistently lose fat but still go out for a meal with the family or have a drink with a mate, without fear of losing muscle gains overnight?

Charles Poliquin, the colourful and recently deceased Canadian strength coach, would say, "the basics are the basics, and you can't beat the basics." *But what are the basics of nutrition for fat loss and building muscle?*

Here, we take our cue from another Eric, Dr Eric Helms, Research Fellow and natural bodybuilder who, in his muscle and strength nutrition pyramid, illustrates a powerful hierarchy of nutritional priorities to achieve our body composition goals (1)

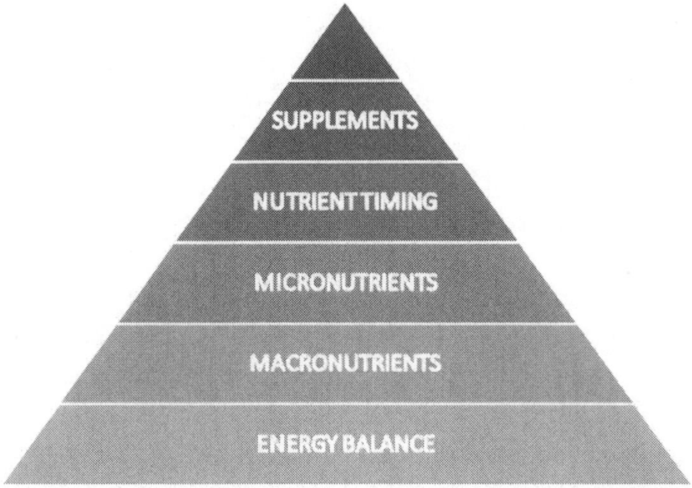

Adapted from The Muscle and Strength Pyramid, March 2019. Dr Eric Helms

Having experienced how difficult it is to make sense of the myriad misconceptions, myths and sometimes blatant *mis*information peddled by the fitness industry, this pyramid cuts through the confusion to provide clarity, structure and purpose. In the chapters that follow, we tackle these topics head on and give the reader a 'paint-by-numbers', guide on how to successfully structure a diet according to individual body composition goals.

Energy Balance

In "*It's the diet, stupid*", we tried to dispel the myth that somehow manages to prevail—namely that calories don't count. Instead, we confirmed a fundamental principle, enshrined in the laws of thermodynamics, that body weight changes are determined by energy balance (2).

Energy balance is the relationship between energy 'in', the food and drink we ingest as measured in calories, and energy 'out', the calories we expend throughout the day whether we are active or spend most of it on the sofa. Total daily energy expenditure (TFEE) includes the maintenance of the brain and the body at rest, the digestion of food, movement and physical activity.

It is important to remember that a calorie is simply a scientific unit for measuring energy. One calorie is the amount of energy required to raise the temperature of one kilogram of water by one degree Celsius. It does not have any magic or health conferring properties. It doesn't change either. 1 gram of protein will always contain 4 calories of energy, whether the source be the chicken or the egg.

First used by engineers in physics, the humble calorie found notoriety in nutrition where it is used to measure the amount of energy food contains. A single calorie, however, is such a small unit, that measuring even one item of food might involve counting into the tens of thousands. The calories you find on food labels are in fact Kilocalories (Kcal), with 1 Kilocalorie the equivalent of 1000 calories.

Energy Balance (CICO)

Energy balance refers to the "Calories in, Calories out" (CICO) equation.

When energy intake equals energy expenditure, the body is said to be in energy balance. For this to happen, an individual will be eating in a state of "maintenance." Maintenance calories are when the number of calories ingested are equal to those expended. Consequently, we remain at the same or current weight.

When energy intake exceeds energy expenditure, a state of *positive* energy balance occurs. In this state, body weight increases. If accompanied by a lack of exercise, increases in body mass can for some, be exponential (3). A positive energy balance requires eating in a calorie surplus. A calorie surplus is when the calories consumed are greater than those expended, leading to weight gain.

Finally, a *negative* energy balance ensues when energy expenditure exceeds energy intake. Consequently, we lose body mass. A negative energy balance is arrived at by eating in a calorie deficit. A calorie deficit is when the calories consumed are less than those expended. The body senses the energy 'deficit', forcing the body to draw upon fat reserves and causing weight loss.

Creating a calorie deficit is essential for weight loss. There are countless ways, diets and exercise regimes to help create a calorie deficit but without one, weight loss is impossible. Individuals respond uniquely to different diets or forms of exercise, but any factor which impacts body weight still acts through one or more component of energy balance (4, 5).

Determining Your Daily Calorie Intake

Our starting point for determining your daily calorie intake is the calculation of maintenance calories – the energy balance that produces no change in current body weight.

Maintenance calories amount to the energy required to fuel your total daily energy expenditure (TDEE). TDEE is made up of various components, the largest (60-80%) being accounted for by Basal Metabolic Rate (BMR). The next largest contributor to TDEE is an individual's activity levels.

Once we have established maintenance calories, we can adjust accordingly, creating a calorie deficit for fat loss or, as in the case for experienced lifters, a moderate calorie surplus to build more muscle.

Calculating your daily calorie intake is therefore a three-step process:

Step 1: Measure Basal Metabolic Rate (BMR)

BMR measures the number of calories burned at rest, to perform all the body's most basic functions such as breathing and circulation. It is sometimes referred to as Resting Energy Expenditure (RRE).

Fortunately, gifted mathematicians before us have devised different formulas and predictive equations to calculate BMR. Calculators for formulas such as the Harris-Benedict, Mifflin St Jeor, and the Katch McArdle, are easily found on the web. There are subtle differences in formulation, but they all provide a baseline target from which we can then estimate daily calorie intake.

In the example below, we use the Revised Harris Benedict formula method to measure BMR.

Revised Harris Benedict (Roza) Formula

This formula for calculating BMR, requires gender, age, height and weight as inputs. It is generally recommended that we measure weight first thing in the morning, having first used the bathroom.

Weight can fluctuate daily, due to water retention, stress or lack of sleep, but being regular about its recording will encourage consistency, along with the ability to monitor weekly and monthly progress, tracking trends over time. Using myself as an example, at the time of writing, I currently weigh 75.5 Kilos, or 166 pounds.

According to the online calculator www.active.com/fitness/calculators/bmr my BMR is 1,598 calories per day.

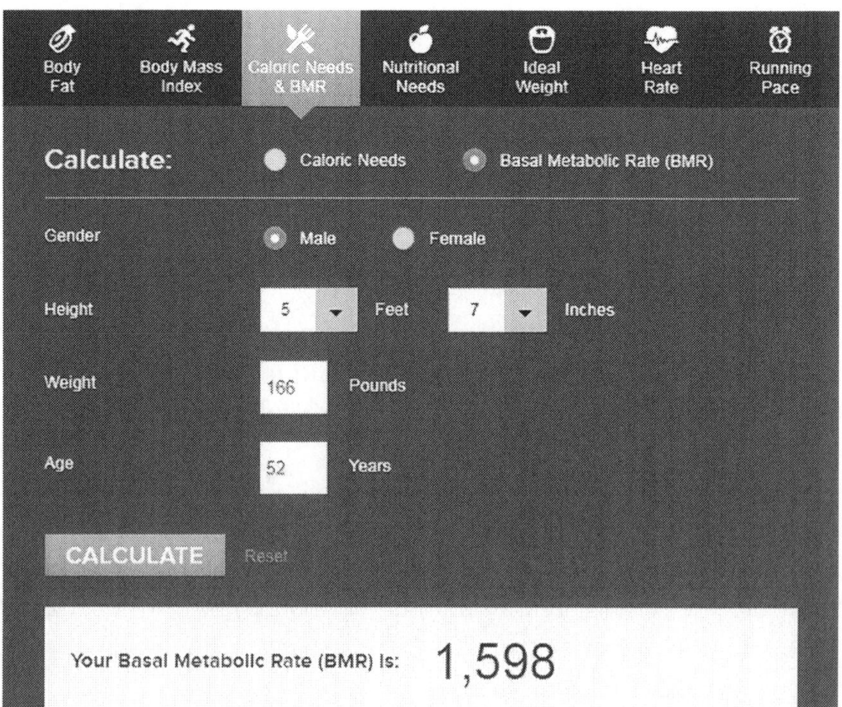

TOTAL DAILY ENERGY EXPENDITURE (TDEE)

TDEE is made up of various components, the largest (60-80%) being accounted for by **Basal Metabolic Rate (BMR).**

BMR measures the energy costs required at rest for metabolism and all the biological processes essential for life itself. Although technically different, BMR is often used interchangeably with the more self-explanatory term, Resting Energy Expenditure (RRE).

Factors which contribute to individual variations in BMR include age, gender, muscle mass, ethnicity, fitness levels, and other genetic and environmental influences (6, 7). The second largest contributor to Total Daily Energy Expenditure (TDEE), is 'non-resting' energy expenditure. This has several subcomponents.

a. Exercise Activity Thermogenesis (EAT)

The purposeful, planned exercise-related activities we engage in, such as going for a jog. This may range anywhere between 15-30% of our TDEE (8).

b. Non-Exercise Activity Thermogenesis (NEAT)

NEAT refers to energy expended by simply living and moving, such as getting up from your desk at work or walking round the supermarket. It also refers to any spontaneous activity beyond our voluntary control, such as fidgeting or toe-tapping. The cumulative impact of NEAT can be significant and may vary substantially between individuals of similar size (9).

c. Thermic Effect of Food (TEF)

The last component of TDEE (approximately 10%) is expended in digesting, absorbing and metabolising food. This process is referred to as the Thermic Effect of Food (TEF) or diet-induced thermogenesis.

Step 2: Calculate Daily Maintenance Calories

To estimate maintenance calories and TDEE, we multiply BMR by an activity multiplier. (See illustration below)

This activity multiplier, which may range from 1.2 b—2.2, considers how many calories are burned through purposeful exercise and physical activity. Occupation, lifestyle, how many times a week you exercise and with what intensity all play a role, but most people will fall into the ranges illustrated in figure 1.

BMR x Activity Multiplier = Daily Maintenance Calories
1,598 x 1.6 = 2,557 Calories

FIG. 1: ACTIVITY MULTIPLIER

Amount of Activity	Description	Activity Multiplier
Sedentary	Little or no exercise/desk job	1.2
Lightly active	Light exercise/ Sports 1-3 days/week	1.375
Moderately active	Regular exercise/ Sports 3-5 days	1.4 -1.6
Very active	Heavy Exercise/ Heavy Training 5-7 days	1.7 -1.8
Extremely active	Very heavy training/physical job/ training x2/day	1.9 -2.2

Step 3: Calculate Total Daily Calories

Having calculated maintenance calories, we can now determine your total daily calorie intake.

If the goal is fat loss, this means creating a caloric deficit. A caloric deficit, sustained over time, is key to any successful fat loss program. The extent of the caloric deficit and rate of weight loss is determined by baseline fat mass levels and body composition goal desired. For most people however, a moderate weekly weight loss target of 1-2 lbs (0.5-1kg) is a good place to start.

My body composition goal is to be stage-ready for a physique competition and lose 6kg (13.2 lbs) over 14 weeks. Whilst this means getting quite lean, I will also want to preserve as much muscle mass as possible. To that end, I will err on the conservative side, with a weekly rate of 1 lb per week or between 0.5-1% of bodyweight, as recommended by Helms et al (10). This rate also gives me some wiggle room to make sure I hit my target!

As a helpful rule of thumb, I lb (0.5 kg) of fat tissue contains approximately 3500 calories.

It follows that to reduce weekly intake by 3,500 calories we need to create a deficit of approximately 500 calories/ day, to lose 1 pound per week (i.e., 3,500 / 7 days = 500 Calories).

Maintenance Calories - Calorie Deficit = Daily Calorie Intake

2,577 Kcal (TDEE)—500 Kcal = <u>2,057 Kcals</u>

Determining Fat Loss rate (Fast v Slow)

My daily calorie intake target of 2057 Kcal amounts to a moderate 20% calorie deficit of maintenance calories.

Studies suggest that for those with a higher baseline fat mass, more aggressive caloric deficits may be advisable. Findings from trials which compared slow with faster weight loss (upwards of 1.5 Lb—2 Lbs/per week) (12, 13), have demonstrated that for the clinically obese larger initial weight losses are linked with greater long-term weight loss success (14—16).

For the very overweight and obese, losing scale weight quickly in the initial stages of a weight control program motivates participants to persevere (17) as they begin to see improvements in general appearance, body image and mobility (18).

Eat big to grow big?

The canon of bodybuilding tradition is full of pithy one-liners, which left unscrutinised, become immutable laws. "Eat big, to grow big" is one such gem. It led however to the widespread custom of 'dirty' bulking, whereby the goal of consuming calories was pursued at any cost, regardless of food quality, body fat gained, or damage done to metabolic health.

The kernel of truth in the phrase is that in order to build muscle, we need some periods where we are eating in a calorie surplus. Building muscle is an energy intensive process. The exception to the rule is the complete beginner, or someone returning to the gym after a long hiatus, when losing fat and building muscle while eating in a calorie deficit, remains a possibility.

Thankfully, fitness professionals now appreciate that gaining fat fast with an unrestricted 'dirty' bulk, while enjoyable at first, comes with unintended consequences such as impaired insulin sensitivity, lower testosterone levels and metabolic dysfunction (19). In this context, I thoroughly recommend a lean or "clean" bulk, where a calorie surplus is capped at 10% more calories than expended. This is the sweet spot for gaining muscle, while minimising unnecessary fat gain (20).

Final Considerations

This notwithstanding, in the final analysis, the calculation of a calorie surplus or deficit, even with sophisticated body fat measurements, is always an estimation. And such calculations are not set in stone. Metabolism is a moveable feast and fat loss, or muscle gain, will never be linear.

Estimations for daily calorie intake help us gather data about our direction of travel and are therefore a great place to start. But they are signposts, not the destination. So, they need to be tracked consistently, paying attention to trends over 1-2 weeks, not daily fluctuations before changing anything when the results we seek aren't forthcoming.

At the same time, we should verify that the data we are recording is correct. It is exceptionally easy to underestimate daily calories, forgetting to track that piece of birthday cake passed around at the office, or the olive oil poured generously over our salads! But we also need other ways of monitoring progress such as taking measurements (waist, chest, etc.) along with progress photos.

For example, it is entirely possible to be losing body fat and need to adjust notches in the trouser belt but see little movement on the scales. At these times, it is important to remember that the goal is not to reach some arbitrary number on the scale. The goal is to improve body composition through building lean muscle and losing body fat.

We are not a weight-watching club and becoming *skinny fat* is not the objective!

SHORT-CUT METHOD TO CALCULATE MAINTENANCE CALORIES

A quick method for estimating maintenance daily calories is to take your current weight in Lbs and multiply by the numbers below, which consider activity levels.

12/13: Sedentary
13/14: Lightly active
15/16: Active/ Very Active (Training 5+ times a week)

Example: (my maintenance calories)
166 lbs x 15 = 2,490 Cals

As you will have noticed, this figure is not a million miles away from the more in-depth calculation we did earlier of 2,577 Cals.

To calculate a deficit or a surplus of approximately 20%, we would simply subtract or add 500 calories to this number.

CHAPTER 13

THEN GOD CREATED PROTEIN

"Life is the mode of action of proteins."

Frederich Engels

"Macros", as we know, are short for macronutrients which are the proteins, fats and carbohydrates the body requires in larger amounts. Having determined our caloric intake in the previous chapter, the next piece of the nutritional puzzle is to partition these calories with optimally allocated grams of protein, carbohydrates and fats.

Anyone starting out seriously on their fitness journey quickly learns the importance of protein to building muscle. Even a cursory glance at fitness magazines reveals the two are practically synonymous. However, the current Recommended Dietary Allowance (RDA) for protein in healthy adults at 0.8 g/kg body weight/day (1), doesn't touch the sides of what is often recommended to build muscle.

Recommended Dietary Intake (RDA)

It is important to qualify that the current RDA of 0.8g protein per kg is an estimate of the *minimum* daily average recommended and was established for the purpose of avoiding protein deficiency. It was also derived from work with sedentary individuals using nitrogen balance (an outdated method for measuring muscle protein status) and not modified for sex, body fat percentage, lean muscle mass or importantly, individual activity levels.

Nor age either. Yet, as we learned in *"Where's the Beef?"*, sarcopenia can lead to the age-related loss of skeletal muscle mass at a rate of 3-8% per decade (2), and is a significant determinant of BMR (basal metabolic rate) (3).

Too much of a good thing?

In contrast, the International Society of Sports Nutrition (ISSN) recommends a much higher protein intake of 1.4- 2.0 g protein/kg bodyweight per day (4). The general population may consider this excessive, yet some bodybuilders—for whom more is often better—have been known to consume up to 4.3 g/kg of protein per day! (5)

So, for the purposes of building muscle, how much protein is too much protein? A recent, exhaustive review and meta-analysis of peer-reviewed research (6) suggests that optimal protein consumption for building muscle with resistance training falls between 1.6g/kg/day -2.2g/kg/day (0.7-1g/lb) (7, 8).

For younger adults, the anabolic effects of protein may begin to taper off at 1.8g/kg (0.82g/lb) (9). However, for older adults engaged in resistance training and seeking to build muscle or preserve it while dieting, it is advisable to shoot for the upper end of the range (2.2g/kg or 1 g/lb). Aging much like dieting is a catabolic, muscle wasting process (10, 11).

BODYWEIGHT V LEAN BODY MASS?

Almost all the research into macronutrient recommendations, calculates intake relative to body weight or as a percentage of total calories. This makes sense for carbohydrates and fats which are first line sources of energy. But protein is a metabolically expensive fuel and more optimally utilised for the repair and building of structural tissue.

In this context, some researchers suggest we calculate protein intake relative to one's own lean body mass. This method is ideal if you are very lean already, or conversely considerably overweight. In the former, protein calculations based on bodyweight may fall short, and in the latter, be unnecessarily high.

A systematic review of dietary protein for resistance trained athletes by Eric Helms et al, recommends 2.3-3.1g/kg of FFM (fat free mass) while dieting, the exact amount dependent on the severity of the caloric deficit and body composition (11). However, a problem for the general population, is that accurate, reliable and inexpensive methods of measuring lean body mass (bodyweight minus body fat) are not readily accessible.

A simple alternative, as suggested by researcher Alan Aragon, is to set protein intake relative to one's target weight, not current body weight, as a "surrogate measure of lean mass plus a small safety buffer" (12).

High protein diets: "*Are they safe*?"

The benefits of a high-protein diet (weight loss, improved body composition) are widely recognised (13, 14). Yet mainstream media consistently questions their safety, particularly with regards to kidney, liver and bone health.

The causes for this confusion are easily identified. Nitrogen, an essential element of amino acids, is derived from dietary protein intake and is excreted by the kidneys. For those already suffering from pre-existing kidney damage and renal disorders, restricted protein diets are sometimes recommended to limit the "energetic cost" to the kidney.

However, for the general population, with an otherwise healthy kidney function, there is simply no data in the literature to support the myth that higher protein diets can *cause* kidney dysfunction (15, 16). Indeed, a series of studies by Antonio et al. with protein intakes as high as 3.4g/kg did not impair renal function (17).

In the same way, there is no scientific evidence to support the contention that high protein diets have a detrimental effect on either liver function or bone health (18, 19).

Protein Absorption (The "Muscle-Full" Effect)

Another prevailing myth still doing the rounds is the body can only absorb a limited amount of protein at any one meal sitting. Around thirty grams seems to be the magic number.

While there is a limit to how fast the body can absorb protein (5-10 grams per hour), in absolute terms, there are no such limitations. The small intestine, where 95% or so of dietary protein is absorbed (20), has a great capacity to absorb and hold onto amino acids, extracting nutrients for its own regeneration, then releasing them into the bloodstream.

There is, however, an anabolic ceiling for muscle protein synthesis (MPS). Having hit this ceiling, protein synthesis then becomes refractory (resistant). And although it may still be absorbed, any protein consumed beyond this amount is surplus to muscle building requirements. This threshold on MPS is termed the "muscle full effect" (21).

But it is not an absolute, one- size-fits-all number. In younger males, 25 grams of protein (0.24g/kg/per meal) may do the job. Whereas, due to a blunted response from anabolic resistance, 0.4-0.6 g/kg of protein per meal (approx. 35-50 grams) may be required to achieve comparable results for those in midlife (22).

Protein Distribution

Amino acids, which are the building blocks of protein, are a potent regulator of muscle protein synthesis (23). In total, there are 20 amino acids. However, essential amino acids (EAA), of which there are nine, cannot be synthesised by the body in any significant amounts. Therefore, they must (essential) be obtained from the diet.

Among the essential amino acids, evidence points to a unique role for leucine. This branch-chained amino acid is responsible for the stimulation of muscle protein synthesis by activating the mTOR signalling pathway (24,25). The minimum threshold of EAAs needed to elicit muscle protein synthesis (MPS) gets higher with age. While 15 g of EAAs stimulates muscle protein anabolism in young and old alike (26), 7 g of EAAs falls short for mature adults (27).

This threshold is dependent on protein quality and its leucine profile, with a higher proportion of leucine required to stimulate muscle protein synthesis in older adults (28). For mature adults, the optimal intake estimated to ensure maximal protein synthesis is between 3-4.2 grams of leucine per meal (29, 30). This corresponds to roughly 35-50 grams of dietary protein, depending on the type and quality of protein ingested (31).

Leucine Content of various protein sources:		
Protein Source	**Leucine % of total protein**	**Required to reach 3-4 g of Leucine**
Whey Protein	12%	25-33 g
Casein	9.3%	32-43g
Egg	8.6%	35-47g
Fish	8.1%	38-50g
Beef	8.0%	38-51g
Chicken	7.5%	41-54g
Wheat	6.8%	44-59g

Adapted from "Optimal protein intake and meal frequency to support maximal protein synthesis and muscle mass", Layne Norton, B.S. University of Illinois. June 14, 2008 (31)

However, muscle protein synthesis is transient in nature. Although blood amino acids may remain elevated for longer, following a meal protein synthesis itself lasts only 3-4 hours. (32). To this end, I recommend 3-5 quality protein meals evenly spread throughout the day (33, 34). This kind of protein dosing provides more opportunities to trigger muscle protein synthesis and help overcome the catabolic effects of anabolic resistance (35).

OPTIMAL PROTEIN RECOMMENDATIONS FOR MUSCLE GROWTH (OVER 40S)

- ✓ Optimal daily protein consumption falls between 1.6g/kg—2.2g/kg/day. Lifters over 40 should target the upper end of this range (1g/lb or 2.2g/kg) for maximising muscle growth and possibly even more, when dieting.
- ✓ The overweight, obese, and very lean individuals might consider setting protein intake relative to lean body mass, not bodyweight.
- ✓ Optimal protein distribution is evenly spread, with 3-5 meals (depending on total protein intake) throughout the day.

✓ Aim for 35-50 grams of a high-quality protein per meal, which will deliver 3-4 grams of leucine—optimal for triggering muscle protein synthesis.

Protein Quality

When it comes to building muscle, not all protein is created equal.

The nutritional value of different proteins may vary quite widely. The important variables are its essential amino acid (EAA) profile and "digestibility." The protein digestibility-corrected amino acid score (PDCAAS) was adopted by the FAO/WHO, as the preferred method for measuring protein value in human nutrition.

In terms of EAA profile, leucine is the master regulator of muscle protein turnover (23, 36), and as such, the ingestion of proteins enriched with this amino acid, should be prioritised. Leucine is critical for kick-starting protein synthesis (37), but its complete metabolism does require the availability of other essential amino acids, such as isoleucine and valine (38).

Quality protein sources that contain high proportions of leucine are beef, lean meats, fish, eggs and dairy-based products such as whey and casein. Indeed, whey has one of the highest percentages of leucine content, with approximately 12% leucine per gram of protein.

Animal products, such as steak, have high levels of leucine.

Plant-based v Animal sources of protein

It is important to note that plant-based sources of protein produce a lower anabolic, protein synthetic response, when compared to animal-based proteins (39, 40). This is largely due to differences in essential amino acid (EAA) profile (Fig. 1). Calorie for calorie, plant-based proteins have lower amounts of leucine, isoleucine and valine (41), which are vital for muscle building.

Plant-based proteins also tend to have "limiting amino acids", EAAs which are present in such small amounts they limit the rates of protein synthesis. Cereal grains, along with nuts and seeds for example, have lysine as a limiting amino acid (42). Beans and legumes on the other hand lack sufficient methionine and cysteine.

FIG 1 EAA concentrations of various protein sources. Differentiation is made between plant- and animal-based proteins.

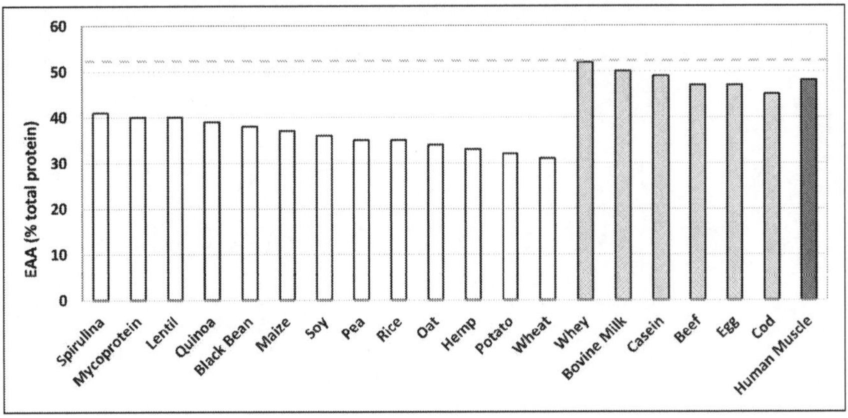

Adapted from The Journal of Nutrition, Volume 145, Issue 9, September 2015, Pages 1981–1991

Plant-based proteins also have lower digestibility than animal-based proteins. The digestibility of the protein source is defined as the proportion of amino acids that can be effectively digested and absorbed by the body (43). Animal based protein sources (eggs, meat, dairy) are highly digestible, with a digestibility rate higher than 90%, but plant-based proteins considerably less so (44).

These differences may limit the anabolic response and lower protein synthesis rates. A randomised crossover trial conducted with middle aged men demonstrated a dairy-protein rich breakfast activates the mTOR signalling pathway essential for triggering muscle anabolism, while a soy-rich breakfast does not (45). More comprehensively, a meta-analysis and systematic review found animal proteins favour greater gains in lean muscle mass over plant-based proteins (46).

This is not to say a plant-based lifestyle is completely incompatible with building muscle. There are workarounds. Combining foods with complimentary essential amino acid profiles is one such method. Supplementation with a protein powder such as pea protein, which is high in leucine and well digested, is another.

Nevertheless, there are some inherent nutritional challenges to this lifestyle which any vegetarian serious about building muscle would do well to recognise.

Digestion Rates

The speed of protein digestion and absorption of amino acids by the gut also varies according to the source of dietary protein. It is common to classify carbohydrates as slow and fast, but the varying speeds of protein absorption may also impact the metabolic, hormonal and anabolic response to a meal (47).

In this context, the digestion and absorption rates of different proteins are a variable we should consider when choosing our protein sources, but especially in midlife, when we may experience an age-related decrease in gastric emptying rates (48). For example, whey protein is more quickly digested and absorbed than casein, stimulating a faster and greater protein synthetic response in older adults (49,50).

Moral of the story?

Understanding exactly how much, but also the quality of protein in your diet is crucial to your success.

CHAPTER 14

FAT: THE GOOD, THE BAD, AND THE VERY UGLY

"Those who think they have no time for healthy eating will sooner or later have to find time for illness."

Edward Stanley

The popularity of the Ketogenic Diet has made dietary fat fashionable. Where once fat was considered the enemy, and "low in fat" was the food label most prized by the health conscious, coffee with melted butter, poached eggs and smashed avocado now adorn the carefully curated Instagram accounts of the "Keto-fit."

The Ketogenic diet is designed to create a state of ketosis, whereby the body, in the absence of glucose, converts fat into compounds known as ketones. After a period of adaptation, these carbon-oxygen molecules when produced by the liver, replace glucose to become the body's primary source of energy.

The ketogenic diet was first proposed by Dr. Henry Geylin, an endocrinologist, at the annual meeting of the American Medical Association in 1921 as a way of treating epileptic seizures (1). Taking his lead from the ancient Greeks who employed fasting to manage epileptic episodes, he discovered that the physiological changes that occur on fast-falling blood glucose levels accompanied by a rise in ketones—can be obtained on a high fat, very low carbohydrate diet.

The ketogenic diet may have other therapeutic uses outside of epilepsy but in recent times it has become popular as an effective diet for weight loss. And make no mistake, as a fat loss diet, it works (2). But not as some would have us believe, due to intrinsic magical properties which somehow confound the laws of thermodynamics, or because fat is non-insulinogenic (which is true) but rather because it facilitates the creation of a calorie deficit. Limiting an entire food group (carbs) to 50 grams will do that for you!

> **Insulinogenic**: stimulating the production of insulin

Similarly, as 20-25% of the diet comes from protein and 70% from fat, the ketogenic diet also produces satiety—the physical feeling of fullness followed by suppression of hunger. Indeed, this appetite-suppressing (3) combination of protein and fat is one reason why fat loss on the ketogenic diet can, for some, feel effortless. Anecdotally, keto lovers also speak of a lifting of mental fogginess and accompanying mental clarity. All good things.

Interestingly, the Keto diet is also protein sparing, which aids the conservation of lean muscle mass (4). The production of ketones spares blood glucose, reducing the need for gluconeogenesis—the conversion of amino acids (protein) to glucose. Ketones, along with oxidised fatty acids, can also be used as fuel for low intensity activities (5, 6).

If the Keto diet is appetite suppressing, elicits fat loss and is muscle sparing, *what's not to like?*

Well, in the first instance, not everyone can adhere to a diet where fat constitutes 70% of the daily calorie intake. That's a whole lot of bacon, cream and cheese! Personally speaking, I develop enormous cravings for fruit. Less obviously, while the Ketogenic diet is effective for fat loss and the preservation of skeletal muscle, its ability to build lean muscle tissue is largely unproven.

The research supporting Keto for building lean body mass is not compelling. To date, there is only one study, much heralded by Keto enthusiasts, which reported gains in lean muscle for resistance trained males (7). It should be noted however, that even these results were reported after the reintroduction of carbohydrates.

On balance, the studies observe fat loss and considerable conservation of muscle, but without significant increases in lean mass (8, 9, 10, 11). Little wonder a recent narrative review concluded, "caution should therefore be taken when maintaining a Ketogenic Diet...*when increases in muscle mass* and performance are sought" (12).

Role of Dietary fat

So, the skinny on Keto aside, what role does dietary fat play in a balanced, healthy diet optimal for building muscle?

Dietary fat is an essential macronutrient. It is a vital form of energy, the most concentrated source of all the macronutrients, providing 9 kcal per gram consumed. If not used, it may be stored in the body as fat tissue, under the skin as subcutaneous fat or around the organs as visceral fat. These fat deposits can then be released as fatty acids to meet energy demands as required.

Fats, however, are not just a source of energy. They are indispensable for the optimal functioning of the human body, its growth and development. They function as structural building blocks of the body. The membranes around the cell, for example, which control the movement and uptake of substances in and out of the cell, are comprised of fat. Dietary fat also serves as a carrier for the fat-soluble vitamins, A, D, E and K, supporting their absorption in the intestine.

SATURATED, POLYUNSATURATED, MONOUNSATURATED...?

Body fat itself comes predominantly in the form of triglycerides which are carried in the blood and stored in fat cells.

Triglycerides are composed of a glycerol backbone, to which three fatty acids are attached. At a chemical level, fatty acids have a similar structure, made up of a chain of carbon atoms bonded together.

The differences in length and shape of the chain determine whether a fatty acid is "saturated" or "unsaturated" and define its characteristics – its form, melting point and digestibility. Butter for example is a saturated fat which is solid at room temperature. It is "saturated" with a maximum number of hydrogen atoms, attached to each carbon atom.

Polyunsaturated fats, (PUFAs) have two or more carbon-to-carbon double bond and are found in high concentrations in fish, walnuts, flax seeds and certain plant oils.

Monosaturated fats on the other hand, are missing a pair of hydrogen atoms. Their chemical structure keeps monounsaturated fats, such as olive oil, liquid at room temperature.

Omega 3s

Polyunsaturated fats, (PUFAs) come in two forms: omega-3 and omega-6 fatty acids.

Both EPA (eicosapentaenoic acid) and DHA (docosahexaenoic acid) are Omega 3 polyunsaturated fats with an abundance of health benefits (13). They play an important role in blood clotting, anti-inflammatory processes (14) and are essential for foetal development and healthy aging

(15). The brain itself is very rich in fat, the Omega-3 docosahexaenoic acid (DHA) being its main structural component (16).

These longer chain Omega 3 fatty acids, EPA and DHA, are not easily synthesised by the body. They are therefore said to be "conditionally essential." For this reason, it is recommended to consume them directly in one's diet. The richest dietary sources of EPA and DHA polyunsaturated fats are marine-based oils from fish such as salmon, tuna, anchovy and mackerel (17).

Western Diets & Inflammation

Unfortunately, while both are important, the typical Western diet has an imbalanced intake of Omega-6 fatty over Omega-3 fatty acids. This can lead to inflammation, as a high omega-6 fatty acid diet inhibits the anti-inflammatory effects of Omega 3 fatty acids (18).

However, rather than purposefully trying to avoid foods with high Omega 6:-3 ratios (e.g., nuts!) as suggested in some quarters, our focus should simply be to increase omega-3 intake from dietary sources and marine-based supplementation. This will help redress any imbalances (19) while positively impacting cognitive function, joint health, cardiovascular health (20) and even body composition (21).

Fish oil consumption has even been shown to stimulate protein synthesis and gains in muscle mass in older adults, by helping overcome age-induced anabolic resistance (22). The cardio-protective benefits of a Mediterranean diet, rich in monounsaturated fats like olive Oil and Omega-3 polyunsaturated fats from oily fish, are similarly well-founded (23, 25).

Staples of the Mediterranean Diet

The C-Word

If Omega-3 monounsaturated and polyunsaturated fats represent the “good”, *what of the bad and the very ugly?*

In 1970, The Seven Countries Study By Ancel Keys (26) Found A Significant Correlation Between High Saturated Fat Intake, High Blood Cholesterol Levels, And Heart Disease Mortality Was Observed (27, 28).

As A Result, Dietary Fat Of All Types Became Indiscriminately Demonised And The Reduction Of *Total* Fat In The Diet Became The Bedrock Of Western Government Recommendations (29) For Both Weight Loss And Reducing The Risk Of Cardiovascular Disease. Saturated Fat And Dietary Cholesterol However Were Reserved A Special Place In The Public's Imagination As “Bad.”

Nevertheless, cholesterol plays a vital role in how the body works. Indeed, 80% of cholesterol is synthesised in the body by the liver and intestines. Cholesterol is found in *every* cell of the body as part of its membrane. It is used to make Vitamin D and bile which helps digest fats. Significantly for the midlife male, cholesterol is the precursor to the synthesis of all steroid hormones, including testosterone.

Cholesterol travels through the blood, attached to proteins known as "lipoproteins." Low-density lipoproteins (LDLs) are the villain of the piece, as they build up on the artery walls of blood vessels as plaque, constricting the vessels which allow blood to pump from the heart and flow to other organs. High-density lipoproteins (HDLs) or 'good' cholesterol absorbs LDL cholesterol, carrying it back to the liver where it can be flushed out of the body (30).

In this context, advice to lower *blood* plasma levels of cholesterol, in particular LDL cholesterol still holds good. Indeed, the Consensus Panel of the European Atherosclerosis Society recently stated that "*consistent evidence from numerous and multiple different types of clinical and genetic studies unequivocally establishes that LDL causes atherosclerotic cardiovascular disease*" (27).

Improving the ratios of HDL to LDL may also help reduce the risk of heart disease (31). Those staples of the Mediterranean diet, such as Olive Oil, oily fish, nuts and high fibre fruit (32) along with unrefined whole grain complex carbohydrates like oatmeal, have been observed to lower LDL levels and improve those ratios. But confusingly, *dietary* cholesterol in and of itself, does not contribute to increases in blood cholesterol levels and the risk of heart disease (33, 34).

The confusion exists because dietary cholesterol is often associated with an increased intake of saturated fatty acids. Saturated fats as we know, *can* increase LDL cholesterol blood plasma levels (35), and therefore are associated with a higher *risk* of heart disease. But eggs and shrimp, for example, are dietary sources of cholesterol which are low in saturated fat.

While not all heart disease mortality is statistically associated with high blood cholesterol levels (36), the evidence that saturated fat may increase the *risk* factors of heart disease is somewhat compelling (37, 38). Therefore, recommendations based on a review by the UK government's Scientific Advisory Committee on Nutrition (SACN) to restrict saturated fats to 10% (39) bear consideration.

But context is everything. Dark chocolate for example is high in saturated fat, but rich in polyphenols, which are antioxidants associated with cardiovascular health. A grass-fed steak, while a source of saturated fat, is quite different to processed meat and is rich in iron, zinc and selenium.

Indeed, a recent meta-analysis showed that even >3 servings of red meat showed no negative effects on blood lipids or LDL cholesterol (40). Similarly, a low carb diet consisting of red meat, nutrient dense foods and high vegetable intake, although consisting of up to 18% saturated fat, improved overall lipid profiles (41).

HEART HEALTHY

The Mediterranean diet is associated with many health benefits, including protection against the development of inflammatory and cardiovascular diseases (42).

A "Mediterranean diet" refers to the traditional way of eating in the olive tree-growing countries of the Mediterranean basin. Whilst it may vary slightly, it involves the generous consumption of fruits, vegetables, legumes, whole grain cereals, fish and moderate amounts of poultry, dairy and meat.

It is also characterised by moderately high fat intake (30-40% of total energy). However, this is derived from a high ratio of monounsaturated fatty acids and *n*-3 PUFAs, relative to saturated fats, due to the liberal use of olive oil, fish, nuts and seeds (43). The cardio-protective effects of Extra Virgin Olive Oil are due to its phenolic compounds, powerful antioxidants such as hydroxytyrosol and oleuropein (44), which are also responsible for its bitter taste.

Central to the heart-healthy credentials of the Mediterranean diet is how it improves high-density lipoprotein (HDL) function. HDLs help absorb and transport "bad" cholesterol (LDL's) to the liver for elimination (45). They are also antioxidative and anti-inflammatory.

Similarly, they stimulate the production of nitric oxide (46) as mediated by endothelial cells (which form the lining of blood vessels). Nitric Oxide is vital for the repair of skeletal muscle and plays an important role in the protection against cardiovascular disease (47).

And replaced with what?

But the review by the SACN (May 2018) entitled, "Saturated Fats and Health" (39) also highlighted the importance of what should replace saturated fat. As a result of the focus to reduce *total* fat for cardiovascular disease, an unforeseen consequence was the increased consumption of *refined* carbohydrates and added sugars (48). Total fat consumption has certainly gone down, but only to be accompanied by increases in both total energy intake and obesity rates (49, 50).

Replacing saturated fat with complex carbohydrates from *whole* grains such as oatmeal, rather than refined grains is on the other hand, associated with a reduced risk of heart disease (51). Similarly, the substitution of saturated fat by polyunsaturated, Omega-3 rich fats to lower blood cholesterol levels and reduce cardiovascular risk is supported by a whole raft of research (52, 53, 54).

Unfortunately, such salutary changes to global eating habits didn't occur. Instead, the market became flooded with cheap, refined carbohydrates and added sugars. And consequently, carbohydrates of all hues and colours (including fruit!) became the macronutrient enemy *du jour.*

The Very Ugly

Incorporating "good" cardio-protective monounsaturated fats (e.g., olive oil) and Omega 3 polyunsaturated fats (e.g., salmon), while keeping an eye on the total intake of potentially "bad" saturated fat, makes for a balanced approach towards dietary fat.

The fats however to be avoided, and the truly ugly are trans-fats. Hydrogenation, which converts liquid unsaturated fat into a solid fat by adding hydrogen, is a process which helps food companies preserve shelf life. But during this process of partial hydrogenation, trans-fats are made.

Trans-fats are found in highly processed foods, the deep fried and battered, baked goods, cakes, pies and margarines. These partially hydrogenated oils affect heart health by increasing LDL "bad" cholesterol, but also by lowering "good" HDL cholesterol. Trans-fats are similarly associated with arrhythmia, systemic inflammation, and insulin resistance (55).

Calculating Total Fat Intake

While keeping saturated fat under 20% of our daily intake seems prudent, what of total daily fat consumption? What should we be aiming for?

Dietary guidelines from the World Health Organization have of late, not set upper limits of total fat intake, but rather placed the emphasis on the types of fat consumed and healthy dietary patterns (56). They do however recommend a minimum intake of 20% for energy production and the ingestion of essential fatty acids. Keeping dietary fat lower than 20% of total daily energy intake is also not advisable as it may lower testosterone levels (57, 58).

Indeed, recent research published in The Journal of Steroid Biochemistry and Molecular Biology found that low fat diets may decrease men's testosterone levels by 10-15% (59). Fatty acids are, if you recall, substrates for cholesterol synthesis, which is the precursor for testosterone production. It makes sense therefore that a diet higher in fat (≥30%) increases testosterone levels (60).

In this context, I always recommend that dietary fat represent at least 30% of total calorie intake for mid-lifers.

CHAPTER 15

CARBOHYDRATES & MIDDLE AGE: FRENEMIES?

"Food is the only beautiful thing that truly nourishes."

Will Keane (Richard Gere) 'Autumn in New York'

When I first set out on the journey to transform my physique, I imitated the nutrition protocols of famous bodybuilders who graced the covers of magazines like Muscle & Fitness. With iron-clad discipline they would eat industrial size portions of carbs, mainly rice and sweet potato, with every Tupperware meal. Post-workout, they would similarly neck down fast-digesting, high-glycemic carb drinks composed of glucose or maltodextrin.

Such practices were founded on the prevailing belief that insulin is anabolic and, as carbs stimulate insulin secretion, the more, the better. The net result for me, however, was fat gain. My own Damascene moment was stumbling upon an article by Dr Layne Norton entitled, "Anabolic eating for your age" (1).

> **Anabolic** growth promoting: the set of metabolic pathways which build larger molecules from smaller ones. Muscle Protein Synthesis is an anabolic process.

The penny dropped. Carbohydrates, while anabolic and growth promoting for the young, become less so with age. Indeed, young people are so receptive to the effects of insulin that ingesting carbohydrates alone (without additional protein) is sufficient to stimulate protein synthesis (2). However, the same anabolic effects are not observed in more mature adults (3).

The difference in anabolic response to carbohydrates is associated with insulin resistance and a so-called, 'carbohydrate intolerance' (4).

Insulin Resistance

In healthy individuals insulin, which promotes the storage of nutrients, helps stabilise blood sugar levels by increasing the uptake of glucose from dietary carbohydrates into fat cells, the liver and muscle. In fact, skeletal muscle accounts for approximately 75% of glucose uptake from the blood after a meal (5). At the same time, insulin supresses glucose production by the liver and inhibits the breakdown of protein and fats into circulation.

However, with age, excess body fat and muscle loss, our ability to regulate blood sugars diminishes (6).

An insulin 'resistance' develops, whereby the body's cells grow less sensitive to the effects of insulin. Glucose uptake into the muscle slows (7), the suppression of liver glucose production is delayed, and as a result, more glucose remains in the blood stream. As blood sugar levels rise, the compensatory increases in insulin production become less and less effective (8). A vicious circle ensues with the body's ability to partition nutrients and store excess fat compromised.

The cause of this decline in carbohydrate metabolism is multifactorial. But a significant factor is muscle loss, having a direct impact on blood glucose control and insulin resistance (9, 10). Conversely, building a greater muscle mass through resistance training is associated with improved insulin sensitivity (11), better glycemic profiles (12) and metabolic health (13).

In a very real sense you can, as the legendary Olympic Coach Charles Poliquin used to say, "earn your carbs."

Carbs. *What are they good for...?*

Followers of the Ketogenic diet adhere to a very low carb regime (under 50g). Diehards of the carnivore diet, however, question the necessity of carbs altogether. And in the strictest sense, they are right. Aside from being less anabolic with age, carbohydrates, unlike proteins and essential fats, are not necessary for survival. The brain and red blood cells undoubtedly require glucose, but this can be derived from protein and fat (triglycerides) via gluconeogenesis.

> **Gluconeogenesis:** the synthesis of glucose from noncarbohydrate precursors, such as amino acids (protein) providing glucose when dietary intake is insufficient or absent.

In this context, national guidelines to structure diet around 50-55% of total daily calories from carbohydrates (14) is counter intuitive, or at the least unhelpful for an aging and sedentary population who needs to lose weight. The same goes for Public Health England's Eatwell Guide (15) and its advice to *"base meals on potatoes, bread, rice, pasta or other starchy carbohydrates."*

When people talk of giving up carbs, they are of course referring to 'starchy carbohydrates' like potatoes, bread and pasta. But they also think of cakes, crisps, donuts and chocolate bars. These, however, are a hedonistic mixture of carbs, fat and added sugars. At the other end of the spectrum, many are unaware that fruits and vegetables contain carbohydrates. Yet these are vital sources of vitamins, antioxidants and minerals, critical to growth, bone health, immune function and energy production.

Consequently carbohydrates, although not essential for survival, do possess unique properties which contribute to our overall health. They also provide readily available energy for strong performances in the gym. These twin criteria—having enough fuel in the tank for training and optimising health—informs my approach to carbs which is moderately low, relative to total calories and strategic in terms of quality and timing. (See Chapter "Nutrient Timing")

CLASSIFYING CARBS: SIMPLE & COMPLEX

Carbohydrates are sugars or saccharides. Depending on their chemical structure and how quickly they are digested and absorbed, they are often classified as simple or complex carbohydrates.

Simple carbohydrates are composed of just one or two sugars:

Monosaccharides, such as the glucose and fructose found in honey and fruits, are single sugars and examples of a simple carbohydrate.

Disaccharides made up of two sugars, such as the lactose found in milk, are also simple carbohydrates. Sucrose, commonly known as table sugar is made up of glucose and fructose, in equal parts.

Glucose is also the building block of starches, joining together in long chains to form complex carbohydrates. **Complex carbohydrates** are composed of three or more sugars.

The most abundant complex carbohydrates found in nature are **polysaccharides** (*many~* sugars). Starch, glycogen and cellulose are common examples.

Starches are found in nutrient-rich foods like oats, root vegetables, beans, lentils, and whole-grain breads and cereals, but also in the highly refined, nutrient-poor foods we love to eat (and overeat) such as crisps, French fries, biscuits and cakes.

Dietary fibre

Generally, carbohydrates are first broken down into single sugars like glucose before entering circulation. All that is, except dietary fibre.

Fibre cannot be broken down by the digestive enzymes of the small intestine. And dietary fibre, such as we find in whole grains, has many proven health benefits including lowering cholesterol levels, improved blood lipid metabolism, greater glycaemic control and insulin sensitivity (16,17), as well as increased satiety (18). It is also associated with a lower risk of both cardiovascular disease and coronary heart disease (19).

Satiety characterised by the absence of hunger; it is defined as the inhibition of further eating following a meal.

Insoluble fibre, of the kind we find in wheat bran, vegetables and wholegrains, adds significant bulk to food and aids regularity of bowel movements. Soluble fibre, the type found in oats, barley, beans and lentils and some fruits, improves blood glucose and insulin sensitivity, delaying the intestinal absorption of the digested sugars.

Additionally, dietary fibre intake may also reduce chronic inflammation, interacting beneficially with the gut. Chronic low-grade inflammation is, as we know, intimately linked to the aging process (20).

High-in-fibre whole-grain foods and fruits are rich in bioactive compounds with anti-inflammatory properties such as antioxidants (21).

Overall dietary intake of fibre for adult males living in Europe averages around 18-24 grams per day. We should be aiming for more like 30-35 grams per day (22).

Oats, high in the soluble fibre beta-glucan, may help reduce cholesterol.

Glycemic Index (GI)

A high dietary fibre content is associated with complex carbohydrates and to a varying degree, low-glycemic (GI) foods.

The glycemic index ranks different foods according to the impact it has on blood sugar levels. The ranking is relative to pure glucose, which has a value of 100, while white bread for example has a high GI value of 75. Dietary glycaemic load (GL) meanwhile, considers both the GI and the serving size, as the total amount of carbohydrate in a food affects blood sugar concentrations and insulin secretion (23).

Originally designed to help with diabetes management, the "GI Diet" encourages the consumption of complex carbohydrates, high in fibre, such as whole grains, oats, lentils and beans. It advises against the overconsumption of more refined "high GI" carbs, such as white bread. Overly processed, refined carbs produce high blood sugar spikes and desensitise the body to the effects of insulin. Over time, these spikes may contribute to oxidative stress and chronic low-grade inflammation (24).

All sound advice. And though by no means conclusive, research has shown this approach may work for the management of type 2 diabetes, by minimising blood sugar fluctuations, enhancing insulin sensitivity and improving glycemic control (25). Replacing refined carbs with slow time-released carbs, can have a profound impact on the energy levels we experience. Feeling lethargic all the time is not an inevitable rite of passage once we hit 40!

The Glycaemic Index, however, does throw up some anomalies. Many low GI foods are minimally processed carbohydrates such as whole grain cereals and vegetables. But this is not always the case. For example, watermelon has a high GI value of 80, but relatively few digestible carbohydrates in a normal serving. Similarly, chocolate has a relatively low GI value due to its high fat content, as fats slow down the rate sugars are released into the intestine.

Therefore, how we combine foods in a meal also makes a difference to blood sugar control, energy levels and satiety. For example, white rice scores high on the GI index. But when paired with a lean chicken breast, fibrous vegetables and an olive oil salad dressing, its sugars are released more slowly.

Carbs & Performance

The role of carbohydrates in athletics and sports has long been considered of vital importance to performance and recovery (27). When exercising at higher intensities especially, carbohydrates are a 'preferential' fuel, as they are readily broken down into glucose for immediate energy production.

But if not required for immediate use, glucose from dietary carbohydrates is stored in the liver and muscles as glycogen. The liver can store up to 100g of glycogen, while skeletal muscle can hold up to approximately 500g of glycogen (28). During exercise, liver glycogen is broken down to help maintain blood sugar levels, whereas muscle glycogen is a localised source of energy for the "working" muscle (29).

During resistance training, glycogen is broken down to provide energy for muscle contractions. The body's stores of glycogen are limited, but the amount used up will depend on the intensity and volume of training (30). Nevertheless, a typical resistance training bout may reduce glycogen stores by 24 to 40% (31). Whilst this does not amount to the kind of glycogen depletion we associate with fatigue and dips in performance, it does suggest a minimum amount of carbs being necessary to lift well (32).

Performance nutrition strategies for endurance athletes are designed to optimise muscle and liver glycogen. In the first instance, this means having high daily carbohydrate intakes (≥8g/kg/day) (33). Yet, similarly high carbohydrate intakes are often recommended for lifters and strength athletes (34). Indeed, competitive bodybuilders report average daily intakes of 5.3 g/kg in off-season (35).

But are these high intakes for non-endurance sports justified?

A recent systematic review (2002) of 49 studies by Henselmans et al suggests otherwise. Despite the weight of tradition, it found that resistance trained athletes performed equally well on lower, more moderate carbohydrate intakes as on higher ones (36). At first sight, this may seem surprising. After all, resistance training is largely anaerobic and uses glycogen as a primary fuel source (37).

And certainly, a high-volume workout with short rest periods creates substantial glycogen depletion (38). However, shorter workouts (such as I recommend) consisting of heavier loads, but less reps and longer rest periods will see energy substrates other than glycogen at work. For example, lifting heavy weights requires the use of intramuscular stores of creatine phosphate. At the same time, longer rest periods (aerobic) will be fuelled by fatty acid reserves.

It is in this context, that while carbs remain important for training, I would limit the upper end of daily carbohydrate intake to 3 g/kg per day, for any man over 40 with the goal of fat loss.

Carbohydrates & Hormones

In mature adults, carbs are not considered strictly anabolic as they do not promote muscle protein synthesis (39). Yet they can prove protein sparing and anti-catabolic. When carb intake is too low the enzyme AMPK, an energy sensor, blunts energy-consuming processes – such as building muscle – and heightens catabolic ones, such as muscle protein breakdown (40).

However, the insulin secreted following carbohydrate ingestion supresses the muscle protein breakdown (41) produced by training (42). In this way, adequate carb consumption, perhaps especially around the workout period, may help dampen these catabolic forces and shift the dial towards a positive protein balance (43).

In fact, in the post workout period, and until a refeeding, it is catabolic, muscle wasting processes which predominate. Insulin remains low, while cortisol the stress hormone and catecholamines are elevated (44). Dietary carbs post-workout can help reduce cortisol levels (45), which in turn improves cortisol-to-free testosterone ratios (46), thereby creating a more favourable anabolic environment for muscle growth.

Interestingly, as little as 30 grams of carbohydrate (e.g., 150g of sweet potato) may be enough to suppress these catabolic, muscle wasting processes (47).

Calculating Daily Carbohydrate Intake

For our purposes, calculating overall daily carbohydrate intake is very simple. It amounts to what remains of total calories, having first determined the other macronutrient priorities, namely protein and fat.

In my case, this amounts to 151 grams, or approximately 30% of my total daily calories (when dieting). Whilst there isn't a strict definition of what constitutes a "low-carb" diet, 151 grams might be considered moderately low, and certainly by comparison to government guidelines in the UK and the USA—which recommend anywhere between 50-60% of total calories.

A low carb diet is thought to be somewhere between 100-130 grams, while under 50g of carbohydrates, qualifies as a Very Low Carbohydrate Ketogenic diet (VLCKD).

Low carb, high protein diets are effective for weight loss and helping to achieve rapid health outcomes for the obese and insulin resistant (48, 49). I certainly do not hesitate to recommend them for some clients—especially in the early phases of a fat loss program. The relatively rapid outcomes achieved, both in terms of scale weight loss, new dietary habits and health markers can prove motivational (50).

In successive phases, having lost some weight and built more muscle tissue, along with the ability to train with more intensity, it becomes possible to introduce more carbs—for example on a more demanding "leg" day.

CALCULATING CARBOHYDRATE INTAKE

Step 1: Determine total daily calories and other macros (protein + fat)

My current weight: 75.5 Kg (166 pounds)
Total Daily Calories: 2,057 Cals (my calorie deficit when dieting)

Protein: 1.1 gram per pound
= **183 grams** (732 Cals)—35% of Total Calories.

Fats: 35% of total calories
= **80 grams** (720 Cals)

Step 2: Subtract total Protein + Fat Cals from total daily calories.

Carbs: Total Calories—Protein + Fat
= 2,057 - 1,452 Cals (732 Cals protein + 720 Cals fat)

= **151 grams** (605 calories / 30% of total calories)

CHAPTER 16

MICRONUTRIENTS

"Let food be thy medicine, and let medicine be thy food."

Hippocrates

Despite the misleading name, the dietary intake of 24 *micronutrients* comprising of vitamins, minerals and trace elements are essential for maintaining normal health. They play a central role in metabolism and energy production, the immune system, bone health and the maintenance of tissue function. But, relative to macronutrients, micronutrients need only be supplied in small amounts with their Recommended Daily Allowance (RDA) measured in milligrams and micrograms.

These days, classic micronutrient deficiency diseases such as scurvy are rare. Nevertheless, inadequate dietary intakes of certain vitamins and minerals are common (1) and most likely due to over consumption of energy-rich nutrient-poor food in the western diet. Having less than optimal intakes of any given micronutrient may result in what is termed a "subclinical" deficiency.

There are also different times in our life cycle when we require more nutrients than are typically provided, such as iron for women during pregnancy or vitamin B_{12} after the age of 50 (2). More topically, the importance of Vitamin D to the immune system post Covid-19, has received media coverage and scientific interest (3).

Vitamins

Vitamins are a group of organic compounds that the body requires for normal metabolism and energy production. Apart from a few exceptions, most notably Vitamin D, the human body does not synthesise vitamins in sufficient amounts and must be provided by the diet. Unlike macronutrients such as carbohydrates or fat, vitamins do not provide energy but rather, act as coenzymes necessary to break down and *release* energy from food.

Vitamins are broadly classified as water-soluble or fat-soluble. Water-soluble vitamins, which include Vitamin C and members of the Vitamin B complex, are carried to the body's tissues but are not stored in the body. We therefore require an almost continuous daily supply and as any excess will be eliminated in urine, toxicity is also rare.

On the other hand, the fat-soluble vitamins A, D, E and K, are absorbed in the intestine in the presence of fat. They play a vital role in many physiological processes including vision, bone health, immune and endocrinal (hormones) function. Fat-soluble vitamins are stored in fatty tissues and the liver, so are eliminated more slowly than water-soluble vitamins. As such, they pose a greater risk of toxicity when consumed in excess (4).

Vitamins & Exercise

Vitamins and minerals are essential for energy metabolism and exercise taxes the metabolic pathways which require micronutrients. During training for example, the rate of energy turnover in skeletal muscle can be anywhere between 20-100 times that of normal resting rate (5). In this context we should be striving for optimal intakes of the micronutrients required for recovery along with the building, repair and maintenance of lean body mass (6) rather than simply avoiding deficiencies.

B-Complex

Many vitamins, particularly the B-complex vitamins, play key roles in building muscle, mitochondrial energy metabolism and forming oxygen-carrying red blood cells (7). Thiamin, riboflavin, $B_{6,}$ pantothenic acid and biotin are directly involved in energy production, acting as coenzymes in the metabolism of fat and carbohydrates (8). Folate and vitamin B_{12} are essential to produce red blood cells, protein synthesis and tissue repair.

Vitamin D

Vitamin D, commonly associated with bone health, enhances the absorption of important minerals such as calcium, magnesium and phosphorous, by up to 30-40% (9). But recent studies have also highlighted its mediating role in immunity, cardiovascular health, neuromuscular function and body composition (10-12). Research has demonstrated that Vitamin D may increase protein synthesis and cellular growth, increasing the size and number of type II muscle fibres (13). Cross-sectional studies have similarly revealed a relationship between Vitamin D levels and various measures of muscle strength with ageing (14, 15).

Vitamin D is unique because we synthesise Vitamin D3 in the skin from exposure to sunlight. For this reason, it is often referred to as the Sunshine Vitamin (16). As few foods contain Vitamin D (oily fish and fish liver oils are among the best sources) (17), the principal cause of Vitamin D deficiency is inadequate sunlight exposure (18). But as we grow older, we lose some of our ability to synthesise Vitamin D in the skin from sunlight (19). In this context, fortified foods and/or supplementation are worth considering, particularly in the long winter months or in countries with temperate climates.

Antioxidants

The antioxidant nutrients, vitamins C, E and β-carotene, play important roles in health, protecting cell membranes from oxidative stress. Oxidative stress is linked to multiple pathologies including heart disease, type 2 diabetes and the ageing process itself (20-22). It is produced by elevated levels of oxidants, free radicals or reactive oxygen species (ROS) which lacking an electron, bind (react) with other molecules in the body, causing cellular damage.

Oxidative stress and low-grade, yet persistent levels of inflammation seem to be a pervasive feature of aging (23). Oxidative stress also appears to contribute to the progressive loss of muscle mass which characterises aging (24). Age-related increases in Reactive Oxygen Species (ROS) production inhibits mTOR and the enzyme p70S6K, both involved in initiating protein synthesis and building muscle (25).

> **Oxidative Stress:** Cellular damage caused by elevated levels of oxidants (free radicals or reactive oxygen species) which bind with other molecules.

Oxidative stress may go some way to explaining "anabolic resistance"—the impaired ability to stimulate protein synthesis from dietary protein intake with age. Anabolic resistance may be mitigated by resistance training and increasing dietary protein (26). But interestingly, some research has shown that by reducing the inflammatory state, the antioxidants Vitamin E, Vitamin A, rutin, zinc and selenium may help restore the anabolic effect of protein in a meal (27).

Sources

We know that a diet rich in fruit and vegetables may reduce the risk of major diseases such as cancer, diabetes and cardiovascular disease (28, 29) and its antioxidant content has been linked to many of these benefits (30). Fruits and vegetables contain many different types of antioxidants.

Indeed, the well-known antioxidants Vitamin C, β-carotene, and α-tocopherol are just a few compared to the many other carotenoids, phenolic acids, flavonoids, and lignans (31).

Many of these antioxidants work in tandem. As such, recent research points to the total value and combinations of antioxidants found in dietary plants rather than individual antioxidants (e.g., vitamin E), as providing much of their protective effects (32). Similarly, the evidence that one antioxidant deficiency adversely affects athletic performance, or that its single supplementation may improve performance is unclear (33, 34).

In this regard, other than perhaps a good multivitamin for the purposes of belt and braces, the priority should be to consume a diet rich in antioxidants, rather than resorting to supplementation.

ANTIOXIDANTS

Vitamins: Vitamin C, E, and B

Minerals: Selenium, zinc, Iron, manganese.

Phytochemicals: Phenolic compound derivatives that are neither vitamins nor Minerals. Examples are carotenoids, flavonoids, catechins, polyphenols, and phytoestrogens.

Carotenoids are antioxidants found in the pigments of plants and are responsible for the different colours found in vegetables and fruits. There are more than 600 carotenoids. They are known to support a healthy immune system along with eye health.

Dietary sources: pumpkins, carrots, spinach, kale, tomatoes

Flavonoids are phytochemicals which contribute to the healthy cell communication which can decrease inflammation and reduce the risk of disease spreading. One of the largest groups of phytonutrients, this compound is rich in antioxidant properties.

Dietary sources: apples, grapefruit, ginger, green tea, onions

Polyphenols are the most abundant antioxidants in the diet. These compounds present different antioxidant properties such as scavenging free radicals.

Dietary sources: fruit, juices, tea, coffee, and red wine.

Everyone's favourite antioxidant (polyphenol)

Minerals

While evidence that a single antioxidant deficiency affects performance is weak, we know with some degree of certainty that a mineral deficiency can impair training and recovery. An iron deficiency, for example, will certainly impair strength and muscle function (35).

There are in fact a few select minerals such as calcium, magnesium, iron and zinc, which we cover in this chapter, whose deficiencies are associated with a decline in strength (36), dieting (37) mitochondrial decay and aging (38).

Iron

Iron is an essential mineral which plays a critical role in oxygen delivery via haemoglobin, a protein in red blood cells which carries oxygen. An iron deficiency can lead to extreme fatigue, weakness, inflammation, cognitive decline and depression. Iron-rich foods are red meat, seafood and dark green leafy vegetables. The iron found in plants, however, are less bioavailable than that found in meat.

In general, a food-first approach is advisable, as toxicity is a concern. Supplementation may also have unpleasant side effects such as nausea and black stools. In this regard, please consult with your GP first if you are experiencing symptoms of a clinical deficiency.

Calcium

Growing up in a pre-lactose intolerant world, milk and being sure to *drink it all up* was synonymous with health, strength and vitality. And with good reason. Calcium is one of the 24 vitamins and minerals required for optimal health and as such is considered a "macromineral."

Commonly associated with bone health, a chronic calcium deficiency may lead to osteoporosis. But calcium is also essential for building muscle, triggering as it does muscle contraction, through its reaction with regulatory proteins (39).

Good sources of dietary calcium are found in dairy, nuts, fruits and vegetables. Broccoli and dark leafy greens such as chard, kale, and spinach are all nutrient dense sources of calcium. Other good, non-dairy sources include almonds, chia seeds and dried figs: all of which are high in fibre and facilitate calcium absorption by decreasing the rate food passes through the intestines. The body also requires vitamin D to absorb calcium.

Guidelines published by Public Health England have set the Recommended Daily Allowance (RDA) for men over 19 years of age at 700 mg per day (40). The National Osteoporosis Foundation recommends that older men take 1,000 mg. Women may need less calcium than men because high estrogen levels will deposit more calcium in the bones.

Recommended dosage

Reaching RDA levels of calcium from dietary sources alone is eminently possible. For example, 250ml of milk contains 250mg. A whey protein shake contains 100 mg per 30g serving. Chia seeds contain 300 milligrams of calcium per 2 ½ tablespoons and one tablespoon of black strap molasses contains 200 mg of calcium.

Good Calcium Sources

Milk, 250ml: 250mg
Whey Protein, 30 g: 100mg
Chia Seeds, 2 ½ tablespoons: 300mg
Black strap molasses, 1 tablespoon: 200mg

Zinc

Zinc, an essential micronutrient, is a trace mineral required in many of our cellular processes, notably in the healthy functioning of the immune system, cell growth and protein synthesis (41). Zinc is also recognised as an important antioxidant with anti-inflammatory properties (42).

Despite being readily found in the diet, with meat, egg and legumes being common dietary sources, zinc deficiency is prevalent, particularly in countries of high cereal consumption (41). While deficiency rates in the western world are between 10-15%, global "insufficiency" rates are at nearly 50%. Similarly, some diets, while not necessarily low in zinc may have its bioavailability restricted by "anti-nutrients" such as phytic acid which is present in cereals and can inhibit its absorption (43).

A zinc deficiency is associated with the aging process (44) insulin resistance, obesity (45) and hypogonadism (low testosterone) in men (46, 47). Excreted through sweat, athletes and those who train frequently may also find themselves prone to a zinc deficiency (48). A fascinating study on wrestlers who trained to exhaustion showed that, following four weeks of zinc supplementation, testosterone levels were restored to normal levels, aiding performance and recovery (49).

Another randomised, double-blind study on trained varsity American Football players found that zinc (30g) and magnesium supplementation increased levels of both free and total testosterone, along with IGF-1 (insulin-like Growth Factor) (50). IGF-1 is another anabolic factor known to enhance muscle function, through the regulation of cellular growth and metabolism, but which decreases with age (Somatopause).

Recommended dosage

The upper tolerable dosage limit for Zinc is 40 mg. Exceeding this can cause nausea, irritation to the gastrointestinal tract or even a copper deficiency. If you eat meat and lead a sedentary lifestyle, supplementation will likely be unnecessary. For those who train regularly, supplementation with 10-25mg/day should be sufficient.

Zinc should be taken with meals, to prevent potential nausea. Avoid taking calcium, iron, magnesium, and zinc at the same time in combinations of 800+ mg, since high amounts of these minerals will compete for absorption.

Magnesium

Magnesium is an essential mineral, involved in more than 300 enzyme reactions, key to many health outcomes. Low intake is often associated with heart disease, type 2 diabetes and metabolic syndrome (51). Fundamental for bone growth, it is also thought to play a role in athletic performance (52) involved in the generation of adenosine triphosphate (ATP) and energy in the cell's mitochondria.

Dietary intake of magnesium is commonly deficient in the Western World (53), which in part is due to a nutrient-poor diet, rich in processed foods and lacking in green vegetables. Natural dietary sources of magnesium are widespread and include whole grains, leafy vegetables, nut and legumes. Nevertheless, per serving, most foods will contain less than 20% of the Recommended Daily Allowance, which for men between the ages of 31-50, is 420mg.

The activity of anabolic hormones such as Testosterone is central to understanding the ageing process. This in turn is influenced by inflammation, caloric and protein intake and mineral status including magnesium. Inadequate intracellular magnesium may increase the production of reactive oxygen species (ROS), oxygen-derived free radicals associated with systemic inflammation. The impaired antioxidant expression negatively influences both testosterone and magnesium levels (54).

Magnesium supplementation can increase total testosterone (55) Importantly, by inhibiting the sex hormone binding globulin (SHBG), which increases with age (56). It can also increase the percentage of free and bioavailable testosterone (57) which is more readily available to leave circulation and enter cells.

Recommended dosage

Like zinc, magnesium is excreted through sweat, so athletes and those who train regularly should consider their magnesium intake. The body only absorbs the magnesium it requires, so the side effects associated with its supplementation are few. The standard dose is 200-400mg. Magnesium citrate as opposed to magnesium oxide, which may cause diarrhoea, is a preferable source.

CHAPTER 17

NUTRIENT TIMING: ANOTHER LOOK

"You don't have to swing hard to hit a home run. If you got the timing, it'll go."

Yogi Berra

Nutrient timing refers to the set of strategies developed by sports nutritionists for the planned ingestion of certain macronutrients at specific times, to better promote performance and recovery. The practice reached the zenith of its popularity at the turn of this century. Some of its leading lights went so far as to suggest that it was more important than the "absolute daily intake of nutrients" (1).

More recently, the research (1) has put the proverbial cart back behind the horse, re-establishing a hierarchy of nutritional priorities. That is, hitting total daily calorie and macronutrient intake targets, irrespective of timing, is the first order of the day to improve performance and training adaptations.

That said, for those mid-lifers seeking to level the playing field and optimise training, nutrition and muscular gains, *is there a place for nutrient timing?*

Anabolic Window?

While enthusiastic proponents of nutrient timing exaggerated its benefits, not least for muscle hypertrophy, the pendulum has swung the other way. The blame—for throwing the baby out with the bathwater—must surely lie with their promotion of a concept known as the "Anabolic Window."

This theory hypothesised a limited timeframe, a small, post-exercise *anabolic window,* when one could take advantage of the synergistic effects of nutrition on exercise (2, 3). The sense of urgency created by such a brief opportunity to progress, ensured a generation never left the gym without first necking a protein shake.

> **Anabolic:** The growth promoting set of metabolic pathways which build larger molecules from smaller ones. Protein synthesis is an anabolic process.

This notwithstanding, the enhanced effects of a protein feeding post-workout on muscle protein synthesis are not in dispute (4, 5). The ingestion of protein following exercise does indeed coalesce to promote further anabolism in young (6) and older adults (7) alike.

The important distinction however, one which belies the idea of a fleeting anabolism, is that post-workout increases in muscle protein synthesis remain elevated for up to 24-48 hours (8). Therefore, while there is undoubtedly an increased sensitivity to nutrient uptake immediately after exercise, a more comprehensive understanding appreciates the post-workout period holds several opportunities for targeted nutrition interventions (9).

Post workout carbs?

Early research into nutrient timing was focused on endurance sports (10, 11). For these athletes, replacing muscle glycogen stores by ingesting carbs following a competition is a priority. And certainly, muscle glycogen is replenished more rapidly when carbohydrates are consumed immediately post-workout. Even delaying consumption by two hours may decrease the rate of muscle glycogen resynthesis by up to 50% (12).

However, for resistance training, while glycogen is broken down to provide energy for muscle contractions, a typical training bout may only deplete glycogen stores by 24-40% (13). Therefore, unless you are training twice daily, the speed of glycogen re-synthesis is irrelevant. If total daily carbohydrate intake is adequate, glycogen levels return to baseline within 24 hours (14). As such, the popular practice by bodybuilders of drinking high-glycemic carbs post-workout, borrowed straight from the playbook of endurance athletes, is superfluous.

On the other hand, some studies have suggested post-workout carbs are beneficial for creating an overall net positive protein balance (15). Further investigation however, reveals this nudging of the dial, while not to be scoffed at, is due to the prevention of muscle protein breakdown (16) and not by increasing muscle protein synthesis. This tallies, as carbs which spike insulin, have muscle-sparing (anti-catabolic) properties which inhibit its breakdown.

However, the time-honoured tradition of a whey protein shake for *immediate* post-workout nutrition is a practice I still recommend clients. In the first instance, with its high leucine content it maximally stimulates muscle protein synthesis (17, 18). But it is also sufficiently insulinogenic to be anti-catabolic. Following consumption, insulin remains at the elevated levels required to optimise net protein balance (15-30 mU/L) for approximately 2 hours (19).

> **Insulinogenic** pertaining to the stimulation of insulin secretion.

In this way, we also do not waste calories on fast-digesting carbs of dubious nutrient value, to inhibit muscle breakdown. Instead, we get to allocate more high-quality carbohydrates for our first sit down, prepared meal after training. I suggest between 30-40% of our daily carb allowance for this mixed meal.

Eating a substantial portion of our carbs after a workout, with its heightened insulin sensitivity, makes for better nutrient partitioning. Nutrient partitioning is the utilisation, storage, and conversion of food to peripheral tissues (20). While elevations in GLUT4 glucose transporter activity (21)—which facilitate the uptake of glucose into muscle—last only 30-40 mins after exercise (22), these acute increases also mediate a greater insulin sensitivity which can last up to 48hrs (23).

Nutrient Delivery

The young perhaps need not concern themselves with the minutiae of nutrient timing. But given the age-related challenges mid-lifers face to build muscle and lose fat, it makes sense to take any opportunity it might offer to level the playing field.

One such age-related challenge, which contributes to a blunted response to the stimuli of exercise and nutrition (anabolic resistance), is decreased blood flow and endothelial dysfunction (24). The blood circulatory (vascular) system is after all, responsible for nutrient delivery. With age, this system becomes impaired due to oxidative stress and inflammation (25).

However, during exercise, blood flow improves as the cardiovascular system redistributes the blood to working muscles, and away from organs such as the digestive system (26). As a result of the improved circulation following exercise, nutrient delivery is greatly enhanced. Exercise, even aerobic exercise, can significantly improve anabolic responses to both protein and carbohydrate consumption through improved nutrient delivery (27).

As we age, we may also experience decreases in gastric emptying rates (28). The rapidity of absorption of nutrients by the gut positively influences postprandial protein synthesis rates (29). In this context, a fast-digesting whey protein again proves a formidable ally to the midlife lifter, as it rapidly empties from the stomach into the duodenum (30).

> **Postprandial** occurring after a meal.

Pre & Intra Training

Discussion around nutrient timing is often centred around the *post-exercise* period. But accounting for the whole peri-workout period, with the practical implications of when we can both train and eat—which will inevitably vary—can help us make informed decisions.

> **Peri-workout Nutrition** nutritional interventions before, during, and after a workout.

For example, you might like to train first thing in the morning and fasted. However, it is noteworthy that muscle protein breakdown is significantly increased following a fasted workout (31) and may last up to 24 hours (32). In this instance, a liquid carbohydrate drink, combined with essential amino acids (EAA's), might be worth ingesting during (intra) training, to suppress cortisol and exert some anti-catabolic effects (33).

On the other hand, if you had a mixed meal with carbohydrates and protein one to two hours before training as I like to recommend where possible, intra-workout nutrition becomes surplus to requirement. Blood and muscle amino acids (the building blocks of protein) remain elevated during the session (34), and the carbohydrates provide easily accessible fuel.

Even though as discussed, glycogen depletion is not a matter for concern when weight training, carbs are still the most efficient energy source. ATP (energy) production from glucose is anywhere between two to five times faster than fat oxidation (35). So, if you are training intensely—as you ought!—blood glucose and muscle glycogen provide the lion share of energy (36).

Unfortunately, research on the ergogenic effects of pre/intra-workout carbohydrate supplementation on resistance training performance is less than exhaustive. However, one instructive study by Krings et al, showed that depending on the exercise, a dosage of 15-30 g/h of carbs with 500ml of fluid, taken at the start of training, led to the greatest overall performance (37).

One fascinating study showed that even a carbohydrate mouth rinsing—without actual ingestion—helped improve performance in resistance training (38).

> **Ergogenic** enhancing energy production, training performance and/or recovery. For example, creatine is an ergogenic aid for strength training.

Optimal Meal (Protein) Distribution

The synergistic effects of nutrition on training are unquestionable. Yet, arguably the most important aspect of nutrient timing is that as muscle is sensitive to a protein feeding and aminoacidemia for at least 24 hours after training, there are several touchpoints during the day when we can trigger muscle protein synthesis.

> **Aminoacidemia**: the presence of amino acids in the blood.

Muscle protein synthesis is transient in nature. In response to a complete meal containing high quality protein the duration of protein synthesis is approximately two to three hours long (39). Blood amino acids remain elevated for some time after that, but there is a ceiling for muscle protein synthesis (MPS), referred to as the "muscle full effect" (40). After reaching this threshold, protein synthesis becomes refractory (resistant).

> **Gluconeogenesis**: the generation of glucose from non-carbohydrate sources, such as protein.

The threshold is both age-related and dose dependent. MPS is maximised in young adults with 20-25 grams of a high-quality protein (or ~0.25 g/kg/meal) (41). However, mature adults require more protein intake in a single meal to maximally stimulate MPS rates (42). The saturable limit for "muscle-full" in older adults is more likely between 35-45 grams per serving (43) or 0.4-0.6g/kg protein per meal (44).

How meals are distributed throughout the day is a matter of some confusion. Perhaps you have heard that regular meals facilitate fat loss because they "stoke the fires of metabolism." This is a myth. Energy balance alone dictates weight loss and meal frequency does not promote greater weight loss (45). When calories are equated, six meals produce no greater effect on fat oxidation than three (46). For the purposes of fat loss, how many meals (and when) is a matter of personal preference.

On the other hand, for building muscle, meal distribution can make a difference. As protein synthesis lasts 3 hours (39), a minimum of 3-5 meals spaced evenly throughout the day is preferable. This kind of eating structure provides greater opportunities to trigger muscle protein synthesis (41) and overcome anabolic resistance (47).

Aside from promoting anabolism, increased meal frequency and protein distribution is associated with other health benefits, such as improved appetite control (48), lower fasting blood glucose levels (49), insulin sensitivity (50) and increased food thermogenesis and fat utilisation (51).

KEY TAKEAWAYS

Meal distribution:

- ✓ 3-5 meals with 35-50grams of high-quality protein spaced evenly throughout the day (delivering 3-4g of the all-important amino acid Leucine)

Pre/Intra Training:

- ✓ Where possible, 30-40% of dietary carbohydrate intake before the workout period, including a mixed protein & complex carbohydrates meal 2-3 hrs before training.
- ✓ If training fasted, an intra-workout of 15-30g/hr fast digesting carbs in 500ml of fluid along with 15 grams of EAA (Essential Amino Acids).

Immediate post-workout nutrition:

- ✓ A fast-digesting whey protein (40-45g) post-workout shake.

Post workout:

- ✓ A mixed meal of protein and carbohydrates, with 30-40% dietary carbohydrate intake in first, sit-down prepared meal after training.

CHAPTER 18

SUPPLEMENTS

"To eat is a necessity, but to eat intelligently is an art."

La Rochefoucauld

It is quite commonplace for 'newbies' to obsess over the minutiae of optimal nutrition and training practices, without having first mastered the basics. Aside from having *'all the gear and no idea'*, this often manifests itself in a kitchen cabinet chock full of supplements. At the opposite end of the spectrum, there are those who insist that unless derived from whole natural food sources, supplements have no place in a healthy diet.

The truth is somewhere in between. While we certainly espouse a "food first" approach, modern farming practices and food processing methods, particularly those involving heat, have undoubtedly induced mineral depletion and changes in the vitamin composition of foods (1). As we learned in the previous chapter on micronutrients, a vitamin or mineral deficiency can lead to disease, possibly even death, and sadly in some corners of the globe remains commonplace.

However, even in developed economies many of us suffer from one macronutrient insufficiency or another (2). These insufficiencies are often related to poor diet, but other factors include age, gender, ethnicity and even athletic performance. Vitamins and minerals mediate a whole host of metabolic and physiologic processes and may become depleted during intense training. Indeed, one surprising study found that professional male athletes had deficiencies in 40% of vitamins and 54% of minerals (3).

This review on supplements is intended to serve as a stand-alone chapter and point of reference, so apologies in advance for the inclusion and repetition of certain vitamins/minerals already covered in the chapter on micronutrients.

In this chapter we mainly concern ourselves with supplementation for age-related issues which inhibit muscle growth and prevent optimal health—such as declining testosterone levels, inflammation and importantly, in this post-Covid 19 world, a compromised immune system. We will also dive into the world of ergogenic aids—those supplements which may improve exercise performance or enhance training adaptations (4).

While general health draws people to consider supplementation, nothing inflames the desire to pop a magic pill quite like the promise of increasing testosterone. Or perhaps more accurately, libido. It is widely known that libido is positively associated with testosterone (5).

Unfortunately, not all libido-enhancing supplements, such as maca, positively affect testosterone levels. Therefore, we limit our discussion here to evidence-based supplements which may support the restoration of healthy levels of testosterone.

General Health/Immunity/Testosterone

Vitamin D

Vitamin D is one of four, fat-soluble vitamins (A, D, E, K). Fat-soluble vitamins are stored in the liver and fatty tissues of the body and are eliminated more slowly than water-soluble vitamins. Vitamin D which exists in two forms, Vitamin D2 and D3, is unique because we can only synthesise Vitamin D3 in the skin from exposure to sunlight (6).

Vitamin D2, which cannot be made by humans, is found in sun-exposed mushrooms, while oil-rich fish such as salmon and mackerel contain some Vitamin D3. Vitamin D is commonly associated with bone health. And with good reason: it can enhance the absorption of the minerals, calcium, magnesium and phosphorous, often by as much as 30-40% (7).

Recent research however has highlighted the mediating role Vitamin D may play in muscle function and metabolism, the immune system, cardiovascular health, neuromuscular function and body composition (8-9). Significantly for muscle building, research has also demonstrated that Vitamin D can increase protein synthesis and cellular growth, increasing the size and number of type II muscle fibres (10).

Reflecting this wider, more holistic role for Vitamin D (outside that of bone health) many of the body's tissues and organs, including the prostate, heart, blood vessels and endocrine glands contain the Vitamin D receptors (VDR's) essential for Vitamin D signalling. These Vitamin D receptors (VDR's) are often near to androgen receptors such as the testes, prostate and seminal vesicles (11).

Perhaps unsurprisingly then, Vitamin D is thought to play a role in male fertility (12). The research supports a positive association between Vitamin D and levels of total and free testosterone levels (13, 14). One study showed that middle aged men with Vitamin D deficiency (hypovitaminosis D) also had low levels of total and free testosterone (15). Another revealed that older men with low testosterone levels, when combined with a vitamin D deficiency, were at greater risk of cardiovascular mortality (16).

A vitamin D deficiency is far more commonplace than one might imagine. An estimated 1 billion people worldwide suffer from a vitamin D deficiency (17), across a variety of age groups and ethnicities. Vitamin D deficiency becomes more prevalent as we age (18) and is often found in the obese and those with limited sun exposure (19). People with a dark complexion also require longer sun exposure to synthesise comparable amounts to someone with a fair or white complexion (20).

Supplementation with 3000 IU vitamin D per day has been proven to restore healthy testosterone levels (21) Significantly, the positive results yielded in the study from Plitz et al followed a year of vitamin D supplementation. This notwithstanding, there are no demonstrable effects from supplementation on healthy men with *normal* levels of testosterone (22). On the other hand, the same study showed that while total testosterone levels did not increase following supplementation, levels of sex hormone binding globulin (SHBG) did decline—resulting in more bioavailable testosterone.

Looking at the body of literature, it is reasonable to assert that vitamin D supplementation is most effective when restoring low testosterone levels to normal levels. Similarly, where there is vitamin D deficiency, supplementation is worth considering, especially in the long winter months or in countries with more temperate climates.

Recommended Dosage

The recommended daily allowance for Vitamin D is currently set at 400-800IU/day and the tolerable upper intake level (UL) is defined as 4000IU/day.

The Endocrine Practice Guidelines Committee however suggests a daily intake of 1500–2000IU of vitamin D3 daily for adults over 18 years up to 70 years. As a rule of thumb, vitamin D supplementation between 1000 to 3000 IUs per day is considered optimal.

Doses of more than 4000 IU/day is not advisable, as vitamin D is fat soluble and may cause toxicity. Vitamin D3 supplementation (cholecalciferol) is recommended over D2 supplementation (ergocalciferol), since D3 is more stable and bioavailable. Vitamin D should be taken daily, with meals, preferably with a source of fat.

Zinc

Zinc is an essential micronutrient, a trace mineral required in many of our cellular processes, notably in the healthy functioning of the immune system, cell growth and protein synthesis (23). Zinc is recognised as an important antioxidant with anti-inflammatory properties (24).

Despite being readily found in the diet, with meat, egg and legumes being common dietary sources, zinc deficiency is prevalent in the world—particularly in countries of high cereal consumption (23). While zinc deficiency rates in the western world are between 10-15%, global insufficiency rates are at nearly 50%.

Similarly, some diets, while not necessarily low in zinc, may have its bioavailability restricted by "anti-nutrients" such as phytic acid which, present in cereals, can inhibit its absorption (25). Zinc deficiency is similarly associated with the aging process (26) insulin resistance, obesity (27) and hypogonadism (low testosterone) in men (28, 29).

Zinc is excreted through sweat, so athletes and those who train frequently may also be prone to a zinc deficiency (30). A fascinating study on wrestlers who trained to exhaustion, showed that following 4 weeks of zinc supplementation, testosterone levels were restored to normal levels, aiding performance and recovery (31).

Another randomised double-blind study on trained, varsity American Football players found that zinc (30g) and magnesium supplementation increased levels of both free and total testosterone, along with IGF-1 (insulin-like Growth Factor) (32). IGF-1 is another anabolic factor known to enhance muscle function through the regulation of cellular growth and metabolism, but which also decreases with age (Somatopause).

Recommended Dosage

The upper tolerable dosage limit for Zinc is 40 mg. Exceeding this can cause nausea, irritation to the gastrointestinal tract or even a copper deficiency.

If you eat meat and lead a sedentary lifestyle, supplementation may likely be unnecessary. But if you train regularly, 15-25 mg/day is considered optimal. Elite athletes, or those who sweat profusely might consider taking higher dosages.

Zinc should be taken with meals to prevent potential nausea. You should also avoid taking calcium, iron, magnesium, and zinc at the same time in combinations higher than 800+ mg, since high amounts of these other minerals compete for absorption.

Magnesium

Magnesium is an essential mineral, involved in more than 300 enzyme reactions and key to many health outcomes. Low intake is often associated with heart disease, type 2 diabetes and metabolic syndrome (33). Fundamental for bone growth, it is also thought to play a role in athletic performance (34) in the pathways for generating energy.

Despite this, dietary intake of magnesium is commonly deficient in the Western World (35). This is in part due to a nutrient poor diet, rich in processed foods and lacking in green vegetables. Like zinc, it can also be lost in sweat with intense physical exercise.

Natural dietary sources of magnesium are widespread and include whole grains, leafy vegetables, nut and legumes. Nevertheless, per serving, most foods will contain less than 20% of the Recommended Daily Allowance which, for men aged 31-50yrs is 420mg.

The activity of anabolic hormones, with Testosterone playing a pivotal role, is central to the ageing process which; is influenced by inflammation, caloric and protein intake and mineral status (magnesium). Inadequate intracellular magnesium may increase the production of reactive oxygen species (ROS), oxygen-derived free radicals, which is associated with systemic inflammation. The impaired antioxidant expression negatively influences both testosterone and magnesium levels (36).

Magnesium supplementation may increase total testosterone (37). By inhibiting the sex hormone binding globulin (SHBG) which increases with age (38), it may also augment the percentage of free and bioavailable testosterone (39), which is more readily available to leave circulation and enter cells.

Recommended Dosage

The RDA for men aged 31-50yrs + is 420mg which is a standard dose, and it should be taken with food.

Toxicity is not an issue as the body absorbs what it needs. Larger doses may however cause gastrointestinal distress and/or diarrhoea. Such side effects are more common with magnesium oxide. As such, magnesium citrate is a preferable choice for supplementation.

Boron

The trace mineral boron is a micronutrient which plays a diverse and vital role, particularly in the metabolism and absorption of other vitamins and micronutrients, including magnesium and Vitamin D (40).

Dietary boron, found in fruit, vegetables and legumes, is essential for the growth and maintenance of bone health. Nevertheless, its daily intake can vary widely depending on boron concentrations in the soil (41). Available food software databases have been shown to greatly overestimate the boron content of foods (42).

Following supplementation, increased levels of testosterone have been demonstrated in both men and women (43,44). In one study in healthy men seven days of supplementation resulted in a significant increase (28%) in free testosterone (45). Indeed, after only six hours' supplementation, there was a significant decrease in levels of sex hormone binding globulin (SHBG) (46).

Another study with 4 weeks of 10mg Boron supplementation noted a trend towards increased testosterone (11%) (47). It is in this context that the author of a review of Boron (48), concluded that supplementation *"may have significant beneficial ramifications, particularly in ageing men, in whom, typically, levels of SHBG increase and levels of FT decrease."*

Although not all studies have established a positive association between boron supplementation and testosterone (49), its positive, synergistic interaction with both Vitamin D metabolism and magnesium absorption should also be considered when thinking about supplementation.

Recommended Dosage

Human requirements for boron remain undefined. The only guideline is a tolerable UL, which for adults aged 18 years or older is approximately 20 mg. In the studies undertaken to reveal a positive association with testosterone levels, 10mg was used.

Omega 3 (Fish Oil)

Excess body fat, poor diet and sedentary lifestyle are all factors which contribute to chronic, systemic, low-grade inflammation (50). But the aging process itself sees increased plasma levels of pro-inflammatory cytokines such as tumor necrosis factor α (TNFα), C-reactive protein (CRP) and interleukins (IL-6, IL-18) (51). An increase in these markers affects muscle protein metabolism and contributes to sarcopenia and the loss of muscle mass and strength (52).

The anti-inflammatory effects of Omega 3 polyunsaturated fatty acids (n-3 PUFA) are well documented (53-55). The main bioactive PUFAs are eicosapentaenoic acid (EPA), and docosahexaenoic acid (DHA). They are found in seafood and the marine oils extracted for supplementation from cold-water fishes such as sardines and salmon, which possess a greater quantity of body fat.

Studies suggest that Omega 3 supplementation may support the immune function, especially post-exercise (56), reduce cardiovascular risk factors such as high cholesterol and high blood pressure (57) as well as lower levels of triglycerides (58). But a recent meta-analysis concluded that n-3 PUFA supplementation may also directly contribute to our efforts to combat anabolic resistance, by helping to increase muscle mass and strength in older adults (59).

Recommended Dosage

500 milligrams to 1.8 grams of EPA and DHA per day. Additional health benefits may be seen with a combined intake of 6 grams per day.

Strength & Muscle Building/Ergogenic Aids

Whey Protein

Perhaps nothing embodies more the image of a serious gym goer intent on building muscle, than necking a protein shake post workout. Of course, hitting optimal protein targets from whole foods alone without resorting to supplementation is entirely possible.

Nevertheless, protein powders are quick to prepare, convenient to carry and easy to consume. They are also typically low in carbohydrates and fats, and easy to digest and absorb.

Whey protein is the most popular of supplemental protein powders. And with good reason. Whey protein has been exhaustively researched in sports nutrition and is considered an optimal source of protein for supporting the addition of lean muscle mass (60-62).

Whey is rated as a high-quality protein source due to its bioavailability, high digestibility and essential amino acid (EAA) profile. Essential Amino Acids (EAAs) cannot be synthesised de novo (from scratch) by the body and must therefore, be provided for by the diet. Whey protein is high in all EAAs, but most notably, leucine (14%). Leucine is the most anabolic of amino acids and is key to stimulating the mTOR pathway and triggering muscle protein synthesis (63,64).

Importantly, for the purposes of building muscle, whey protein is also quickly digested and absorbed. Following resistance training, rapid increases in EAA's in the blood stream have been shown to produce greater Muscle Protein Synthesis (MPS) than a more slowly digested protein source such as casein (65, 66). In young people a fast-digesting whey protein does not stimulate any greater muscle gains in the way it does with older adults (67, 68).

Whey protein is also a source of bioactive peptides. These are small chains of amino acids that can't be completely broken down by digestive enzymes. These peptides regulate important bodily functions and offer a whole host of health promoting benefits through activities which positively impact the cardiovascular and immune systems (69).

Whey protein concentrate (WPC) is particularly rich in these bioactive peptides (70). Whey protein isolate (WPI) on the other hand, passes through a further filtration process which removes biproducts such as lactose and extra fat, making it a more suitable choice for the lactose intolerant.

Whey protein hydrolysates (WPH) are more rapidly digested than WPC (71) as the protein is broken into peptides through enzymatic means. Depending on the type of enzymes used, WPH may have lower bioavailability of these health promoting bioactive peptides (72). Importantly, studies report that both whey concentrates, and whey hydrolysates led to similar increases in muscle mass with resistance training (73).

Recommended Dosage

Depending on the type and quality of whey protein, individual serving sizes may vary from 25-35 grams. The most important number to look out for, however, is grams of leucine per serving. This needs to be at least 3-4.2 grams per serving to optimally stimulate protein synthesis in more mature adults.

Creatine

In the early 1990's Creatine Monohydrate became a popular supplement among athletes. Since then, it has become the most well researched and probably most effective of all ergogenic (performance enhancing) aids in sports.

While purported to provide an array of physiological, health and even cognitive (74) benefits, creatine proves especially beneficial in sports performance, most notably in high-intensity intermittent activities (75, 76), improving strength outputs (77), increasing lean muscle (78), and aiding the recovery process (79).

Creatine is a naturally occurring compound, made up of the amino acids L-arginine, glycine and methionine. Our bodies can synthesise creatine naturally, primarily in the liver, as well as in the kidneys and pancreas. It is also found in the diet, primarily in eggs, red meat and seafood (80). Most of the creatine (~95%) is stored in skeletal muscle with smaller amounts found in the brain and testes. Approximately two thirds of intramuscular creatine are stored as creatine phosphate, or phosphocreatine.

The muscles of our body power up muscle contractions with Adenosine Triphosphate, or ATP, which is often referred to as the body's energy currency. But the body has a limited supply of ATP which may be quickly used up in training, breaking down ATP to produce energy. ATP is most quickly regenerated by means of an enzymatic reaction with creatine phosphate (phosphocreatine).

Utilisation of creatine phosphate is rapid during the first few seconds of high-intensity exercise, where it is also thought to act as a buffer to the delay in energy provision from glycogenolysis (81). Supplementing with creatine increases creatine phosphate stores (82) which translates to higher rates of phosphocreatine re-synthesis and improved training performance (83).

Creatine Monohydrate, which is creatine with one molecule of water attached to it, is the most common form of supplementation. Supplement companies have experimented with other forms such as creatine ethyl ester, but none have proved more effective than creatine monohydrate (84).

But despite the abundance of research, or perhaps because of its association with enhancing sports performance, creatine remains largely misunderstood by the public and myths still abound as regards to its supplementation. It is not, as sometimes believed, a steroid. Similarly, while creatine may increase levels of creatinine in the body—which is a marker of existing poor kidney function—it does not affect renal function in healthy populations (85-87).

Indeed, the only consistently reported side effect from creatine supplementation is weight gain (88,8 9). However, it is important to note that this is not increased fat mass but increased water weight from inside the cell. The increased cellular hydration from creatine supplementation may also contribute to creating that "fuller" muscle look and "pump" during a workout.

Recommended Dosage

The most effective way to increase muscle creatine stores is to ingest 5g of creatine monohydrate (or approximately 0.3 g/kg body weight) four times daily for 5–7 days, followed by 3–5 g/day thereafter to maintain elevated stores. This is known as creatine loading.

Ingesting smaller amounts of creatine monohydrate (e.g., 3–5 g/day) will also increase muscle creatine stores over a 3–4 weeks period. However, the initial performance effects of this method of supplementation are less supported in the literature.

Citrulline (Malate)

Age-related inflammation leads to arterial stiffness and vascular, endothelial dysfunction. Endothelial dysfunction which impairs the functioning of the endothelium – which lines the circulatory system—is characterised by a decrease in blood flow (90), which in turn contributes to anabolic resistance.

The mechanisms of endothelial dysfunction relate to a reduction in the production and bioavailability of nitric oxide (91). Nitric oxide is a signalling molecule associated with cardiovascular health and a prominent role as a vasodilator, helping to relax and widen blood vessels and improve blood flow (92).

Nitric oxide supplements have become popular among gym-goers. At a basic level, wider blood vessels increase the delivery of nutrients and oxygen to working muscles during exercise. They also facilitate the "pump", whereby muscles engorged with blood and intracellular fluid produce cell swelling and initiate protein synthesis (93).

Citrulline is a nonessential amino acid, which after supplementation is converted to L-arginine, the precursor for nitric oxide production.

Recommended Dosage

For circulatory health 2,000 mg of citrulline, three times a day with meals, for a total daily dose of 6,000 mg.

Citrulline supplementation is often sold as Citrulline Malate, in which case, take 1.76g of citrulline malate for every 1 gram of citrulline.

Supplementation often recommended in combination with 200mg/d of Glutathione (GSH) as it may extend the half-life of nitric oxide, resulting in greater vasodilation.

Caffeine

For enhancing exercise performance in the gym, caffeine is one of the most studied and effective of ergogenic aids, consistently improving performance across a wide range of sporting outcomes, including strength, endurance and anaerobic power.

Apart from attenuating fatigue and stimulating cognitive awareness, it stimulates beta-endorphins which lower perception of pain and effort. It can also be glycogen sparing and so encourage the oxidation of fatty acids as an energy source.

The growing energy and sports drink industry relies heavily on caffeine as its main ingredient, so be sure to check dosages. As a benchmark, one cup of coffee provides approximately 100mg of caffeine.

Recommended Dosage

The ISSN (International Society of Sports Nutrition) recommends doses of 3–6 mg/kg body mass, 60 min pre-exercise (94).

PART FOUR
MINDSET

"Every battle is won before it is ever fought."

Sun Tzu, Art of War

CHAPTER 19

ALL IN THE MIND?

If my mind can conceive it, and my heart can believe it—then I can achieve it."

Muhammed Ali

Fat loss and building muscle is often likened to running a marathon. Presumably to emphasize the fact that it takes time. And it does. But unlike a marathon, the finishing line is not marked, and the journey resembles more of a hike, complete with rocky terrain. In that regard, this book has been written as a map.

In earlier chapters, we learned of some of the age-related physiological and sociological roadblocks to be negotiated en route. The biggest obstacles, however, are to be found in the mind.

"*The map is not the territory*" was a term first coined by the philosopher and semantic specialist Alfred Korzybski, to convey the idea that our minds are distinct from reality; that the mental maps we create to navigate life, drawn from experience and imprinted neurologically into patterns, are merely models of reality (1).

Indeed, maps, whilst useful, are only ever a static snapshot of reality. The territory itself (life!) is dynamic and ever-changing. Moreover, the mental maps we draw are prone to cognitive bias, distortions and deletions.

They may prove accurate at one point in time, but they can also quickly become outdated.

The term ("the map is not the territory") is a foundational principle of Neurolinguistic Programming (NLP) and the brainchild of John Grinder, a linguistics professor at University of California, Santa Cruz, and Richard Bandler, a psychology student. NLP studies how language impacts our thoughts, nervous system, and physical responses to external stimuli. Its most famous student is Anthony Robbins, the peak performance expert and coach.

Focus

Cognitive science teaches us that we have a limited capacity for processing information. In fact, we are only capable of focusing on five to nine things at any one time (2). The world is certainly rich with infinite possibility but given these limitations, we have an overwhelming need to simplify reality. The information we perceive with our senses must therefore be filtered.

We use senses outwardly to perceive the world but also inwardly to interpret what we learn. Information is represented, coded and stored through our senses alongside the feelings we have about this knowledge. But whilst we use *all* our senses, when filtering information one sense tends to predominate. In NLP, this is referred to as the preferred or primary representational system.

This preference is reflected in our language and communication. A predominantly visual person, who consistently makes pictures in his mind's eye, will often uses phrases such as *"I see what you mean,"* or *"the future looks bright."* The kinesthetic person speaks of *"grasping an idea,"* or feeling *"under pressure."* The auditory minded understands *"loud and clear"* and creates rapport with others who are *"on the same wavelength."*

Identifying one's primary representational system can help us understand how we communicate, or indeed miscommunicate, with ourselves and others. It is also a powerful tool for goal setting and sustaining motivation. "Words can change your brain" as Dr Andrew Newberg writes in his fascinating book of the same title (3). The language we use to set goals can be more compelling, and the "self-talk" we employ to inspire action more incisive, when peppered with sensory-based words from our own, preferred representational system.

When describing a "beach body" transformation goal for example, someone with a preferred auditory system might set the scene referring to the *"sound of the waves."* The predominantly visual person will see themselves in brightly coloured swimming trunks, inspiring admiring "*looks*" from passers-by.

Primary Representational System

To determine your own primary representational system, state your preference in the following scenarios:

1. When vacationing at the beach, the first thing that makes me glad to be there is:
   a. __ The feel of the cool sand, the warm sun or the fresh breeze on my face.
   b. __ The roar of the waves, the whistling wind or the sound of birds in the distance.
   c. __ This is the type of vacation that makes sense, or the cost is reasonable.
   d. __ The scenery, the bright sun, and the blue water.

2. When overwhelmed, I find it helps if:
   a. __ I can see the big picture.
   b. __ I can hear what's going on.
   c. __ I can get in touch with what is happening.
   d. __ I make sense of things in my head.

3. When given an assignment at work, it is easier to carry out if:
   a. __ I can picture what is required.
   b. __ I have a feeling for what is required.
   c. __ I understand what is required.
   d. __ I have tuned into what's required.

4. I find it easier to follow a presentation if:
   a. __ I feel in touch with the presenter and the material is within my grasp.
   b. __ There is a visual display so that I can visualize the concepts.
   c. __ The presentation is based on facts and figures and is logically presented.
   d. __ The presenter speaks clearly with varying tonality or uses sound to emphasize message.

5. When buying a car, I make my decision on:
   a. __ The purchase price, gas mileage, safety features, etc.
   b. __ How comfortable the seats are or the feeling I get when I test drive it.
   c. __ The colour, styling or how I would look in it.
   d. __ The sound of the engine or stereo system.

6. I communicate my thoughts through:
   a. __ My tone of my voice.
   b. __ My words.
   c. __ My appearance.
   d. __ My feelings.

7. When I am anxious, the first thing that happens is:
   a. __ Things begin to sound different.
   b. __ Things begin to feel different.
   c. __ Things begin to look different.
   d. __ Things begin to not make sense.

8. During a discussion, I am most often influenced by:
    a. __ The other person's logic.
    b. __ The other person's tone of voice.
    c. __ The energy I feel from the other person.
    d. __ Seeing the other person's body language or being able to picture the other person's viewpoint.

9. I assess how well I am doing at work based on:
    a. __ My understanding of what needs to be done.
    b. __ How I see myself making progress.
    c. __ How things sound.
    d. __ How satisfied I feel.

10. One of my strengths is my ability to:
    a. __ See what needs to be done.
    b. __ Make sense of new facts and data.
    c. __ Hear what sounds right.
    d. __ Get in touch with my feelings.

11. I enjoy:
    a. __ Choosing a piece of music to listen to.
    b. __ Making a logical, compelling point.
    c. __ Choosing clothes that are comfortable.
    d. __ Choosing clothes that look good.

12. If you agree with someone, you are more likely to say:
    a. __ That feels right.
    b. __ That looks right.
    c. __ That sounds right.
    d. __ That makes sense.

Now add up your answers in the columns below. The comparison of totals will reveal your relative preference—the higher the score, the higher your preference.

Question Number	Visual	Auditory	Kinesthetic	Digital
1	d	b	a	c
2	a	b	c	d
3	a	d	b	c
4	b	d	a	c
5	c	d	b	a
6	c	a	d	b
7	c	a	b	d
8	d	b	c	a
9	b	c	d	a
10	a	c	d	b
11	d	a	c	b
12	b	c	a	d
Total	V =	A =	K =	D =

Limiting Beliefs

Aside from the five senses, the mental maps we draw of the world are further filtered by our experiences, values and beliefs. A frequently held but mistaken belief, one all too readily promoted on social media by the legions of charlatans selling "replacement" shakes or fat burning supplements, is that fat loss can be quick and easy. This expectation alone sets up the rules of the game to lose.

Then there are so called 'limiting beliefs'. Beliefs can be invaluable, but some people put unnecessary boundaries on what we consider *reasonable* behaviour (4). One common limiting belief is that it is 'too late', or they are 'too old' to build an amazing physique. Having tried and failed so many times they don't believe it is even possible.

Undoubtedly, they will try again at some point in the future but the first hurdle,—a weekend of bingeing, or the weight scale not moving in the right direction—and their resolve is weakened. The *stacking* up of failed diets and cancelled gym memberships has provided for many reference points which confirm this belief.

One way to overcome a limiting belief which is holding us back is to simply question its veracity. Sowing the seeds of doubt about a limiting belief will open the pathways of possibility to adopting new, more empowering beliefs.

3 Step process to breaking down limiting beliefs.

1. Identify the limiting belief that is holding you back from achieving a specific goal.
2. Play devil's advocate and challenge its assumptions, one by one.
3. Write down what you could do *if* your limiting belief wasn't true? What might be possible?

What 3 actions could you take right NOW to start the ball rolling?

1.
2.
3.

Meta Programs

Every year millions of us invest in gym memberships. Having started so promisingly, why do these determined New Year resolutions to lose weight and build their dream physique come asunder by March?

Why is it that our actions don't match our good intentions?

The discrepancy, referred to as "the intention-behaviour gap" (4), is pervasive when it comes to health and lifestyle factors, with the intention to exercise or eat more healthily predicting a lacklustre 30-40% of actual change (5).

Human beings are certainly capable of goal-directed, long-term, reward-based behaviours. People do, after all, succeed in some endeavours. But, while possible, it is not easy nor straight forward. For a start our good intentions compete with conditioned associations. For example, the painful memories of being rubbish at school PE prevents us from joining a gym. Not to mention Pavlovian-like stimulus-responses, such as our favourite chocolate bar strategically placed at the supermarket checkout counter.

Then again, perhaps we are not 'driving the bus' quite as much as we think. The study of NLP reveals that human behaviour is often overrun by unconscious "meta-programs." As with a computer, meta-programs act like operating software, running in the background, but which oversee, guide and direct many other mental processes.

These meta-programs can drive behaviour at an unconscious level, filtering information, generalising experience into recognisable patterns and determining who and what we pay attention to. Sometimes they act like a thermostat, kicking the air conditioning into action when the room gets too hot or too cold...whether we like it or not!

As it happens, many of us have such a thermostat for being overweight, a number on the scales, beyond which *'enough is enough'.* At this point, we are impulsively driven to act and begin some diet or exercise regime. The problem is, we also have a thermostat, a number on the scale we are comfortable with; one that is some way off from our goal, but one we can live with. Predictably, we take our foot off the gas and slide back into the old ways... and so the yo-yo cycle continues.

There are well over 50 meta-programs. I have identified those that more obviously pertain to motivation and ability to follow through with our goals.

Match/Mismatch

Look at the shapes above. What do you see? How do they relate to each other?

Perhaps your eye was first drawn to the similarities between the shapes. The fact that they are *all* rectangles. Or was it their differences that you noticed? For example, the fact that one rectangle is horizontal and lying down. Perhaps you concluded there was no way of knowing how they are related, unless you were able to measure them first.

In the match/mismatch metaprogram, "Matchers" respond to the world by seeking out sameness or patterns. Another type of Matcher will see the similarities first, then the exception. "Mis-matchers" on the other hand will tend to focus on what is different.

This metaprogram has, as you might imagine, an important influence on our personal relationships. As a coach, knowing whether a client is a Matcher or Mis-matcher ahead of time, is enormously beneficial to understanding their reactions to training programs, their progress over time, or lack thereof.

Getting lean, losing weight and building muscle takes time. It requires consistency, patience, the forging of daily and weekly habits and the repetition of the basics, both with nutrition and training. Doing the same things, week in week out, might come more naturally to a Matcher. Sometimes, however, it is important to show Matchers new distinctions and that a program has different phases. Attachment to routines and comfort zones can also hinder progress.

The Mis-matcher, on the other hand, tends to see the flaws in any system and instinctively seeks out variety. They balk at any semblance of 'Groundhog Day' and grow impatient quickly. With Mis-matchers it is important to embed some variety or the unusual, while not veering from the essential tenets of the program. This might mean, for example, asking them to experiment with new and differently coloured vegetables every week.

Move Away/Move Toward

Human behaviour is driven by an urge to gain pleasure and avoid pain. At root and crop, this is how we learn. The child refrains from sticking his finger in the electric socket for fear of being scolded again. We order the gourmet pizza because it tastes delicious.

But the human spirit can prevail and, where human motivation and drive is powerful, everything is possible. And our destinies are greater than the accumulation of animal-like, conditioned associations. This is what makes us unique in the animal kingdom. And nuanced. One athlete will train hard for the glory of an Olympic medal. Another for fear of disappointing his father.

In the first example, the athlete is said to be *moving towards* the pleasure of winning. In the latter, his actions are inspired by *moving away* from pain—the fear of letting down a loved one. As with all metaprograms we do not have one absolute strategy but rather, one that predominates. Those who generally *move towards* come across as positive and enthusiastic people because they tend to couch life in terms of what they want. Those that *move away* can appear negative at times, as they frame choice in terms of what they *don't* want.

Neither is wrong. The important thing is to notice your dominant metaprogram and use it consciously to achieve your objectives, rather than be driven *by* it to a place you might not want to go. The pain of being ridiculed or bullied at school has provided many a young man with *move away* motivation to hit the gym and take up the iron game. This is not to be scoffed at. Make use of whatever force you find within to instill the necessary desire and discipline to train frequently.

The study of Neuroscience reveals in fact that change can happen by enhancing rewards for new behaviours which align towards our goals (6), reduce the value of old behaviours that run counter or away from them (7), or a combination of both.

Take some time now to draw up a list of as many positive reasons and benefits which will help move you towards your physique transformation goals. Then jot down another set of reasons which you want to move away from; those things you may stand to lose, should you not achieve your objective.

Here are examples of both:

Move Towards

1. Build optimal health and a muscular, ripped body.
2. Look great on the beach.
3. Attract the partner of my dreams.

Move Away

1. Prevent ill-health and disease.
2. Not feel so embarrassed to take my top off at the poolside.
3. Stop my body being the deal-breaker in finding a partner.

Push V Pull (Necessity v Possibility)

The Push v Pull metaprogram is similar in spirit to the Move Away/ Towards metaprogram and identifies whether you are "pushed" to take action out of necessity or "pulled" by the sense of possibility.

People with a strong "Push" metaprogram speak in terms of "having to," should," "must". They value procedures, security and permanence. Those with a "Pull" prefer options, opportunities, discovery and the chance for reinvention.

Internal/External

One metaprogram that strikes to the core of our identity is whether we have an internal or external frame of reference.

Those with an internal metaprogram have internalised a set of standards against which they judge themselves. The externally motivated enjoy meeting standards set by others, or better yet an officially recognised body or authority. As a coach, those with external frames of reference are, on the surface, a joy to work with. They respond well to praise and encouragement or equally when required, some cajoling. Those with an internal metaprogram may have difficulty accepting instruction or man-management.

The research shows however, that we are more likely to succeed in our goals when they are also tied to a sense of *intrinsic* motivation and driven by internal rewards. Even more so if this intrinsic motivation is linked to self-identity, rather than identity-irrelevant ones (8). Goals based purely on *extrinsic* motivation, such as losing weight for a partner or validation from social media fame, may not provide sufficient staying power to stick at it when the going gets tough.

Examples of Intrinsic/Extrinsic Motivation:

1. Intrinsic motivation: "I want to be the very best that I can be."
2. Extrinsic motivation: "I want to look attractive for my Instagram page."

Know Thyself

The obstacles on a fat-loss or muscle building journey are not merely physiological. They are often found in the mind and affect our ability to act.

Motivation provided by the enthusiasm of the moment is short-lived.

But motivation for consistent, goal-directed action is possible when focused on the *delayed gratification* of a long-term reward (e.g., health). Nevertheless, the levers of motivation are not always apparent. In some cases, they are hard-wired by overarching meta-programs, beliefs and values.

Extoling the virtues of planning and preparation, Sun Tzu writes in "The Art of War", that "every battle is won *before* it is ever fought." Paradoxically, preparation for a body transformation program must in the first instance be psychological. Reflecting on why we have failed in the past, unpacking some limiting belief, or finding what really drives us will help us become more completely aligned with our goals.

Then we may find our behaviours finally match our intentions and unlike Oscar Wilde, we *will* be able to resist everything, *including* temptation!

CHAPTER 20

HACKING THE POWER OF HABIT

"We are what we repeatedly do. Excellence, then, is not an act, but a habit"

Aristotle

In an interview with Vanity Fair in 2012, former US President Barack Obama revealed, "you'll see I wear only gray or blue suits." Richard Branson has confessed to wearing "the same pair of jeans every day," no matter the occasion, and Facebook's Mark Zuckerberg famously pairs almost everything with his signature grey T-shirt. Apart from a passing interest in fashion, these global movers and shakers share a desire to avoid 'decision fatigue'.

Whilst this might on first hearing sound like more eccentric musings from the rich and powerful, the idea finds support in the research which shows that making many decisions a day impairs executive function and subsequent self-control (1). Self-control, willpower and the ability to resist short-term temptation to meet long-term goals are it appears, not unlimited resources but may become drained with use (2, 3).

Other models to explain 'ego-depletion' have been proposed, but at a very real physiological level, we know that acts of willpower and self-control consume glucose (4). While constituting only 2% of our body's weight, the human brain uses up about 20% of our daily calorie intake (5). It stands to reason that the greater the task the more willpower required to overcome an impulse and so the more susceptible we become to fluctuations in blood-glucose levels (6).

Framed in this physiological context, it is easy to understand why people find dieting so hard. Even a modest and sustainable calorie restriction diet plan inevitably involves some form of self-denial, depleting the very resource which fuels our willpower—glucose! Coaches and Personal Trainers of the 'go hard or go home' school of thought, who grow impatient with clients who can't muscle their way through a diet would do well to remember this.

The good news is that willpower can be learned with the regular practice of small acts of self-control (7). Repetition, as they say, is the mother of all learning. But it is also the foundation of successful habit formation and long-lasting behavioural change.

Neuroplasticity, a term first used by Polish neuroscientist Jerzy Konorski in 1948 (8), defines the nervous system's ability to form new connections and pathways and effectively re-wire the brain's circuits. However, this re-wiring takes time and is only possible through the repetition and practice of new habits.

Research has shown that it takes on average, 66 days (9) for a simple habit such as eating a piece of fruit with lunch or doing 50 sit ups upon waking to become automatic. Aside from time and patience, the early stages of habit formation require conscious effort and willpower. As leadership expert, Robin Sharma, is fond of saying, *"All change is hard at first, messy in the middle, and so gorgeous at the end."*

As willpower is not an unlimited resource, focusing on acquiring one or two habits fundamental to the success of your ultimate outcome is smart thinking. For example, planning to run a marathon may be a laudable goal but if you find training after work too tiring, then embedding another habit first—such as rising with sufficient time for a run—makes more sense. When a certain degree of 'automaticity' is reached, the next stage of the training program can begin in earnest.

When a habit becomes automatic it no longer requires conscious effort or thought and willpower is not expended (10). Importantly, habits are also not dependent on motivation (11). Once you are in the gym, motivation to train harder than last time may be the next step but acquiring the habit to consistently show up regardless of mood is half the battle.

Getting lean, building muscle and the creation of good health will obviously necessitate the adoption of a healthy lifestyle. Decisions to change unhelpful habits such as smoking, excessive drinking or avoiding foods that trigger overeating will be entirely personal. Nevertheless, there are some key habits revolving around diet, exercise and sleep, which are universally applicable.

Dietary habits

Although the nation's obesity statistics suggest otherwise, people do lose weight. And on a variety of diets. Keeping it off is another matter. Successful, long term weight loss of 10% or more of one's body weight is not a frequent occurrence. In fact, one study showed that 80% of individuals will put it all back on after 1 year (12).

On the other hand, those who successfully maintain weight loss for two years are more likely to do so for the next five to ten years (13). So, as Anthony Robbins is fond of saying, what is the "difference that makes the difference" between these people?

Perhaps surprisingly for diet zealots, long term success is not associated with any one diet (14). The keys to success are the subject matter of these chapters; the possession of both intrinsic and extrinsic motivation; monitoring and tracking progress; the acquisition of habits which facilitate a lifestyle and characteristics which form a new identity, involving dietary control and exercise.

In previous chapters we discussed the importance of both monitoring food intake and tracking progress. Tracking body composition progress should not be limited to the scale, however, but also include measurements and photos. Of course, monitoring food intake need not involve a food diary or tracking calories but might simply be exercising restraint through portion control and limiting snacks.

Nevertheless, I will recommend clients undertake a period of tracking calories with an app such as MyFitnessPal. The process of tracking and weighing food, especially for the first time, is an invaluable education in nutrition and an exercise in mindfulness. Very often we engage in mindless, or binge eating, then either pretend it didn't happen or indulge in a spot of guilt-ridden self-flagellation. Committing to track daily food intake, irrespective of the foods we eat or even how much, is a process which provides pause for thought and self-reflection.

Mindful eating

Mindful eating habits have been shown to increase adherence and reduce craving-related eating behaviours (15). Mindful, purposeful eating, paying attention to the present moment, has also been shown to reduce self-criticism after temporary lapses and help with the resumption of dietary adherence (16).

One habit we should consider adopting which facilitates mindful eating is to simply chew our food longer. Chewing one's food is also a crucial element of digestion which starts in the mouth with the release of salivary enzymes. This pre-digestion of food before it reaches the pancreas and gallbladder minimises digestive stress caused by having to deal with larger, less digested food (17).

Ayurvedic practitioners recommend chewing each bite up to 30-40 times and, while this might sound impractical for time-poor Westerners, becoming aware of the need to masticate food into smaller particles before swallowing constitutes progress. Research also shows that chewing one's food thoroughly improves dietary adherence from a greater sense of satiety (18) and may lead to less calorie consumption (19).

Exercise habits

We know that regular exercise and physical activity facilitates healthy aging, improves functional capacity and prevents disease (20). Other studies have shown that good exercise habits, including cardio and resistance training help maintain physical performance (21) and muscle strength (22) with age. Significantly, the formation of good exercise habits is also associated with good dietary habits (23).

So, what can help us with the formation of good exercise habits? Establishing strong cue-response associations are of course vital for embedding any new habit (24). This might involve placing your trainers next to your bed if you plan to run upon waking or playing a motivational playlist on the way to the gym. Incorporating a social component to your workout, such as training with a friend or a group class (25) can also positively affect behavior frequency.

Interestingly, perhaps the strongest predictor of exercise habits is sticking to the same workout time and schedule. Regardless of the specific time of day, consistency of exercise time is a distinguishing characteristic which promotes adherence to both regular physical activity and the maintenance of weight loss (26).

Sleep habits

Most people will have heard that eight hours sleep a night is optimal for health. Previous studies have certainly shown that both less than seven hours sleep a night and prolonged sleep of more than 8 hours are associated with increased mortality (27), diabetes (28), and obesity (29).

Margaret Thatcher famously got by on four hours of sleep a night. Nevertheless, both she and Ronald Reagan, another light sleeper, developed dementia in their later years. A 2017 study by Stanford University found that even two nights of poor sleep increased levels of proteins associated with Alzheimer's disease (30). While no one lays claim to a scientific association, it does suggest that regularly burning the candle at both ends—as these leaders did—is not advisable.

Getting enough restorative sleep to have sufficient energy to train regularly and recover adequately also just makes commons sense. *But does sleep have any effect on building muscle?*

In a word, yes. And the answer lies again with hormones.

Testosterone, an anabolic hormone, is a powerful regulator of muscle protein synthesis (31) and a lack of sleep can decrease its production. One study found that after only 8 days of 5.5 hours sleep participants showed a 10-15% decline (32). Another found that even one night of sleep deprivation can result in an acute reduction of testosterone levels (33). IGF-1 (Insulin-like growth factor), another anabolic hormone which plays an important role in protein synthesis and the maintenance of muscle mass (34), also becomes rapidly reduced in conditions of sleep deprivation (35).

The anabolic hormonal environment favourable to muscle building is similarly diminished by the effects a lack of sleep has on increasing cortisol, the stress hormone, which is catabolic (muscle wasting). Cortisol while being lower at night, follows a circadian rhythm of being high in the morning which aids our ability to wake up. A lack of sleep dysregulates these rhythms, reducing morning cortisol but increasing overall exposure throughout the whole day (36).

What are the good sleep habits we should try to encourage?

As with exercise, perhaps the first habit we need to get right concerns timing and the need to sleep and rise at the same time every day. Again, having a pleasing night-time ritual, an order of doing things which helps build the cue-response relationship is vital for establishing a habit (24).

One habit to consider adopting is having a warm bath or shower a while before bed. Besides comfort and good personal hygiene (!), it paradoxically allows for our core body temperature to drop which is important for effective and deep sleep (37).

Avoiding coffee in the afternoon—as caffeine has a half-life of about five to six hours (38)—is another sensible habit. As is limiting the use of light-emitting electronic devices at bedtime which may contribute to fitful sleep patterns (39). Even if the next episode of your favourite box set is especially riveting, the exposure to blue-wavelength light from your device can suppress melatonin and cause neurophysiologic stimulation.

Sleep and its many benefits for physical and mental wellbeing are a fascinating topic to which we couldn't begin to do justice here. For anyone interested in aging well and longevity, I thoroughly recommend reading Matthew Walker's, "*Why we sleep: The New Science of Sleep and Dreams*" for a deeper dive (39).

CHAPTER 21

THE BIG VISION

"Where there is no vision, the people perish."

Proverbs 29:18

Goal setting is widely considered an effective means to increase motivation (1). However, in his autobiography, *Total Recall*, Arnold Schwarzenegger writes about first creating a big vision before drilling down to the time-sensitive, specific goals needed to achieve it. Arnold's own vision involved following in the footsteps of Reg Park, the former Mr. Universe, who went on to become an actor and whom he saw play Hercules in the movies.

Arnold's big vision for achieving success chimes with goal setting tools central to the process in Neurolinguistic Programming (NLP). One such tool is known as "chunking." Borrowed from computer terminology, "Chunking" refers to clusters or chunks of information we may group together in a broad or narrow sense to create patterns that help make sense of the world.

To "chunk up" is to take the 1000 ft helicopter ride and look at something with distance and perspective. For example, *"only the northeast part of the wood is on fire."* To "chunk down", on the other hand, is the view from the trenches which is focused and more granular in detail: *"the fire is raging here... we can't see the wood for the trees."*

As personalities, we tend to default to one or the other. Former UK Prime Minister, Tony Blair for example, concerned himself with the 'big picture' of policy making. Teresa May, in contrast, preferred grappling with the details. To be truly successful in any endeavour we need both.

Nevertheless, as world-renowned business management theorist, Peter Drucker was fond of saying, "management is doing things right; leadership is doing the right things" (2). In this context, before chunking down to the details of "how", the process of goal setting should begin with the creation of a big, compelling vision.

And when you consider Arnold was born in a small, parochial village in southeast Austria and not Venice Beach, California, you begin to understand the scale of how "big" his vision was. But knowing what success looks like to you is very personal and often values-driven. Nevertheless, I encourage you to get real clarity on this and to be ambitious! Vague goals such as "I want to lose a bit of weight" do not have the "pull" to sustain the necessary drive, determination and discipline to transform a body—something which requires time, patience and consistency.

Modelling

Having an idol, like Arnold found in Reg Park or someone who has achieved what you want is also a very powerful tool. In NLP this is referred to as "modelling": the process of recreating and replicating excellence. If, like me, your fitness journey begins in your forties or later (I was 43 years old and 30kg overweight) aspirations to excellence may seem like delusions of grandeur.

Indeed, when I decided to retrain as a Personal Trainer, classmates shot each other incredulous looks when I said I wanted to compete on stage at the Miami Pro Fitness Model Championships. At that time, I had lost some weight and built some muscle but was a long way off from lean and light years away from stage-ready!

Nevertheless, I was driven. I had seen a behind-the-scenes video of James Alexander Ellis at the Miami Pro Championships and something about his swagger, the music and the applause from the crowds lit the fires of my ambition. A year after qualifying as a PT, and 18 months after my mother had died, I placed third in the fitness model category for Over 35's.

The Big Why

I don't mention this to impress you, but to impress upon you the need to find that big, ambitious vision. Grant Cardone refers to this as a 10x vision. But once you have this big vision, you must then take the time to imbue the goal with a sense of meaning, leveraging "the power of why" (3).

Getting in shape for a beach holiday may, for some, be a very powerful 'why'. Building an extraordinary physique to create an online dating profile and attract the woman of your dreams might help you find an extra gear. It may have the intrinsic "pull" to get you up in time to train, or the discipline to go to bed early and ensure restorative sleep.

In some respects, having goals is the easy part. Who doesn't want to look good in a T-shirt or on the beach? The real question is what are you prepared to do for them? Are you ready for the inevitable tradeoffs or even sacrifice that comes with the territory?

What is undeniable is that with such a quest, there is the need to forge a new lifestyle and going to the pub every night (probably) won't make the cut! Muhammed Ali encapsulated this idea best when he said: *"I hated every minute of training, but I said to myself, 'Don't quit. Suffer now and live the rest of your life as a champion" (4).*

A Purposeful Life

We know that achieving our goals provides a sense of achievement. Perhaps, just as importantly, seeing the daily progress we can make towards them gives life a sense of purpose. And, in fact, this sense of purpose is not only rewarding, but a lot healthier for us. A purposeful life has been shown to be associated with a reduced risk of mortality and cardiovascular events (5).

Those with a higher sense of purpose live longer and have a reduced risk of other debilitating conditions such as stroke, loss of physical function, depression and even Alzheimer's disease (6). Interestingly, this sense of meaning need not be overtly spiritual but can come from anywhere, be that gardening or birdwatching! (6).

Purpose, as defined by McKnight and Kashdan, is "a central, self-organizing life aim that organizes and stimulates goals, manages behaviors, and provides a sense of meaning" (7). But this sense of life purpose and meaningfulness can be greatly enhanced when it is aligned or imbued with one's own identity (8) core values and passions (9, 10).

The sense of ongoing purpose I personally derive from my "big vision" of building a physique to the lofty aspirations of the Grecian Ideal continues to surprise me. But this meaningfulness is greatly enhanced by the need to overcome age-related challenges in order to achieve it, as the 'Rocky' persona of 'winning against the odds' is a deeply embedded aspect of my psyche.

Goal setting

Big, purposeful vision in hand, the next step involves identifying the specific goals we need to set to make it a reality. Goals, as defined by Locke and Latham (1991) are "the object or aim of an action, for example, to attain a specific standard of proficiency, usually within a specified time limit" (11).

All well and good. But how do we go about setting them up?

There exists a wealth of research in the area of goal setting—mostly from the field of business management—as to what constitutes successful goal setting, but there is some broad agreement as to some of its underlying principles.

1. They must be written down.

A 2007 study by Dr Gail Matthews (12) showed that people were on average 42% more likely to achieve their goals when they wrote them down.

At the most basic level, it stands to reason that having a visual cue such as a post-it note on your mirror or refrigerator will remind you of the importance of your goal. It can also provide you with the chance to reconnect with your 'why' at a more emotional level, fanning the flames of desire.

But neuroscience has also demonstrated that a phenomenon known as the "generation effect" (13) is responsible for more effective hard wiring of these goals when written down. The "generation effect" demonstrates that when individuals generate material for themselves, rather than simply thinking about them, it becomes more deeply embedded in the memory, contributing to greater attention and cognitive efforts.

2. They must have clarity.

Once you have committed to writing your goals down, take the time to get absolute clarity about what it is you want and why you want it.

Many of you will have attended a workshop or received a goal setting presentation about the importance of having SMART goals. The S (Specific), M (Measurable) and T (Time bound) elements of this acronym are all concerned with achieving this kind of clarity.

S (Specific) M (Measurable) A (Achievable) R (Realistic) T (Time bound)

For example, *"I want to lose some weight"* is vague and directionless in comparison to the unambiguous clarity of *"I want to lose 14 Lbs. in 12 Weeks for my wedding day."*

In this last example, the 'why' is also charged with emotional significance.

3. They must have feedback systems.

When a goal is measurable, we can monitor its progress. Progress, in turn, can provide a new sense of impetus and energy to achieve even more.

Having proper systems in place to provide feedback such as weighing ourselves weekly or taking progress photos every month will also allow us to change tack if what we are doing isn't working.

A goal, according to Napoleon Hill, is "a dream with a deadline" and, while sometimes our dreams may be delayed, setting dates and timelines to achieve them provides both a sense of urgency and the backdrop for measuring progress and taking feedback.

4. They must be challenging.

According to Locke and Latham's goal setting theory (14) to provide motivation a goal must also be challenging.

This, in my opinion, is where the paradigm of SMART goals falls short.

A (achievable) and R (realistic) goals do not set the world alight or produce Elon Musk-like ambition. "Big, hairy audacious goals," according to '*Built to Last*' by Jim Collins, on the other hand, will do that (15).

In the context of both the human spirit and the pace of modern technological change, defining what is achievable and realistic also doesn't lend itself to clarity. These concepts are relative, personal and influenced largely by beliefs and values. Running a four-minute mile or developing an effective vaccine for Covid-19 in 9 months was conceivably neither achievable nor realistic at the time.

At the other end of the spectrum, if you have never managed successfully to lose a lot of weight you may have limiting beliefs about what is realistic. Modelling others who have succeeded, adopting their belief systems and mindset, is a powerful way of overcoming such psychological obstacles.

Big Goals. Small wins.

Big wins, or even a big breakthrough, on the way to achieving our goals are sometimes few and far between. Yet these big wins are always built on the shoulders of small, incremental wins. Breaking your goals down into smaller weekly sub-goals and monthly milestones is one way of ensuring that we experience the uplifting power of progress more frequently.

After the initial phase of a fat loss program, where the pounds fall off more easily, clients sometimes complain of *only* losing a pound a week. The long-term goal being some way off, their exclusive focus on the outcome doesn't allow them to celebrate the small wins. This, even though a pound a week amounts to 52 pounds in one year!

Tracking that extra rep in the logbook, the kilo in micro weights added to a lift, progress photos, taking measurements and not just recording scale weight are all different ways of appreciating the small wins. Compounded, these small wins on sub-goals are powerful and should be celebrated as signposts that you are heading in the right direction.

AFTERWORD

Thank you for buying my book.

I hope it has both inspired and encouraged you to take action, leaving you in no doubt that fat loss, radically transforming your physique and achieving optimal health in your 40s and 50s is not only entirely possible, but in many ways, an imperative.

From its inception, the book's objective was to educate, through evidence-based research, on the importance of a muscle-centric approach to fat loss, and consequently to demystify the principles of training and nutrition, as applied to men over 40. "Teach a man to fish..." etc.

The book was never designed as a generic, "8 weeks to a Fitter You" cookie-cutter program, or worse still, a pale imitation of a Jamie Oliver cookbook. This is because as a Personal Trainer, I understand the primacy of the principle of individualisation for successful, long-term physique transformations. And this is where a good coach makes art out of the science.

In this context, I encourage you to visit my website, www.themidlifealpha.com or write to me personally at anthony@themidlifealpha.com to find out more about my Online Coaching services, or the fully personalised (training, nutrition, lifestyle) 90 Day Plans from my "Dad Bod to Greek God" program.

That said, I want to make sure you receive as much value from your purchase. Accordingly, in the pages that follow, there are examples of the free bonus resources which accompany the book, such as a calorie counted, macro-friendly sample meal plan, high protein recipes and a beginners training program.

Please email bonus@themidlifealpha.com to claim the bonus and access the full PDF versions, stating which resource you require in the subject line.

RESOURCES

Beginner Program: Full Body (3-Day Weekly Split)

WEEK 1, DAY 1:

Exercise	Set	Rep	Rest *(mins)*	Notes
Body Squat	3	12	3	Feet shoulder-width apart. Breathe and brace core. Look straight ahead, torso upright. Push hips back and bend knees simultaneously to sit down into the squat. Avoid knees caving inwards. Drive heels into ground, push floor away, and accelerate through the lift to return to starting position.
Bodyweight Lunges	3	12	3	Feet shoulder-width apart. Engage core and drive front knee forward in controlled fashion, while bending back knee towards the floor. Push through ball of front foot, contracting glutes and quads, to drive back upwards to starting position, by extending the front knee.

Press Ups	3	12	3	Arms slightly wider than shoulder width and placed directly under shoulders. With soft elbows close to body, descend towards floor until chest and thighs touch the ground. Push back up through chest and triceps to ascend to starting position.
Lat Pulldown (Machine)	3	12	3	Lean slightly back, brace core and with palms faced down, pull bar down to chest. Drive elbows into hips. Maintain feet on the floor at times, with glutes glued to the seat!
Standing Biceps Curls (Dumbbells)	3	12	3	Begin with palms face upward and curl dumbbell towards shoulder, keeping shoulder still. Bring forearm into contact with upper arm. Finish curl by supinating at the wrist and squeezing little finger. Controlled eccentric.

WEEK 1, DAY 2:

Exercise	Set	Rep	Rest (Mins)	Notes
Body Squat	3	12	3	Feet shoulder-width apart. Breathe and brace core. Look straight ahead, torso upright. Push hips back and bend knees simultaneously to sit down into the squat. Avoid knees caving inwards. Drive heels into ground, push floor away, and accelerate through the lift to return to starting position.

Romanian Deadlifts (Dumbbells)	3	12	3	Drive hips back behind and into hip flexion. Lower weights with soft break at the knees. Torso upright, chin tucked in. Brace core and maintain neutral spine.
Assisted Pull UPs (Machine) (Use resistance band to assist if gym doesn't have machine)	3	12	3	With neutral grip (palms facing each other) place knees on the kneepad. Pull body and chin towards the bar, initiating with lats, engaging and keeping neutral spine. Drive elbows back and down towards torso. Lower body down in slow, controlled manner. *The machine is weight adjusted and adding weight to the machine reduces the amount of bodyweight require to pull up.
Press Ups	3	12	3	Arms slightly wider than shoulder width and placed directly under shoulders. With soft elbows close to body, descend towards floor until chest and thighs touch the ground. Push back up through chest and triceps to ascend to starting position.
Triceps Pushdown (Ropes)	3	12	3	Chest up, lock elbows into sides, brace core and drive ropes towards waist. When fully extended, pause and maximally contract triceps.

WEEK 1, DAY 3:

Exercise	Set	Rep	Rest *(mins)*	Notes
Goblet Squat (Dumbbells)	3	12	3	Position dumbbell vertically on chest, bending elbows to hold dumbbells like a goblet. Feet shoulder-width apart. Breathe and brace core. Look straight ahead, torso upright. Push hips back and bend knees simultaneously to sit down into the squat. Avoid knees caving inwards. Drive heels into ground, push floor away, and accelerate through the lift to return to starting position.
Dumbbell Lunges	3	12	3	Feet, shoulder-width apart, a set of dumbbells in each arm. Engage core and drive front knee forward in controlled fashion, while bending back knee towards the floor. Push through ball of front foot, contracting glutes and quads, to drive back upwards to starting position, by extending the front knee.
Standing Shoulder Press (Dumbbells)	3	12	3	Stand with feet shoulder-width apart. Brace core. Contract glutes. Press up dumbbells above shoulders, pushing upper arms towards your ears. DO NOT fully straighten arms or touch dumbbells together. Keep dumbbells parallel with floor. Lower weights in controlled fashion.

Leg Extension (Machine)	3	12	3	Squeeze handles and drive glutes into pad. Don't throw weight up. Focus on contracting the whole quad from origin to point of insertion.
Standing Biceps Curls (Dumbbells)	3	12	3	Begin with palms face upward and curl dumbbell towards shoulder, keeping shoulder still. Bring forearm into contact with upper arm. Finish curl by supinating at the wrist and squeezing little finger. Controlled eccentric.

SAMPLE MEAL PLAN (Cals: 2,032)

Total Cals: 2,032
Macros: Protein: 35% Fat: 35% Carbs: 30%

MEAL 1	FOOD	PORTION	Protein (g)	Carbs (g)	Fat (g)	Cals
Breakfast	Scrambled Eggs, Smoked Salmon w/ Avocado on Toast Eggs					
	Egg Whites	2 (Large)	12.6	0	9.6	140
	Smoked Salmon	50g	5.4	0.4	0	24
	(Wild Alaskan)	100g	24.3	0.6	2.7	123
	Avocado	1/4	1.2	2.95	5.1	65
	Sourdough Toast	50g	4.1	26	0.4	125
Sub total			**47.6**	**29.95**	**17.8**	**477**

MEAL 2	FOOD	PORTION	Protein (g)	Carbs (g)	Fat (g)	Cals
Lunch	Walnut Chicken, w/ Yogurt Dressing & Rice					
	Chicken Breast	150g	33.6	0	0.4	153
	Walnuts (crushed)	2	1.2	1.1	5.2	52
	Greek Yogurt	100g	10.1	4	9	95
	Olive Oil	1 tbsp	0	0	14	120
	Baby Spinach Leaves	100g	1.5	0.5	0	19
	White Rice	120g	4.2	38	0.6	160
Sub total			**50.6**	**43.6**	**29.2**	**599**

MEAL 3	FOOD	PORTION	Protein (g)	Carbs (g)	Fat (g)	Cals
Lunch	Walnut Chicken, w/ Yogurt Dressing & Rice					
	Chicken Breast	150g	33.6	0	0.4	153
	Walnuts (crushed)	2	1.2	1.1	5.2	52
	Greek Yogurt	100g	10.1	4	9	95
	Olive Oil	1 tbsp	0	0	14	120
	Baby Spinach Leaves	100g	1.5	0.5	0	19
	White Rice	120g	4.2	38	0.6	160
Sub total			**50.6**	**43.6**	**29.2**	**599**

MEAL 3	FOOD	PORTION	Protein (g)	Carbs (g)	Fat (g)	Cals
Pre-Workout	**Large Banana**	1	1.5	31	0.4	121
Intra-Workout	**Lucozade Low Cal Drink**	1	0	10	0	50
Sub total			**1.5**	**41**	**0.4**	**171**

MEAL 4	FOOD	PORTION	Protein (g)	Carbs (g)	Fat (g)	Cals
Pre-Workout	**Whey Protein Drink**	1.25 Scoop	30	3.8	1.5	150
Sub total			**30g**	**3.8**	**1.5**	**150**

MEAL 5	FOOD	PORTION	Protein (g)	Carbs (g)	Fat (g)	Cals
Dinner	Sirloin Steak, Sweet potatoes and Coleslaw					
	Sirloin Steak	155g	42.8	0	17.7	325
	Sweet Potatoes	130g	3.8	32.1	0.7	155
	Coleslaw	50g	0.6	1.5	13.5	130
	Cherry Tomatoes	100g	1.1	3.4	0	25
Sub total			**48.3**	**37**	**31.9**	**635**

Total			Protein	Carbs	Fat	Cals
			176.5	155.3	80.4	2,032

Examples of High Protein (35g-45g) Meals

Greek Scrambled Eggs

1 tbsp. olive oil
1 garlic clove minced
1 tomato, cored, grated
1 tbsp. dried oregano
3 eggs, beaten
Egg Whites (100g)
(30g) feta, crumbled
Salt & pepper

Per Serving: 507 Cals / 41g Protein / 35g Fat / 8g Carbs

Parmesan Chicken Alfredo

Chicken Breast, 200g
1 Tsp (heaped) garlic powder
1 Tsp (heaped) Italian herbs
1 Tsp (heaped) paprika
1 Tsp salt & Pepper
1 Tsp Olive Oil
120 g uncooked pasta (240 g cooked weight)

Creamy Sauce:

100 ml low fat milk
30 g light cream cheese
20 g parmesan
1 Tsp Italian herbs
Garnish with Parsley & Parmesan

Per Serving: 553 Cals / 55g Protein / 15g Fat / 47g Carbs

Herb & garlic baked cod with romesco sauce & spinach

200g skinless cod fillets
1 tbsp rapeseed oil
1 tsp fresh thyme leaves l
1 large garlic clove, finely grated
½ lemon
1 large red pepper
2 leeks, well washed and thinly sliced
2 tbsp flaked almonds
1 tbsp tomato puree
¼ tsp vegetable bouillon powder
1 tsp apple cider vinegar
100g baby spinach, wilted in a pan or the microwave

Per Serving: 450 Cals / 43g Protein / Fat 24g / Carbs 11g

Moroccan Meatballs and Couscous

30 x 20g Beef meatballs
½ Onion, chopped
3 x Garlic Cloves, finely chopped
1 x Red Onion, chopped
Pinch of Fresh Parsley
1 Tsp Cumin
3 x Sprigs Coriander
6 x Mint Leaves, Chopped
Couscous,300g
1 x Spring Onion, Finely chopped
¼ Sweet Red Pepper
150g Fresh Kale Handful, dried cranberries

Per Serving: 457 Cals / 40g Protein / 15g Fat / 30.6g Carbs

Sticky Teriyaki Salmon Rice

1 Salmon Fillet
1 tbsp teriyaki sauce
1 tbsp sweet chilli sauce
1 salmon fillet
50g wholemeal basmati rice
1 head Pak choi, halved
1 tsp sesame seed oil
2 spring onions, finely chopped
small bunch coriander, roughly chopped
squeeze of lime

Per Serving: 558 Cals / 40 g Protein / Fat 21g / Carbs 53g

Chicken Satay Salad

1 chicken breast, 200g skinless
1 tbsp. tamari soy sauce
1 tsp. medium curry powder
¼ tsp. ground cumin
1 garlic clove—finely grated
1 tsp. clear honey
1 tbsp. crunchy peanut butter
1 tbsp. sweet chilli sauce
1 tbsp. lime juice
2 Little Gem lettuces hearts—cut into wedges
¼ cucumber—halved and sliced
1 banana shallot—halved and thinly sliced
Generous handful coriander—chopped
Seeds from ½ pomegranate

Per Serving: 353 Cals / 40 g Protein / Fat 24g / Carbs 10g

REFERENCES

PART ONE: THE CHALLENGES

CHAPTER 1: I COULDA BEEN A CONTENDER

1 **Nie, Y., Ma, Y., Wu, Y., Li, J., Liu, T., Zhang, C., Lv, C., & Zhu, J.** (2021). Association Between Physical Exercise and Mental Health During the COVID-19 Outbreak in China: A Nationwide Cross-Sectional Study. *Frontiers in psychiatry, 12*, 722448.

2 **Schuch FB, Vancampfort D.** Physical activity, exercise, and mental disorders: it is time to move on. Trends Psychiatry Psychother. 2021 Jul-Sep;43(3):177-184.

3 **Carraro, A. Scarpa, S. Ventura, L.** (2010) Relationships between physical self-concept and physical fitness in Italian adolescents. Percept Mot Skills 110: 522-530.

4 **García-Sánchez, A. Burgueño-Menjibar, R. López-Blanco, D. Ortega, F.B.,** (2013) Condición física, adiposidad y autoconcepto en adolescentes. Estudio piloto. Revista de Psicología del Deporte 22: 453-461.

5 **Grogan, S. Richards, H.** (2002) Body image: Focus groups with boys and men. Men and Masculinities 4(3): 219–232.

6 **Centre for Appearance Research, UWE.** https://info.uwe.ac.uk/news/uwe-news/news.aspx?id=2178

7 **Maisey, D.S., Vale, E.L., Cornelissen, P.L., Tovée, M.J.,** Characteristics of male attractiveness for women. *Lancet*. 1999;353(9163):1500.

8 **Sell, A. Lukazsweski, A.W., Townsley, M.** Cues of upper body strength account for most of the variance in men's bodily attractiveness. *Proc Biol Sci*. 2017;284(1869):20171819.

9 **Jeukendrup A. E. (2017)**. Training the Gut for Athletes. *Sports medicine (Auckland, N.Z.)*, *47*(Suppl 1), 101–110.

10 **Chen, N. Zhou, M. Dong, X. Qu, J. *et al*;** Epidemiological and clinical characteristics of 99 cases of 2019 novel coronavirus pneumonia in Wuhan, China: a descriptive study. *The Lancet*. 2020. (395) 10223. 507-513

11 **Global, regional, and national incidence**, prevalence, and years lived with disability for 354 diseases and injuries for 195 countries and territories, 1990–2017: a systematic analysis for the Global Burden of Disease Study 2017. *Global Health Metrics*. 2018. (392) 10159 1789-1858

12 **Demasi M**. COVID-19 and metabolic syndrome: could diet be the key? *BMJ Evidence-Based Medicine* 2021; 26:1-2.

13 **Wu S, Zhou K, Misra-Hebert A, Bena J, Kashyap SR.** Impact of Metabolic Syndrome on Severity of COVID-19 Illness. *Metab Syndr Relat Disord*. 2022 May;20(4):191-198

14 **Kim G, Kim JH.** Impact of Skeletal Muscle Mass on Metabolic Health. *Endocrinol Metab (Seoul)*. 2020 Mar;35(1):1-6

15 **Gil S, Jacob Filho W, Shinjo SK, Ferriolli E. *et al;*** HCFMUSP COVID-19 Study Group. Muscle strength and muscle mass as predictors of hospital length of stay in patients with moderate to severe COVID-19: a prospective observational study. J *Cachexia Sarcopenia Muscle*. 2021 Dec;12(6):1871-1878

CHAPTER 2: THE REAL MIDLIFE CRISIS

1 https://www.ons.gov.uk/peoplepopulationandcommunity/wellbeing/articles/measuringnationalwellbeing

2 https://www.ons.gov.uk/peoplepopulationandcommunity/birthsdeathsandmarriages/deaths/bulletins/suicidesintheunitedkingdom/2018registrations

3 https://media.samaritans.org/documents/Men-and-Suicide-Report-Samaritans.pdf

4 **Munoz-Reyes, J. Polo, P. Rodriguez-Sickert, C. Pavez, P. Valenzuela N. Ramirez-Herrera, O.** Muscularity and Strength Affect Individual Variation in Self-Perception of Fighting Ability in Men. *Front. Psychol.* 22 January 2019.

5 **Gentil P, Steele J, Pereira MC, Castanheira RP, Paoli A, Bottaro M.** Comparison of upper body strength gains between men and women after 10 weeks of resistance training. *PeerJ*. 2016 Feb 11;4: e1627

6 **Ogden, C.L., Fryar, C.D., Carroll, M.D., Flegal, K.M.,** Mean body weight, height, and body mass index, United States 1960--2002. Advance data from vital and health statistics; no 347. Hyattsville, MD: US Department of Health and Human Services, CDC, National Center for Health Statistics; 2004

7 https://www.gov.uk/government/news/modern-life-responsible-for-worrying-health-in-middle-aged

8 **Travison, T.G., Araujo, A.B., O'Donnell, Kupelian, V. McKinlay, J.B**. A population-level decline in serum testosterone levels in American men. *J Clin. Endocrinol Metab*. 2007;92(1):196-202.

9 **Moffat, S.D., Zonderman, A.B., Metter, E.J., *et al*;** Longitudinal assessment of serum free testosterone concentration predicts memory performance and cognitive status in elderly men. *J Clin Endocrinol Metab.* 2002; 87:5001–5007.

10 **Finas, D., Bals-Pratsch, M., Sandmann, J., *et al*;** Quality of life in elderly men with androgen deficiency. *Andrologia.* 2006; 38:48–53

11 **Berglund, L.H., Prytz, H.S., Perski, A. Svartberg, J.** Testosterone levels and psychological health status in men from a general population: the Tromsø study. *Aging Male.* 2011; 14: 37–41.

12 https://www.drinkaware.co.uk/professionals/press/half-of-uk-middle-aged-men-drinking-above-guidelines

13 https://www.mind.org.uk/news-campaigns/news/mind-survey-finds-men-more-likely-to-experience-work-related-mental-health-problems/

14 **Shor, E. Roelfs D.J. Davidson, K. W. Schwartz, J.E.** Losing Life and Livelihood: A Systematic Review and Meta-Analysis of Unemployment and All-Cause Mortality. *Social Science Medicine* 72(6):840-54

CHAPTER 3: WHO MOVED MY TESTOSTERONE?

1 **Richter, E.A., Derave, W., Wojtaszewski J.F.P.,** Glucose, exercise and insulin: emerging concepts *J Physiol.* 2001 Sep 1; 535(Pt 2): 313 322

2 **Van den Beld, A.W., Kaufman, J.M., Zillikens, M.C., et al**; the physiology of endocrine systems with ageing. *Lancet Diabetes Endocrinol.* 2018 Aug; 6(8): 647–658.

3 **Harman SM, Metter EJ, Tobin JD, *et al*;** Longitudinal effects of aging on serum total and free testosterone levels in healthy men. Baltimore Longitudinal Study of Aging. *J Clin Endocrinol Metab.* 2001; 86:724–31.

4 **Feldman, H. A., Longcope, C, Derby C. A., Johannes, C.B., *et al;*** Age trends in the level of serum testosterone and other hormones in middle-aged men: longitudinal results from the Massachusetts male aging study. *J Clin Endocrinol Metab.* 2002 Feb; 87(2):589-9

5 **Khosla, S., Melton, L. J., Atkinson, E.J., *et al.*** Relationship of serum sex steroid levels and bone turnover markers with bone mineral density in men and women: a key role for bioavailable estrogen. *J Clin Endocrinol Metab.* 1998 Jul; 83(7):2266-74.

6 **Roy, T. A., Blackman, M. R., Harman, S.M., *et al.*** Interrelationships of serum testosterone and free testosterone index with FFM and strength in aging men. *Am J Physiol Endocrinol Metab.* 2002 Aug; 283(2): E284-94.

7 **Zitzmann M.** Testosterone, mood, behaviour and quality of life. Andrology. 2020 Nov;8(6):1598-1605.

8 **Kelly, D.M., Jones, T.H.,** Testosterone: a metabolic hormone in health and disease. *Journal of Endocrinology.* 2013 Apr 29; 217(3): R25-45

9 **Goodale, T, Sadhu, A. Steven Petak, S. Robbins, R**. Testosterone and the heart. Methodist Debakey Cardiovasc J. 2017 Apr-Jun; 13(2): 68–72.

10 **Nur-Vaizura M, Ima-Nirwana S, Kok-Yong C**. A concise review of testosterone and bone health. *Clin Interv Aging*. 2016; 11: 1317–1324.

11 **Cherrier M.M., Craft S, Matsumoto A.H.**, Cognitive changes associated with supplementation of testosterone or dihydrotestosterone in mildly hypo gonadal men: a preliminary report. *J Androl*. 2003 Jul-Aug; 24(4):568-76

12 **Barrett-Connor E, Von Mühlen D.G., Kritz-Silverstein, D.** Bioavailable testosterone, and depressed mood in older men: The Rancho Bernardo Study. *J Clin Endocrinol Metab. 1999 Feb; 84(2):573-7.*

13 **Rizk, P.J., Kohn T.P., Pastuszak, A.W., Khera, M.** Testosterone Therapy Improves Erectile Function and Libido in Hypo gonadal Men. *Curr Opin Urol*. 2017 Nov; 27(6): 511–515.

14 **Guyton ACHJ.** Textbook of Medical Physiology. 11th. Elsvevier Inc; Philadelphia: 2006.

15 **Griggs, R.C., Kingston, W, Jozefowicz, R. F., *et al*;** Effect of Testosterone on Muscle Mass and Muscle Protein Synthesis. *J Appl Physiol* (1985).1989 Jan; 66(1):498-503.

16 **Rossetti M.L., Steiner J.L., Gordon B.S**. Androgen-mediated regulation of skeletal muscle protein balance. *Mol Cell Endocrinol. 2017 May 15; 447():35-44.*

17 **Urban R.J.** Growth hormone and testosterone: anabolic effects on muscle. *Horm Res Paediatr. 2011; 76 Suppl 1():81-3.*

18 **Rivas, A. M., Mulkey, Z., Lado-Abeal, J, Yarbrough, S.** Diagnosing and managing low serum testosterone. *Proc (Bayl Univ Med Cent)* 2014 Oct; 27(4): 321–324.

19 **Travison, T.G., Araujo, A.B., O'Donnell, A.B., Kupelian, V, McKinlay, J.B.,** 2007 A population-level decline in serum testosterone levels in American men. *J Clin. Endocrinol Metab. 2007.* 92 (1): 196–202

20 **Meeker, J.D., Ferguson, K.K.,** Phthalates: human exposure and related health effects. In: Schecter A, ed. *Dioxins and Health: Including Other Persistent Organic Pollutants and Endocrine Disruptors*. 3rd ed. Hoboken, NJ: John Wiley and Sons, Inc; 2012; 415–443.

21 **Meeker, J.D., Sathyanarayana, S., Swan, S.H.,** Phthalates and other additives in plastics: human exposure and associated health outcomes. *Philos Trans R Soc Lond B Biol Sci*. 2009.364(1526):2097–2113.

22 **Brownlee K.K., Moore, A.W., Hackney A.C.,** Relationship between Circulating Cortisol and Testosterone: Influence of Physical Exercise. *J Sports Sci Med*. 2005 Mar; 4(1): 76–83.

23 **MacKelvie KJ, Taunton JE, McKay HA, *et al.*** Bone mineral density and serum testosterone in chronically trained, high mileage 40–55-year-old male runners *British Journal of Sports Medicine* 2000; 34:273-278.

24 **McDonald, C. Moore J. Mcintryre, A. Carmody, K. Donne B.** Acute Effects of 24-h Sleep Deprivation on Salivary Cortisol and Testosterone Concentrations and Testosterone to Cortisol Ratio Following Supplementation with Caffeine or Placebo. *Int J Exerc Sci.* 2017; 10(1): 108–120.

25 **Fryar, C.D., Gu, Q, Ogden, C.L., Flegal, K. M.,** Anthropometric reference data for children and adults: United States, 2011–2014. National Center for Health Statistics. Vital Health Stat 3(39). 2016.

26 **Mathis Grossmann, Alvin M. Matsumoto.** A Perspective on Middle-Aged and Older Men With Functional Hypogonadism: Focus on Holistic Management, *The Journal of Clinical Endocrinology & Metabolism*, Volume 102, Issue 3, 1 March 2017, Pages 1067–1075

27 **Wu, F.C., Tajar, A. Pye, S, R., Silman, A.J, Finn, J.D., O'Neill, T.W., *et al.*** Hypothalamic-pituitary-testicular axis disruptions in older men are differentially linked to age and modifiable risk factors: the European Male Aging Study. *J Clin Endocrinol Metab.* 2008 Jul; 93(7):2737-45.

28 **Katznelson, L. Finkelstein, J.S., Schoenfeld, D.A., Rosenthal, D.I., Anderson, E.J., Klibanski, A.** Increase in Bone Density and Lean Body Mass During Testosterone Administration in Men With Acquired Hypogonadism. *J Clin Endocrinol Metab.* 1996 Dec; 81(12):4358-65.

29 **Kelly D.M., Jones, T.H.,** Testosterone and Obesity. *Obes Rev.* 2015 Jul; 16(7):581-606.

30 **Ding, E.L., Song, Y. Malik, V.S., Liu, S**. Sex differences of endogenous sex hormones and risk of type 2 diabetes: a systematic review and meta-analysis. *JAMA*. 2006; 295:1288–99.

31 **MacDonald, A.A., Herbison, G.P., Showell, M., Farquhar, C, M.**, The impact of body mass index on semen parameters and reproductive hormones in human males: a systematic review with meta-analysis. *Hum Reprod Update.* 2010 May-Jun; 16(3):293-311.

32 **Santen, R.J.,** Is aromatization of testosterone to estradiol required for inhibition of luteinizing hormone secretion in men? *J Clin Invest.* 1975 Dec; 56(6): 1555–1563.

33 **Aesthetic Plastic Surgery National Databank.** 2019. The Aesthetic Society.

34 **British Association of Aesthetic Plastic Surgeons. 2019.** Baaps.org.uk/media/press-releases/1708/cosmetic_surgery_stats

35 **Kraemer WJ, Ratamess NA, Hymer WC, Nindl BC, Fragala MS.** Growth Hormone(s), Testosterone, Insulin-Like Growth Factors, and Cortisol: Roles and Integration for Cellular Development and Growth with Exercise. Front Endocrinol (Lausanne). 2020 Feb 25; 11:33.

36 **Herbert P, Hayes LD, Sculthorpe NF, Grace FM**. HIIT produces increases in muscle power and free testosterone in male masters' athletes. *Endocr Connect.* 2017;6(7):430-436.

37 **Longcope C, Feldman HA, McKinlay JB, Araujo AB.** Diet and sex hormone-binding globulin. J Clin Endocrinol Metab. 2000 Jan;85(1):293-6.

38 **McAlindon TE, Gulin J, Chen T, Klug T, Lahita R, Nuite M.** Indole-3-carbinol in women with SLE: effect on estrogen metabolism and disease activity. *Lupus* 2001;10:779–83

39 **Whittaker J, Wu K.** Low-fat diets and testosterone in men: Systematic review and meta-analysis of intervention studies. *J Steroid Biochem Mol Biol.* 2021 Jun; 210:105878.

40 **Whittaker J, Harris M.** Low-carbohydrate diets and men's cortisol and testosterone: Systematic review and meta-analysis. Nutr Health. 2022 Mar 7:2601060221083079.

41 **Hernán Iturriaga, Ximena Lioi, Luis Valladares.** Sex hormone-binding globulin in non-cirrhotic alcoholic patients during early withdrawal and after longer abstinence. *Alcohol and Alcoholism*, Nov 1999; 34 (6): 903-9

42 **Wittert G.** The relationship between sleep disorders and testosterone in men. *Asian J Androl.* 2014;16(2):262-265.

43 **Holt R, Juel Mortensen L, Harpelunde Poulsen K et al;** Vitamin D and sex steroid production in men with normal or impaired Leydig cell function. *J Steroid Biochem Mol Biol.* 2020 May;199:105589

44 **Santos HO, Teixeira FJ.** Use of medicinal doses of zinc as a safe and efficient coadjutant in the treatment of male hypogonadism. *Aging Male.* 2020 Dec;23(5):669-678.

45 **Cinar, V., Polat, Y., Baltaci, A. K. & Mogulkoc, B**. (2011, April). Effects of magnesium supplementation on testosterone levels of athletes and sedentary subjects at rest and after exhaustion [Abstract]. *Biological Trace Element Research, 140*(1), 18–23

46 **Abbott K, Burrows TL, Acharya S, Thota RN, Garg ML.** Dietary supplementation with docosahexaenoic acid rich fish oil increases circulating levels of testosterone in overweight and obese men. *Prostaglandins Leukot Essent Fatty Acids.* 2020 Dec;163:102204

CHAPTER 4: ITS THE DIET, STUPID

1 **Ludwig, D.S., Ebbeling, C.B.,** the Carbohydrate-Insulin Model of Obesity: Beyond "Calories In, Calories Out". *JAMA Intern Med.* 2018; 178(8):1098-1103.

2 **Park, M.** "Twinkie Diet Helps Nutrition Professor Lose 27 pounds," CNN November 8, 2010. www.cnn.com/2010/HEALTH/11/08/twinkie.diet.professor/index.html

3 **Howell, S.** Calories in, calories out" and macronutrient intake: the hope, hype, and science of calories. *Endocrinology and metabolism.* 2017. 313 (5) 608-612.

4 **Hall, K.D.** Quantification of the effect of energy imbalance on bodyweight. 2011. *The Lancet. 378* (9793), 826-837.

5 **Livesey, G.** Estimation of energy expenditure, net carbohydrate utilization, and net fat oxidation and synthesis by indirect calorimetry: evaluation of errors with special reference to the detailed composition of fuels. (1988). *Am J Clin Nutr.* (47), 608-28.

6 **Hall, K.** What is the Required Energy Deficit per unit Weight Loss? *Int J Obes.* (Lond) (2008) 32 (3), 573-576.

7 **Grimm, E.R., Steinle, N.I.**, Genetics of eating behavior: established and emerging concepts. *Nutr Rev.* 2011; 69(1):52-60.

8 **Ballesteros, F.J., Martinez VJ, Luque B, Lacasa L, et al.** "On the thermodynamic origin of metabolic scaling". *Scientific Reports.* 2018. 8 (1): 1448:1–1448:10

9 **Bytomski, J.R.,** Fuelling for Performance. *Sports Health.* 2018;10(1):47-53.

10 **Dulloo, A.G, Jacquet, J**. Adaptive reduction in basal metabolic rate in response to food deprivation in humans: a role for feedback signals from fat stores. *Am J Clin Nutr.* 1998; 68:599–606

11 **Maclean, P.S., Bergouignan, A. Cornier, M.A., Jackman, M.R.,** Biology's response to dieting: the impetus for weight regain. *Am J Physiol Regul Integr Comp Physiol.* 2011; 301: R581–R600.

12 **Ryan, D.H., Yockey, S.R.,** Weight Loss, and Improvement in Comorbidity: Differences at 5%, 10%, 15%, and over. *Curr Obes Rep.* 2017;6(2):187-194.

13 **Nauli, A.M., Matin, S.,** Why Do Men Accumulate Abdominal Visceral Fat? *Front Physiol.* 2019; 10:1486.

14 **Holt, S.H., Miller, J.C., Petocz, P. Farmakalidis, E.** A satiety index of common foods. *Eur J Clin Nutr.* 1995; 49(9):675-690.

15 **Acheson, K.J.,** Influence of autonomic nervous system on nutrient-induced thermogenesis in humans. *Nutrition.*1993, 9 (4): 373-80.

16 **Barr, S. B., Wright, J.C.,** Postprandial energy expenditure in wholefood and processed-food meals: implications for daily energy expenditure. *Food Nutr Res.* 2010 Jul 2;54.

17 **Westerterp-Plantenga, M.S., Rolland, V. Wilson, S.A., Westerterp, K.R.,** Satiety related to 24 h diet-induced thermogenesis during high protein/carbohydrate vs high fat diets measured in a respiration chamber. *Eur J Clin Nutr.* 1999 Jun;53(6):495-502.

18 **Lejeune, M.P., Westerterp, K.R., Adam, T.C., *et al;*** Ghrelin and glucagon-like peptide 1 concentrations, 24-h satiety, and energy and substrate metabolism

during a high-protein diet and measured in a respiration chamber. *Am J Clin Nutr.* 2006 Jan;83(1):89-94

19 **Layman, D.K., Evans, E. Baum, J.I., *et al*;** Dietary protein and exercise have additive effects on body composition during weight loss in adult women. J Nutr. 2005 Aug; 135(8):1903-10.

20 **Feinman, R.D., Fine, E.J.,** Thermodynamics and metabolic advantage of weight loss diets. *Metab Syn Relat Dis.* 2003. 1:209-219.

21 **Brehm, B.J., Seeley, R.J., Daniels, S.R., D'Alessio, D.A.** A randomized trial comparing a very low carbohydrate diet and a calorie-restricted low-fat diet on body weight and cardiovascular risk factors in healthy women. *J Clin Endocrinol Metab.* 2003 Apr; 88(4):1617-23.

22 **Haff, G.G., Koch, A.J., Potteiger, J.A., Kuphal, K.E., Magee, L.M., Green SB, Jakicic, J.J.**

23 attenuates muscle glycogen loss during acute bouts of resistance exercise. *Int J Sport Nutr Exerc Metab.* 2000 Sep; 10(3):326-39.

24 **Baron A.D., Brechtel G., Wallace P., Edelman S.V.** Rates and tissue sites of non-insulin- and insulin-mediated glucose uptake in humans. *Am. J. Physiol.* 1988;255:E769–E774

25 **Goodpaster, BH, Park, SW, Harris, TB et al.** (2006) The loss of skeletal muscle strength, mass, and quality in older adults: the health, aging and body composition study. *J Gerontol Ser A, Biol Sci Med* 61, 1059–1064.

26 **Rudrappa, SS, Wilkinson, DJ, Greenhaff, PL et al.** (2016) Human skeletal muscle disuse atrophy: effects on muscle protein synthesis, breakdown, and insulin resistance – a qualitative review. *Front Physiol* 7, 361.

27 **Volpi E, Mittendorfer B, Rasmussen BB, Wolfe RR.** The response of muscle protein anabolism to combined hyperaminoacidemia and glucose-induced hyperinsulinemia is impaired in the elderly. *J Clin Endocrinol Metab.* 2000 Dec;85(12):4481-90.

28 **Hämäläinen, E.K., Adlercreutz, H. Puska, P. Pietinen, P.** Decrease of serum total and free testosterone during a low-fat high-fibre diet. *J Steroid Biochem.* 1983 Mar; 18(3):369-70.

29 **Di Pasquale M.G.,** The essentials of essential fatty acids. *J Diet Suppl.* 2009;6(2):143-61

CHAPTER 5: WHERE'S THE BEEF?

1 **NHS, Digital, Health Survey for England, 2019** https://digital.nhs.uk/data-and-information/publications/statistical/health-survey-for-england/2019

2 **Häkkinen, K. Alen, M. Kraemer, W.J., *et al.*** Neuromuscular adaptations during concurrent strength and endurance training versus strength training. *Eur J Appl Physiol.* 2003;89(1):42-52.

3 **Brillon, D.J, Zheng, B., Campbell, R.G., Matthews, D.E.,** Effect of cortisol on energy expenditure and amino acid metabolism in humans. *Am J Physiol.* 1995;268(3 Pt 1): E501-E513.

4 **Melton LJ 3rd, Khosla, S. Crowson, C.S., O'Connor, M.K., *et al;*** Epidemiology of sarcopenia. *J Am Geriatr. Soc.* 2000 Jun; 48(6):625-30.

5 **Holloszy, J.O.** The biology of aging. *Mayo Clin Proc.* 2000 Jan; 75 Suppl: S3-8; discussion S8-9.

6 **Evans, W.J.,** What is sarcopenia? *J Gerontol A Biol Sci Med Sci.* 1995 Nov;50 Spec No:5-8.

7 **Roubenoff, R. Castaneda, C.J.,** Sarcopenia-understanding the dynamics of aging muscle. 2001 Sep 12; 286(10):1230-1

8 **Yang J, Christophi CA, Farioli A, et al.** Association Between Push-up Exercise Capacity and Future Cardiovascular Events Among Active Adult Men. *JAMA Netw Open. 2019; 2 (2):* e188341.

9 **Lera L, Angel B, Marquez C, Saguez R, Albala C.** Besides Sarcopenia, Pre-Sarcopenia Also Predicts All-Cause Mortality in Older Chileans. *Clin Interv Aging.* 2021 Apr 15;16:611-619

10 **Xue, Q.L., Walston, J.D., Fried, L.P., Beamer, B.A.,** Prediction of risk of falling, physical disability, and frailty by rate of decline in grip strength: the women's health and aging study. *Arch Intern Med. 2011 Jun 27; 171(12):1119-21.*

11 **Kraemer William J., Ratamess Nicholas A., Hymer Wesley C., Nindl Bradley C., Fragala Maren S.** Growth Hormone(s), Testosterone, Insulin-Like Growth Factors, and Cortisol: Roles and Integration for Cellular Development and Growth with Exercise. *Frontiers in Endocrinology* 2020; 11: 1664-2392

12 **Powers ML, Florini JR.** A direct effect of testosterone on muscle cells in tissue culture. *Endocrinology. 1975 Oct;* 97(4):1043-7.

13 **Møller N, Copeland KC, Nair KS.** Growth hormone effects on protein metabolism. Endocrinol Metab Clin North Am. 2007 Mar;36(1):89-100

14 **Urban, R.J.** Growth hormone and testosterone: anabolic effects on muscle. *Horm Res Paediatr.* 2011; *76 Suppl 1():81-3.*

15 **Clemmons DR.** Role of IGF binding proteins in regulating metabolism. *Trends Endocrinol Metab* 27: 375–391, 2016.

16 **Qin LL, Li XK, Xu J, Mo DL, Tong X, Pan ZC, Li JQ, *et al;*** Mechano growth factor (MGF) promotes proliferation and inhibits differentiation of porcine satellite cells (PSCs) by down-regulation of key myogenic transcriptional factors. *Mol Cell Biochem.* 2012 Nov;370(1-2):221-30.

17 **Watson, K. Baar, K.** mTOR and the health benefits of exercise. *Seminars in Cell & Developmental Biology.* 2014; 36: 130-139.

18 **Morley JE, Kaiser FE, Perry HM 3rd, Patrick P, Morley PM, et al;** Longitudinal changes in testosterone, luteinizing hormone, and follicle-stimulating hormone in healthy older men. *Metabolism.* 1997 Apr; 46(4):410-3.

19 **Mulligan T, Frick MF, Zuraw QC, Stemhagen A, McWhirter C.** Prevalence of hypogonadism in males aged at least 45 years: the HIM study. *Int J Clin Pract.* (2006) 60:762–9.

20 **Ajdžanovic VZ, Trifunovic S, Miljic D, et al.** Somatopause, weaknesses of the therapeutic approaches and the cautious optimism based on experimental ageing studies with soy isoflavones. *EXCLI J.* 2018; 17: 279-301. Published 2018 Mar 21.

21 **Bian, A., Ma, Y., Zhou, X.** ***et al.*** Association between sarcopenia and levels of growth hormone and insulin-like growth factor-1 in the elderly. *BMC Musculoskelet Disord* **21,** 214 (2020)

22 **Rasmussen BB, Fujita S, Wolfe RR, et al.** Insulin resistance of muscle protein metabolism in aging. FASEB J.

23 **Stokes T, Hector AJ, Morton RW, McGlory C, Phillips SM.** Recent Perspectives Regarding the Role of Dietary Protein for the Promotion of Muscle Hypertrophy with Resistance Exercise Training. *Nutrients.* 2018;10(2):180. Published 2018 Feb 7.

24 **Witard, O. C., Bannock, L., & Tipton, K. D. (2022).** Making Sense of Muscle Protein Synthesis: A Focus on Muscle Growth During Resistance Training, *International Journal of Sport Nutrition and Exercise Metabolism, 32*(1), 49-61

25 **Daniel Tome,** Efficiency of Free Amino Acids in Supporting Muscle Protein Synthesis, *The Journal of Nutrition,* Volume 152, Issue 1, January 2022, Pages 3–4.

26 **Paulussen Kevin J. M., McKenna Colleen F., Beals Joseph W., Wilund Kenneth R., Salvador Amadeo F., Burd Nicholas A;** Anabolic Resistance of Muscle Protein Turnover Comes in Various Shapes and Sizes. *Front. Nutr.,* 05 May 2021. Volume 8.

27 **Beals JW, Skinner SK, McKenna CF, Poozhikunnel EG, Farooqi SA, et al;** Altered anabolic signaling and reduced stimulation of myofibrillar protein synthesis after feeding and resistance exercise in people with obesity. *J Physiol. 2018 Nov; 596(21):5119-5133.*

28 **Kumar V, Selby A, Rankin D, Patel R, Atherton P, Hildebrandt W, et al.** Age-related differences in the dose-response relationship of muscle protein synthesis to resistance exercise in young and old men. *J Physiol.* 2009 Jan 15;587(1):211-7

29 **Gorissen SH, Trommelen J, Kouw IW, Holwerda AM, Pennings B, Groen BB, et al.** Protein type, protein dose, and age modulate dietary protein

digestion and phenylalanine absorption kinetics and plasma phenylalanine availability in humans. *J Nutr.* (2020) 150:2041–50

30 **Breen L, Phillips SM.** Skeletal muscle protein metabolism in the elderly: Interventions to counteract the 'anabolic resistance' of ageing. *Nutr Metab (Lond).* 2011 Oct 5;8:68

31 **Wolfe RR**. The underappreciated role of muscle in health and disease. Am J Clin Nutr. 2006 Sep;84(3):475-82.

32 **Morgan J, Partridge T.** Skeletal muscle in health and disease. Dis Model Mech. 2020 Feb 6;13(2): dmm042192

33 **Gil S, Jacob Filho W, Shinjo SK, Ferriolli E, Busse AL, et al**; HCFMUSP COVID-19 Study Group. Muscle strength and muscle mass as predictors of hospital length of stay in patients with moderate to severe COVID-19: a prospective observational study. J Cachexia Sarcopenia Muscle. 2021 Dec;12(6):1871-1878

34 **Pereira CT, Barrow RE, Sterns AM, et al**. Age dependent differences in survival after severe burns: a unicentric review of 1674 patients and 179 autopsies over 15 years. *J Am Coll Surg* 2005

35 **Afzali A.M. Muntefering T. Wiendl H. Meuth S.G. Ruck T.** Skeletal muscle cells actively shape (auto) immune responses. *Autoimmun Rev.* 2018; **17**: 518-529

36 **Nelke C, Dziewas R, Minnerup J, Meuth SG, Ruck T.** Skeletal muscle as potential central link between sarcopenia and immune senescence. *EBioMedicine.* 2019 Nov; 49:381-388

37 **Leal LG, Lopes MA, Batista ML Jr.** Physical Exercise-Induced Myokines and Muscle-Adipose Tissue Crosstalk: A Review of Current Knowledge and the Implications for Health and Metabolic Diseases. Front Physiol. 2018 Sep 24; 9:1307

38 **DeFronzo R. A., Ferrannini E., Sato Y., Felig P., Wahren J.** (1981a). Synergistic interaction between exercise and insulin on peripheral glucose uptake. *J. Clin. Invest.* 68, 1468–1474

39 **Frayn KN, Arner P, Yki-Järvinen H**. Fatty acid metabolism in adipose tissue, muscle and liver in health and disease. Essays Biochem. 2006;42:89-103

40 **Baron A.D., Brechtel G., Wallace P., Edelman S.V.** Rates and tissue sites of non-insulin- and insulin-mediated glucose uptake in humans. *Am. J. Physiol.* 1988;255:E769–E774

41 **Shou, J., Chen, PJ. & Xiao, WH.** Mechanism of increased risk of insulin resistance in aging skeletal muscle. *Diabetol Metab Syndr* **12,** 14 (2020)

42 **Pontzer, H. Yamada, Y. Sagayama, H. Ainslielene P, N. Anderson F. et al;** Daily energy expenditure through the human life course. *Science.* 13 Aug 2021. Vol 373, Issue 6556 pp. 808-812.

43 **Zurio, F, Larson, K, Bogardus, C et al.** (1990) Skeletal muscle metabolism is a major determinant of resting energy expenditure. *J Clin Invest* 86, 1423–1427

44 **Shimokata H, Kuzuya F.** [Aging, basal metabolic rate, and nutrition]. Nihon Ronen Igakkai Zasshi. 1993 Jul;30(7):572-6.

45 **Willoughby D, Hewlings S, Kalman D.** Body Composition Changes in Weight Loss: Strategies and Supplementation for Maintaining Lean Body Mass, a Brief Review. Nutrients. 2018 Dec 3;10(12):1876.

46 **Liu, D., Zhong, J., Ruan, Y. *et al.*** The association between fat-to-muscle ratio and metabolic disorders in type 2 diabetes. *Diabetol Metab Syndr* **13,** 129 (2021

47 **Nishikawa H, Asai A, Fukunishi S, Nishiguchi S, Higuchi K**. Metabolic Syndrome and Sarcopenia. *Nutrients.* 2021 Oct 7;13(10):3519.

48 **Villegas R. Perry, I,J. Creagh D. Hinchion R. O'Halloran D.** Prevalence of the Metabolic Syndrome in Middle-Aged Men and Women *Diabetes Care* 2003;26(11):3198–3199

49 **Chen L, Deng H, Cui H, et al**. Inflammatory responses and inflammation-associated diseases in organs. *Oncotarget.* 2017;9(6):7204-7218.

50 **Lilja M, Mandić M, Apró W, Melin M, Olsson K, Rosenborg S, Gustafsson T, Lundberg TR.** High doses of anti-inflammatory drugs compromise muscle strength and hypertrophic adaptations to resistance training in young adults. *Acta Physiol (Oxf).* 2018 Feb;222(2).

51 **Furman, David et al.** "Chronic inflammation in the etiology of disease across the life span." *Nature medicine* vol. 25,12 (2019): 1822-1832.

52 **Ellulu MS, Patimah I, Khaza'ai H, Rahmat A, Abed Y.** Obesity and inflammation: the linking mechanism and the complications. *Arch Med Sci.* 2017;13(4):851-863.

53 **Khanna D, Khanna S, Khanna P, et al**. (February 28, 2022) Obesity: A Chronic Low-Grade Inflammation and Its Markers. Cureus 14(2): e22711.

54 **Dalle S, Rossmeislova L, Koppo K**. The Role of Inflammation in Age-Related Sarcopenia. Front Physiol. 2017 Dec 12;8:1045

55 **Giugliano D, Ceriello A, Esposito K.** The effects of diet on inflammation—Emphasis on the metabolic syndrome. *J Am Coll Cardiol.* 2006;48:677–85

56 **Calder PC, Albers R, Antoine JM, Blum S, *et al;*** Inflammatory disease processes and interactions with nutrition. *Br J Nutr.* 2009;101 1:S1–4

57 **Esposito K, Nappo F, Giugliano F, Giugliano G, Marfella R, Giugliano D**. Effect of dietary antioxidants on postprandial endothelial dysfunction induced by a high-fat meal in healthy subjects. *Am J Clin Nutr.* 2003;77:139–43.

58 **Jackson, M.J.; McArdle, A**. Age-related changes in skeletal muscle reactive oxygen species generation and adaptive responses to reactive oxygen species. J. Physiol. 2011, 589, 2139–2145.

59 **Lian, D. Chen, M, M. Wu, H. Deng, S. Hu, X.** The Role of Oxidative Stress in Skeletal Muscle Myogenesis and Muscle Dis Myogenesis and Muscle Disease. *Antioxidants* 2022, 11, 755
60 **Chung HY, Kim DH, Lee EK, et al.** Redefining Chronic Inflammation in Aging and Age-Related Diseases: Proposal of the Senoinflammation Concept. *Aging Dis.* 2019;10(2):367-382. Published 2019 Apr
61 **Toda, N.** Age-related changes in endothelial function and blood flow regulation. *Pharmacol Ther.* 2012 Feb; 133(2):159-76.
62 **Mozos I, Luca CT.** Crosstalk between Oxidative and Nitrosative Stress and Arterial Stiffness. *Curr Vasc Pharmacol.* 2017; 15(5):446-456
63 **J S Stamler, G Meissner.** Physiology of nitric oxide in skeletal muscle. *Physiol Rev* (2001)
64 **Schoenfeld, B, J., Contreras, B.** The Muscle Pump: Potential Mechanisms and Applications for Enhancing Hypertrophic Adaptations. *Strength and Conditioning Journal.* 2014. (36) 3: 21-25
65 **Donato, A. Rivas, SJ Lessard NP, Rice MS et al**; Diminished skeletal muscle microRNA expression with aging is associated with attenuated muscle plasticity and inhibition of IGF-1 signaling. *FASEBJ.* Sept 2014 (28) 9: 4133-4147
66 **Dennis, R. A., Przybyla, B., Gurley, C., Kortebein, P. M., Simpson, P., Sullivan, D. H., and Peterson, C. A.** (2008) Aging alters gene expression of growth and remodeling factors in human skeletal muscle both at rest and in response to acute resistance exercise. *Physiol. Genomics* **32**, 393–400

PART TWO: THE SCIENCE OF MUSCLE-BUILDING

CHAPTER 6: THE GRECIAN IDEAL

1 **Kadi, F. Bonnerud, P. Eriksson, A. Thornell, L.E.,** The expression of androgen receptors in human neck and limb muscles: effects of training and self-administration of androgenic-anabolic steroids. *Histochem Cell Biol.* 2000; 113(1):25-29.
2 **Baggish, A.L., Weiner, R.B., Kanayama, G.** ***et al.*** Long-term anabolic-androgenic steroid use is associated with left ventricular dysfunction. *Circ Heart Fail.* 2010;3(4):472-476.
3 **Hartgens, F. Kuipers, H.** Effects of androgenic-anabolic steroids in athletes. *Sports Med.* Auckland, NZ. 2004;34:513–554.
4 **Sullivan, M.L., Martinez, C.M., Gennis, P. Gallagher, E.J.** The cardiac toxicity of anabolic steroids. *Prog. Cardiovasc. Dis.* 1998;41:1–15.
5 **Payne, J.R., Kotwinski, P.J., Montgomery, H.E.,** Cardiac effects of anabolic steroids. *Heart.* 2004 May; 90(5):473-5.

6 **Pope, H.G., Katz, D.L.**, Psychiatric effects of exogenous anabolic-androgenic steroids. In: Wolkowitz OM, Rothschild AJ, editors. *Psychoneuroendocrinology:* The scientific basis of clinical practice. American Psychiatric Press; Washington, DC: 2003. pp. 331–358.

7 **Papazisis, G. Kouvelas, D. *et al;*** Anabolic androgenic steroid abuse and mood disorder: a case report. *Int. J. Neuropsychopharmacol. / official scientific journal of the Collegium Internationals Neuropsychopharmacologicum* (CINP) 2007;10:291–293

8 **Smit, D.L., Nuijens, J.H., de Ronde W**. Spontaneous haemorrhage of hepatic adenoma in a patient addicted to anabolic steroids. *Netherlands Journal of Medicine 2019.* 77 261–263.

9 **Randy Roach.** Muscle, smoke and mirrors. Author house, 2008.

CHAPTER 7: SKELETAL MUSCLE, UNDER THE BONNET

1 **Kim, J Wang, Z., Heymsfield, S. B., Baumgartner, R. N., and Gallagher, D.** (2002). Total-body skeletal muscle mass: estimation by a new dual-energy X-ray absorptiometry method. *Am. J. Clin. Nutr.* 76, 378–383.

2 **Zurlo F, Larson K, Bogardus C, Ravussin E.** Skeletal muscle metabolism is a major determinant of resting energy expenditure. J Clin Invest. 1990 Nov;86(5):1423

3 **DeFronzo R.A., Ferrannini E., Sato Y., Felig P., Wahren J.** Synergistic interaction between exercise and insulin on peripheral glucose uptake. *J Clin Invest.* 1981; 68:1468–1474

4 **Robert R Wolfe.** The underappreciated role of muscle in health and disease, *The American Journal of Clinical Nutrition*, Volume 84, Issue 3, December 2006, Pages 475–482

5 **Frontera, W.R., Ochala, J**. Skeletal Muscle: A Brief Review of Structure and Function. *Calcif Tissue Int* 96, 183–195 (2015)

6 **Tsintzas K, Jewell K, Kamran M, Laithwaite D, Boonsong T, et al**; (2006) Differential regulation of metabolic genes in skeletal muscle during starvation and refeeding in humans. *J Physiol* 575, 291

7 **R. D. Fell J. A. McLane W. W. Winder. J. O. Holloszy.** Preferential resynthesis of muscle glycogen in fasting rats after exhausting exercise. *American Journal of Physiology.* May 1980.

8 **West MD, Sternberg H, Labat I, Janus J, Chapman KB, Malik NN, de Grey AD, Larocca D.** Toward a unified theory of aging and regeneration. *Regen Med.* 2019 Sep;14(9):867-88

9 **Weismann A.** Essays Upon Heredity and Kindred Biological Problems (2nd Edition). Clarendon Press, Oxford, UK (189

10 **Johnston AP, De Lisio M, Parise G.** Resistance training, sarcopenia, and the mitochondrial theory of aging. *Appl Physiol Nutr Metab.* 2008; 33:191–199.

11 **Frontera, W.R., Ochala, J.** Skeletal Muscle: A Brief Review of Structure and Function. *Calcif Tissue Int* 96, 183–195 (2015)

12 **Farup, J., Rahbek, S. K., Riis, S., Vendelbo, M. H., de Paoli, F. V., Vissing, K.** (2014b). Influence of exercise contraction mode and protein supplementation on human skeletal muscle satellite cell content and muscle fibre growth. *J. Appl. Physiol.* 117, 898–909.

13 **Menon, M. K., Houchen, L., Singh, S. J., Morgan, M. D., Bradding, P., Steiner, M. C.** (2012). Inflammatory and satellite cells in the quadriceps of patients with COPD and response to resistance training. *Chest* 142, 1134–1142

14 **Verdijk, L. B., Gleeson, B. G., Jonkers, R. A., Meijer, K., Savelberg, H. H., Dendale, P., et al.** (2009). Skeletal muscle hypertrophy following resistance training is accompanied by a fibre type-specific increase in satellite cell content in elderly men. *J. Geront. Ser. A Biol. Sci. Med. Sci.* 64, 332–33

15 **Buchthal F, Schmalbruch H.** Motor unit of mammalian muscle. Physiol Rev. 1980 Jan;60(1):90-14

16 **Enoka RM, Duchateau J.** Rate Coding and the Control of Muscle Force. *Cold Spring Harb Perspect Med.* 2017;7(10): a029702. Published 2017 Oct 3.

17 **Henneman, E, Somjen G, Carpenter, D.O.** Functional significance of cell size in spinal motoneurons. *J Neurophysiol.* 1965. 28: 560-5

18 **Enoka RM, Duchateau.** Neural control of lengthening contractions. January 2016. *Journal of Experimental Biology* 219(2):197-20

19 **Costal, D.L., Daniels, J, Evans, W, Fink, W, Krahenbuhl, G, Saltin, B.** Skeletal muscle enzymes and fibre composition in male and female track athletes. *J Appl Physiol.* 40: 149–154, 197

20 **Trappe, T.A., Carroll, C.C., Tesch, P.A.** Human soleus muscle protein synthesis following resistance exercise. *Acta Physiol Scand.* 182: 189-196, 2004

21 **Powers, S.K., Howley, E.T.,** (2012). Exercise Physiology: Theory and Application to Fitness and Performance, (8th Edition). New York, NY: McGraw Hil

22 **Kosek, D.J., Kim, J.S., Petrella, J.K., Cross, J.M., Bamman, M.M.** Efficacy of 3 days/wk. resistance training on myofiber hypertrophy and myogenic mechanisms in young vs. older adults. J Appl Physiol. 101: 531-544, 2006.

23 **Miljkovic N, Lim JY, Miljkovic I, Frontera WR.** Aging of skeletal muscle fibers. Ann Rehabil Med. 2015 Apr;39(2):155-62.

24 **Reid, K. F., and Fielding, R. A. (2012).** Skeletal muscle power: a critical determinant of physical functioning in older adults. *Exerc. Sport Sci. Rev.* 40, 4–12.

25 **Mastrocola R, Collino M, Nigro D, Chiazza F, D'Antona G, Aragno M, et al.** Accumulation of advanced glycation end-products and activation of the

SCAP/SREBP lipogenetic pathway occur in diet-induced obese mouse skeletal muscle. *PLoS One* (2015) 10(3): e0119587.

26 **Tuttle LJ, Sinacore DR, Mueller MJ.** Intermuscular adipose tissue is muscle specific and associated with poor functional performance. *J Aging Res* (2012) 2012:172957

27 **Miljkovic, I., and Zmuda, J. M.** (2010). Epidemiology of myosteatosis. *Curr. Opin. Clin. Nutr. Metab. Care* 13, 260–264.

28 **Mackey, A. L., Esmarck, B., Kadi, F., Koskinen, S. O., Kongsgaard, M., Sylvestersen, A., et al.** (2007a). Enhanced satellite cell proliferation with resistance training in elderly men and women. *Scand. J. Med. Sci. Sports* 17, 34–42

29 **Egan B, Zierath JR** (2013) Exercise metabolism and the molecular regulation of skeletal muscle adaptation. *Cell Metab* 17(2):162–184

30 **Lee S, Libman I, Hughan K, Kuk JL, Jeong JH, Zhang D, Arslanian S**. Effects of Exercise Modality on Insulin Resistance and Ectopic Fat in Adolescents with Overweight and Obesity: A Randomized Clinical Trial. *J Pediatr.* 2019 Mar; 206:91-98.

31 31.**Shepherd SO, Cocks M, Tipton KD, Witard OC, Ranasinghe AM, Barker TA, Wagenmakers AJ, Shaw CS.** Resistance training increases skeletal muscle oxidative capacity and net intramuscular triglyceride breakdown in type I and II fibres of sedentary males. *Exp Physiol.* 2014 Jun;99(6):894-908

32 **Akasaki, Y, Ouchi, N, Izumiya, Y, Bernardo, B, LeBrasseur, N, Walsh K**. (2013). Glycolytic fast-twitch muscle fibre restoration counters adverse age-related changes in body composition and metabolism. *Aging Cell.* 13:80-91

CHAPTER 8: THE MECHANICS OF MUSCLE BUILDING

1 **Schoenfeld, Brad J.** The Mechanisms of Muscle Hypertrophy and Their Application to Resistance Training. *Journal of Strength and Conditioning Research:* October 2010—Volume 24—Issue 10—p 2857-2872

2 **Monaghan L.** Looking good, feeling good: The embodied pleasures of vibrant physicality. *Sociol. Health Illness* 23: 330- 356, 2

3 **Brad, J. Schoenfeld. Bret Contreras**. The Muscle Pump: Potential Mechanisms and Applications for Enhancing Hypertrophic Adaptations. June 2014. *Strength and Conditioning Journal* 36(3):21-25

4 **Sjøgaard G, Adams RP, Saltin B.** Water and ion shift in skeletal muscle of humans with intense dynamic knee extension. *Am J Physiol.* 1985 Feb;248(2 Pt 2): R190

5 **Allen DG, Lamb GD, Westerblad H.** Skeletal muscle fatigue: cellular mechanisms. *Physiol Rev* 88: 287–332, 2008.

6 6.**Dankel SJ, Mattocks KT, Jessee MB, Buckner SL, Mouser JG, Loenneke JP**. Do metabolites that are produced during resistance exercise enhance muscle hypertrophy? *Eur J Appl Physiol* 117: 2125–2135, 2017

7 **Wackerhage H, Schoenfeld B, J, Hamilton D, L, Lehti M, Hulmi J, J.** Stimuli and sensors that initiate skeletal muscle hypertrophy following resistance exercise. *J Apply Physiol.* 09. Jan 2019.

8 **McDougal, J. D., Sale, D. G., Elder, G. C., and Sutton, J. R**. (1982). Muscle ultrastructural characteristics of elite powerlifters and bodybuilders. *Eur. J. Appl. Physiol. Occup. Physiol.* 48, 117–126.

9 **Haun CT, Vann CG, Osburn SC, Mumford PW, Roberson PA, et al**; Muscle fiber hypertrophy in response to 6 weeks of high-volume resistance training in trained young men is largely attributed to sarcoplasmic hypertrophy. *PLoS One.* 2019 Jun 5;14(6): e0215267.

10 **Roberts MD, Haun CT, Vann CG, Osburn SC, Young KC**. Sarcoplasmic Hypertrophy in Skeletal Muscle: A Scientific "Unicorn" or Resistance Training Adaptation? *Front Physiol.* 2020 Jul 14:11: 816

11 **Moritani, T., deVries, H.A.,** Neural factors versus hypertrophy in the time course of muscle strength gain. *Am J Phys Med.* 1979;58(3):115–30.

12 **Rindom E, Vissing K.** Mechanosensitive molecular networks involved in transducing resistance exercise-signals into muscle protein accretion. *Front Physiol* 7: 547, 2016.

13 **Hornberger TA**. Mechanotransduction and the regulation of mTORC1 signaling in skeletal muscle. *Int J Biochem Cell Biol* 43: 1267–1276, 2011

14 14.**Vandenburgh, H.H.,** Motion into mass: how does tension stimulate muscle growth? *Med Sci Sports Exerc.* 1987 Oct;19(5 Suppl): S142-9

15 **Russell, B., Motlagh, D., and Ashley, W. W.** (2000). Form follows function: how muscle shape is regulated by work. *J. Appl. Physiol.* 88, 1127–1132

16 **Fenwick, A.J., Wood, A, M., Tanner, B.C.W.**, Effects of cross-bridge compliance on the force-velocity relationship and muscle power output. *PLoS One.* 2017; 12(12): e0190335

17 **Mitchell C.J., Churchward-Venne T.A., West D.W.D., Burd N.A., Breen L., Baker S.K., Phillips S.M.** Resistance exercise load does not determine training-mediated hypertrophic gains in young men. *J. Appl. Physiol.* 2012;113

18 **Schoenfeld, Brad J; Grgic, Jozo; Ogborn, Dan; Krieger, James W.** Strength and Hypertrophy Adaptations Between Low- vs. High-Load Resistance Training: A Systematic Review and Meta-analysis, Journal of Strength and Conditioning Research: December 2017—Volume 31—Issue 12—p 3508-3523

19 **Schoenfeld BJ, Grgic J, Van Every DW, Plotkin DL**. Loading Recommendations for Muscle Strength, Hypertrophy, and Local Endurance: A Re-Examination of the Repetition Continuum. *Sports.* 2021; 9(2):32.

20 **Sampson JA, Groeller H**. Is repetition failure critical for the development of muscle hypertrophy and strength? *Scand J Med Sci Sports*. 2016 Apr;26(4):375-83

21 **Morán-Navarro R, Pérez CE, Mora-Rodríguez R, de la Cruz-Sánchez E, González-Badillo JJ, Sánchez-Medina L, Pallarés JG**. Time course of recovery following resistance training leading or not to failure. *Eur J Appl Physiol*. 2017 Dec;117(12):2387-2399

22 **Helms, E.R.; Byrnes, R.K.; Cooke, D.M.; Haischer, M.H.; Carzoli, J.P.; Johnson, T.K.; Cross, M.R.; Cronin, J.B.; Storey, A.G.; Zourdos, M.C**. RPE vs. Percentage 1RM Loading in Periodized Programs Matched for Sets and Repetitions. *Front. Physiol*. 2018, 9, 247.

23 **Steele J, Endres A, Fisher J, Gentil P, Giessing J**. Ability to predict repetitions to momentary failure is not perfectly accurate, though improves with resistance training experience. *Peer J*. 2017;5: e4105. Published 2017 Nov 30.

24 **Zhousheng, X, Darryl, Quarles, L**. Physiological mechanisms and therapeutic potential of bone mechanosensing. *Rev Endocr Metab Disord*. 2015 Jun; 16(2): 115–129.

25 **Mattocks, KT; Buckner, SL; Jesse, MB; Dankel, SJ; Mouser, J. Grant; Loenneke, JP.** Practicing the test produces strength equivalent to higher volume training. Medicine & Science in Sports & Exercise: September 2017, Vol 49, 9. P1945-1954

26 **Schoenfeld BJ.** Does exercise-induced muscle damage play a role in skeletal muscle hypertrophy? ***J Strength Cond Res*** 26: 1441–1453

27 **Evans WJ, Cannon JG**. The metabolic effects of exercise-induced muscle damage. ***Exerc Sport Sci Rev*** 19: 99–126, 1991.

28 **McHugh, M. P.** (2003). Recent advances in the understanding of the repeated bout effect: the protective effect against muscle damage from a single bout of eccentric exercise. *Scand. J. Med. Sci. Sports* 13, 88–97.

29 **Peake, J. M. Neubauer, O. Della Gatta, P.A. Nosaka, K**. Muscle damage and inflammation during recovery from exercise. *J Apply Phyisol*. 2017; 122 (3)

30 **Russell B, Dix DJ, Haller DL, Jacobs-El J.** Repair of injured skeletal muscle: a molecular approach. *Med Sci Sports Exerc* 24: 189–196, 1992.

31 **Franchi MV, Reeves ND, Narici MV**. Skeletal Muscle Remodeling in Response to Eccentric vs. Concentric Loading: Morphological, Molecular, and Metabolic Adaptations. *Front Physiol*. 2017; 8:447

32 **Finni T, Ikegawa S, Lepola V, Komi PV.** Comparison of force-velocity relationships of vastus lateralis muscle in isokinetic and in stretch-shortening cycle exercises. *Acta Physiol Scand* 177: 483–491, 2003

33 33.**McCarthy JJ, Esser K A.** Anabolic and catabolic pathways regulating skeletal muscle mass. *Curr Opin Clin Nutr Metab Care*. 2010 May; 13(3): 230–235.

34 **Verbrugge SAJ, Schönfelder M, Becker L, Yaghoob Nezhad F, Hrabě de Angelis M, Wackerhage H.** Genes whose gain or loss-of-function increases skeletal muscle mass in mice: a systematic literature review. ***Front Physiol*** 9: 553, 2018

35 35.**Yoon, M. S.** (2017). mTOR as a Key Regulator in Maintaining Skeletal Muscle Mass. Front Physiol, 8, 788.

36 36.**Bodine SC, Stitt TN, Gonzalez M, Kline WO, *et al***; Akt/mTOR pathway is a crucial regulator of skeletal muscle hypertrophy and can prevent muscle atrophy in vivo. *Nat Cell Biol.* 2001. 3: 1014–1019.

37 **Glass DJ.** Skeletal muscle hypertrophy and atrophy signalling pathways. *Int J Biochem Cell Biol.* 2005 37: 1974–1984.

38 **Hornberger TA, Stuppard R, Conley KE, *et al;*** Mechanical stimuli regulate rapamycin-sensitive signalling by a phosphoinositide 3-kinase-, protein kinase B- and growth factor-independent mechanism. *Biochem J.* 2004. 380: 795–804

39 **Hameed, M, Lange, KH, Andersen, JL, Schjerling, *et al;*** The effect of recombinant human growth hormone and resistance training on IGF-I mRNA expression in the muscles of elderly men. *J Physiol. 2004.* 555: 231–240, 2004.

40 **Barton-Davis, E, R., Shoturma, D, I., Sweeney, H, L.,** Contribution of satellite cells to IGF-I induced hypertrophy of skeletal muscle. *Acta Physiol Scan. 1999.* 167: 301–305.

41 **Evans, W. E.,** (2010) Skeletal muscle loss: cachexia, sarcopenia, and inactivity. *Am J Clin Nutr* 91(Suppl):1123S–1127S

42 **Atherton, P.J., Smith K.** Muscle protein synthesis in response to nutrition and exercise. *J Physiol. 2012 Mar 1; 590(Pt 5): 1049–1057*

43 **Burd, N.A., Tang, J.E., Moore, D.R., *et al.*** Exercise training and protein metabolism: influences of contraction, protein intake, and sex-based differences. *Journal of applied physiology*, 2009. 106(5): p. 1692-701.

44 **Philips SM, Tipton KD, Aarsland A, Wolf SE, Wolfe RR.** Mixed muscle protein synthesis and breakdown after resistance exercise in humans. *Am J Physiol.* (1997) 273 (1 Pt 1): E99-107

45 **Pasiakos SM, Carbone JW.** Assessment of skeletal muscle proteolysis and the regulatory response to nutrition and exercise. *IUBMB Life.* 2014; 66: 478-484

46 **Biolo G, Tipton KD, Klein S, Wolfe RR.** An abundant supply of amino acids enhances the metabolic effect of exercise on muscle protein. *Am J Physiol.* (1997) 273 (1 Pt 1) E122-9

CHAPTER 9: FREQUENCY: THE SECRET SAUCE

1 **Schoenfeld BJ, Contreras B, Krieger J, Grgic J; *et al.*** Resistance Training Volume Enhances Muscle Hypertrophy but Not Strength in Trained Men. *Medicine & Science in Sports & Exercise. 51: 94-103, 2019.*

2 2.**Brigatto FA, Lima LEM, Germano MD, Aoki MS, Braz TV, Lopes CR.** High Resistance-Training Volume Enhances Muscle Thickness in Resistance-Trained Men. *J Strength Cond Res.* 2019 Dec 20.

3 3.**Schoenfeld BJ, Ogborn D, Krieger J.** A dose-response Relationship Between Weekly Resistance Training Volume and Increases in Muscle Mass: A Systematic Review and Meta-Analysis. *J Sports Sci* 2017 Jun; 35(11):1073-1082

4 **Krieger, J.W.** (2010) Single vs. multiple sets of resistance exercise for muscle hypertrophy: A meta-analysis. *J Strength and Cond Res.* 24: 1150-1159, 2010

5 **Schoenfeld B.** Science and development of muscle hypertrophy. 2020. Human Kinetics, Inc. ISBN 10: 1492597678 ISBN 13: 9781492597674

6 **Kumar V, Selby A, Rankin D, Patel, Atherton P; *et al.*** Age-related differences in the dose-response relationship of muscle protein synthesis to resistance exercise in young and old men. *J Physiol.* 587: 211-217, 2009.

7 **Wernborm M, Augustsson J, Thomee R.** The influence of frequency, intensity, volume and mode of strength training on whole muscle cross-sectional area in humans. Sports Med. 37: 225-264, 2007.

8 **Morton RW, Sonne MW, Zuniga AF, Mohammad, IYZ**; ***et al.*** Muscle fibre activation is unaffected by load and repetition duration when resistance exercise is performed to task failure. 2019. *The journal of physiology.* Sep; 597 (17): 4601-4613, 2019

9 **Netreba Ai, Popov DV, Bravyi I, Misina SS, Vinogradova OL.** Physiological effects of low-intensity strength training without relaxation. *Fiziol Cheloveka.* 35: 97-102, 2009

10 **Holm L, Reitelseder S, Pedersen TG, Doessing S; *et al.*** Changes in muscle size and MHC composition in response to resistance exercise with heavy and light loading intensity. *J Appl Physiol.* 105: 1454-1461, 2008 4.

11 **Kraemer WJ, Ratamess NA.** Fundamentals of resistance training. Progression and exercise prescription. *Med Sci Sports Exerc.* 36: 674-688, 2004.

12 **Rutherford, O. M., and D. A. Jones**. The role of learning and coordination in strength training. *Eur. J. Appl. Physiol.* 55: 100–105, 1986.

13 **Dankel SJ, Mattocks, K.T., Jessee MB;** ***et al.*** Frequency: The Overlooked Resistance Training Variable for Inducing Muscle Hypertrophy? *Sports Med* (2017) 47: 799

14 **Schoenfeld BJ, Grgic J, Krieger J.** (2019) How many times per week should a muscle be trained to maximize muscle hypertrophy? A systematic review

and meta-analysis of studies examining the effects of resistance training frequency, Journal of Sports Sciences, 37:11, 1286-1295

15 **Schoenfeld, B.J., Ogborn, D. & Krieger**. Effects of Resistance Training Frequency on Measures of Muscle Hypertrophy: A Systematic Review and Meta-Analysis. *J.W. Sports Med* (2016) 46: 1689

16 **Gomes, G.K., Franco, C.M., Nunes, P.R.P., & Orsatti, F.L.** High-frequency resistance training is not more effective than low-frequency resistance training in increasing muscle mass and strength in well-trained men. *The Journal of Strength & Conditioning Research. 2018.*

17 **Yoon T, Schlinder Delap B, Griffith EE, Hunter SK**. Mechanisms of fatigue differ after low- and high-force fatiguing contractions in men and women. *Muscle Nerve.* 2007 Oct;36(4):515-24.

18 **Thomas K, Goodall S, Stone M, Howatson G, St Clair Gibson A, Ansley L**. Central and peripheral fatigue in male cyclists after 4-, 20-, and 40-km time trials. *Med Sci Sports Exerc.* 2015 Mar;47(3):537-46

19 **Beiner JM, Jokl P, J Cholewicki J, Panjabi MM.** The Effect of Anabolic Steroids and Corticosteroids on Healing of Muscle Contusion Injury. *Surg Gynecol Obstet.* (1993) Jan; 176(1):73-9.25.

20 **Fell J, Williams D**. The Effect of Aging on Skeletal-Muscle Recovery from Exercise: Possible Implications for Aging Athletes. *J Aging Phys Act.* 2008 Jan;16(1):97-115

21 **Christiansen JJ, Djurhuus CB, Gravholt CH, Iversen P, Christiansen JS, Schmitz O.** Effects of cortisol on carbohydrate, lipid, and protein metabolism: studies of acute cortisol withdrawal in adrenocortical failure. *J Clin Endocrinol Metab.* 2007;92(9):3553. et al

22 **Healy ML, Gibney J, Pentecost C, Wheeler MJ, Sonksen PH**. Endocrine profiles in 693 elite athletes in the post competition setting. *Clin Endocrinol (Oxf)* 2014;81(2):294

23 **Bartolomei S, Malagoli Lanzoni I, Di Michele R.** Two vs. One Resistance Exercise Sessions in One Day: Acute Effects on Recovery and Performance. *Res Q Exerc Sport.* 2022 Jan 4:1-6

24 **Moffat SD, Yang An, MS, Resnick SM, Diamond MP, Ferrucci L**. Longitudinal Change in Cortisol Levels Across the Adult Life Span, *The Journals of Gerontology: Series A*, Volume 75, Issue 2, February 2020, Pages 394–400

25 **Rahimi R, Rohani H, Ebrahimi M**. Effects of very short rest periods on testosterone to cortisol ratio during heavy resistance exercise in men. *Apunts medicina de l'esport.* 2011 July; 46: 145-49.

26 **Smeuninx B, Mckendry J, Wilson D, Una Martin U, Breen L**. Age-Related Anabolic Resistance of Myofibrillar Protein Synthesis Is Exacerbated in Obese Inactive Individuals. *J Clin Endocrinol Metab.* 2017 Sep 1; 102(9): 3535–3545.

27 **Chesley A, MacDougall JD, Tarnopolsky MA, Atkinson SA, Smith K.** Changes in human muscle protein synthesis after resistance exercise. A. Chesley, J.D. MacDougall, M.A. Tarnopolsky S.A. Atkinson, and K. Smith. *J Appl. Physiol.*1992.73.4.1383.

28 **MacDougall DJ, Gibala MJ, Tarnopolsky MA, MacDonald JR; *et al.*** The time course for elevated muscle protein synthesis following heavy resistance exercise. *Canadian Journal of Applied Physiology*, 1995, 20(4): 480-486.

CHAPTER 10: PRINCIPLES OF PROGRAM DESIGN

1 **Williams TD, Tolusso DV, Fedewa MV, Esco MR**. Comparison of Periodized and Non-Periodized Resistance Training on Maximal Strength: A Meta-Analysis. *Sports Med. 2018 Feb;* 48(2):495-496.

2 **Plisk SS, Stone MH**. Periodization strategies. *Strength Cond. J.* 2003. 25 19–37

3 **Rhea MR, Alderman BL**. A meta-analysis of periodized versus non-periodized strength and power training programs. *Res Q Exerc Sport. 2004* Dec; 75(4):413-2

4 **Diem, C.** (1966). Historia de los deportes (Vol. 1). Barcelona: Luis de Caralt

5 **Matveyev L.** (1981). Fundamentals of Sports Training. Moscow: Progress Publishers.

6 **Sale, D. G.** Neural adaptation to strength training. In: Strength and Power in Sport, P. V. Komi (Ed.). 2nd Ed. Malden, MA: Blackwell

7 **Clark MA, Lucett SC, Sutton BG**, eds. NASM. Essentials of Personal Fitness Training, 4th Edition, p.607. Philadelphia Lippincott Williams & Wilkins, 2012

8 **Issurin V.** Block Periodization Versus Traditional Training Theory: A Review *J Sports Med Phys Fitness* 2008 Mar;48(1):65-75.

9 **Rhea MR, Ball SD, Phillips WT, Burkett LN**. A Comparison of Linear and Daily Undulating Periodized Programs with Equated Volume and Intensity for Strength. *J Strength Cond Res.* 2002 May;16(2):250-5

10 **Graham J.** Periodization: research and an example application. *Strength Cond J.* 2002;24(6):62–70.

11 7**Stone MH, O'Bryant HS, Schilling BK, et al**. Periodization part 2: effects of manipulating volume and intensity. Strength Cond J. 1999;21(3):54–60

12 **Kiely J.** Periodization Paradigms in the 21st Century: Evidence-Led or Tradition-Driven? *International Journal of Sports Physiology and Performance*; 2012, 7, 242-250

13 **Kraemer WJ, Ratamess NA.** Fundamentals of resistance training: progression and exercise prescription. *Med Sci Sports Exerc. 2004 Apr; 36(4):674-88*

CHAPTER 11: ANYONE FOR CARDIO?

1 **Wang B, Li R, Lu Z, Huang Y**. Does comorbidity increase the risk of patients with COVID-19: evidence from meta-analysis. *Aging* (Albany NY). 2020 Apr;12(7):6049–57.

2 **Reis Gonçalves C.T., Reis Gonçalves C.G., de Almeida F.M.** Protective effects of aerobic exercise on acute lung injury induced by LPS in mice. *Critical Care*. 2012;16(5): R199

3 **Blair SN, Kampert JB, Kohl HW III, Barlow CE**, *et al.* Influences of cardiorespiratory fitness and other precursors on cardiovascular disease and all-cause mortality in men and women. J Am Med Assoc. 1996;276: 205–210.

4 **Schuch FB Vancampfort D. Richards J, Rosenbaum S Ward PB, Stubbs B** Exercise as a treatment for depression: A meta-analysis adjusting for publication bias. *J Psychiatr Res.* 2016 Jun; 77:42-51

5 **Dorling J, Broom DR, Burns SF, Clayton DJ** *et al.* Acute and Chronic Effects of Exercise on Appetite, Energy Intake, and Appetite-Related Hormones: The Modulating Effect of Adiposity, Sex, and Habitual Physical Activity. *Nutrients.* 2018 Sep; 10(9): 1140

6 **Lee DC, Sui X, Church TS, Lavie CJ, Jackson AS, Blair SN**. Changes in fitness and fatness on the development of cardiovascular disease risk factors: Hypertension, metabolic syndrome, and hypercholesterolemia. *J Am Coll Cardiol.* Elsevier Inc.; 2012;59: 665–672

7 **Cox C.E;** Role of Physical Activity for Weight Loss and Weight Maintenance *Diabetes Spectr.* 2017 Aug; 30(3): 157–160

8 **Donnelly JE, Honas JJ, Smith BK, Mayo MS, Gibson CA,** *et al.* Aerobic exercise alone results in clinically significant weight loss for men and women: Midwest exercise trial 2. *Obesity (Silver Spring).* 2013 Mar;21(3): E219-28.

9 **Thomas DM, Bouchard C, Church T, Slentz C, Kraus WE,** *et al.* Why do individuals not lose more weight from an exercise intervention at a defined dose? An energy balance analysis. *Obes Rev.* 2012 Oct; 13(10):835-47.

10 **Nelson MB, Kaminsky LA, Dickin DC, Montoye AH**. Validity of Consumer-Based Physical Activity Monitors for Specific Activity Types. *Med Sci Sports Exerc.* 2016 Aug;48(8):1619-28

11 **Woo R, Pi-Sunyer FX**. Effect of increased physical activity on voluntary intake in lean women. *Metabolism.*1985; 34:836–84119.

12 **Ravussin E, Lillioja S, Knowler WC, Christin L,** *et al.* Reduced rate of energy expenditure as a risk factor for body-weight gain. *N Engl J Med.* 1988 Feb 25; 318(8):467-72.

13 **Vincent J. L.** (2008). Understanding cardiac output. *Critical care (London, England), 12*(4), 174.

14 **Klausen K, Andersen LB, Pelle I.** Adaptive changes in work capacity, skeletal muscle capillarization and enzyme levels during training and detraining. *Acta Physiol Scand.* 1981; 113:9 –16.

15 **Timmerman KL, Volpi E.** Endothelial function and the regulation of muscle protein anabolism in older adults. *Nutr Metab Cardiovasc Dis.* 2013;23 Suppl 1(0 1): S44-S50.

16 **Short KR, Bigelow ML, Kahl J**, *et al.* Decline in skeletal muscle mitochondrial function with aging in humans. *Proc Natl Acad Sci USA*. 2005; 102:5618–23.

17 **Schwerzmann K, Hoppeler H, Kayar SR, Weibel ER**. Oxidative capacity of muscle and mitochondria: correlation of physiological, biochemical, and morphometric characteristics. *Proc Natl Acad Sci USA* 86: 1583–1587, 1989.

18 **Steele J, Fisher J, McGuff D, Bruce-Low S, Smith D.** Resistance Training to Momentary Muscular Failure Improves Cardiovascular Fitness in Humans: A Review of Acute Physiological Responses and Chronic Physiological Adaptations. *Journal of Exercise Physiology. 2012;* 15: 3

19 **Hickson R.C**. Interference of strength development by simultaneously training for strength and endurance. *European Journal of Applied Physiology and Occupational Physiology.* (1980) 45, 255-263

20 **Kraemer WJ Patton JF, Gordon SE, Harman EA**, *et al.* Compatibility of high-intensity strength and endurance training on hormonal and skeletal muscle adaptations. *J Appl Physiol (1985).* 1995 Mar;78(3):976-89

21 **Coffey V.G., Hawley J.A.** Concurrent exercise training: do opposites distract? *Journal of Physiol.* 595, 2883-2896. (2017)

22 **Methenitis, S.** A Brief Review on Concurrent Training: From Laboratory to the Field. *Sports (Basel).* 2018 Dec; 6(4): 127.

23 **Wilson JM, Marin PJ, Rhea MR, Wilson SM, Loenneke JP, Anderson JC**. Concurrent training: a meta-analysis examining interference of aerobic and resistance exercises. *J Strength Cond Res.* 2012 Aug;26(8):2293-307

24 **Lundberg T.R., Fernandez-Gonzalo R., Gustafsson T., Tesch P.A.** (2013) Aerobic exercise does not compromise muscle hypertrophy response to short-term resistance training. *Journal of Applied Physiology* (1985)114, 81-89

25 **Tsitkanou S., Spengos K., Stasinaki A.N., Zaras N., Bogdanis G., Papadimas G., Terzis G.** (2016) Effects of high-intensity interval cycling performed after resistance training on muscle strength and hypertrophy. *Scandinavian Journal of Medicine & Science in Sports* 27, 1317-1327.

26 26.**Ryu JH, Paik IY, Woo JH, Shin KO, Cho SY, Roh HT.** Impact of different running distances on muscle and lymphocyte DNA damage in amateur marathon runners. *J Phys Ther Sci.* 2016;28(2):450-455.

27 **Robineau J., Babault N., Piscione J., Lacome M., Bigard A.X**. (2016) Specific Training Effects of Concurrent Aerobic and Strength Exercises Depend

on Recovery Duration. *Journal of Strength and Conditioning Research* 30, 672-683.

28 **Bell GJ, Petersen SR, Quinney HA, Wenger HA.** Sequencing of endurance and high-velocity strength training. Can J Sport Sci 13: 214–219, 1988.

29 **Cadore EL, Izquierdo M, Albertson CL, Pinto RS**, *et al.* Strength prior to endurance intra-session exercise sequence optimizes neuromuscular and cardiovascular gains in elderly men. Exp Gerontol 47: 164–169, 2012.

30 **Okamoto T, Masuhara M, Ikuta K**. Combined aerobic and resistance training and vascular function: Effect of aerobic exercise before and after resistance training. J Appl Physiol 103: 1655–1661, 2007.

31 **Romijn, J.A.**, et al., Regulation of endogenous fat and carbohydrate metabolism in relation to exercise intensity and duration. *Am J Physiol,* 1993. 265(3 Pt 1): p. E380-9

32 **Carey DG.** Quantifying differences in the "fat burning" zone and the aerobic zone: implications for training. *J Strength Cond Res.* 2009;23(7):2090-5.

33 **Hall KD, Heymsfield SB, Kemnitz JW, Klein S, Schoeller DA, Speakman JR.** Energy balance and its components: implications for body weight regulation.

34 **Vieira AF, Costa RR, Macedo RC, Coconcelli L, Kruel LF.** Effects of aerobic exercise performed in fasted v. fed state on fat and carbohydrate metabolism in adults: a systematic review and meta-analysis. Br J Nutr. 2016 Oct;116(7):1153-1164.

35 **Manore M, Larson-Meyer D, Lindsay A, Hongu N, Houtkooper L.** Dynamic Energy Balance: An Integrated Framework for Discussing Diet and Physical Activity in Obesity Prevention—Is it More than Eating Less and Exercising More? *Nutrients* 9(8):905 · August 2017

36 **de Venne WP V, Westerterp KR**. Influence of the feeding frequency on nutrient utilization in man: consequences for energy metabolism. *Eur J Clin Nutr.* 1991;45(3):161–169.

37 **Keating SE, Johnson NA, Mielke GI, Coombes JS**. A systematic review and meta-analysis of interval training versus moderate-intensity continuous training on body adiposity. *Obes Rev.* 2017 Aug;18(8):943-964.

38 **Ross, A., Leveritt, M**. Long-Term Metabolic and Skeletal Muscle Adaptations to Short-Sprint Training. *Sports Med* **31,** 1063–1082 (2001)

39 **Wilson JM, Loenneke JP, Jo E, Wilson GJ, Zourdos MC, Kim JS,** *et al.* The effects of endurance, strength, and power training on muscle fibre type shifting. *J Strength Cond Res.* 2012; 26:1724–9.

40 **Hejazi SM.** Effects of High Intensity Interval Training on Plasma Levels of GH and IGF-I. International Journal of Medical Research & Health Sciences, 2017, 6(4): 55-59

41 **Hayes L, Herbert P, Sculthorpe N, Grace F.** Exercise training improves free testosterone in lifelong sedentary aging men. Endocrine Connections 2017. 6 306-310.

42 **Hackney AC, Hosick KP, Myer A, Rubin DA, Battaglini CL.** Testosterone responses to intensive interval versus steady-state endurance exercise. *J Endocrinol Invest.* 2012 Dec;35(11):947-50.

43 **Herbert P, Hayes LD, NF Sculthorpe NF Grace FM.** HIIT produces increases in muscle power and free testosterone in male masters' athletes. ***Endocr Connect.*** 2017 Oct; 6(7): 430–436.

44 **Nevill ME, Holmyard DJ, Hall GM,** *et al.* Growth hormone responses to treadmill sprinting in sprint- and endurance-trained athletes. *European Journal of Applied Physiology and Occupational Physiology.* 1996;72(5-6):460–467.

45 **Zouhal H, Jacob C, Delamarche P, Gratas-Delamarche A.** Catecholamines and the effects of exercise, training and gender. *Sports Medicine.* 2008;38(5):401–423

46 **Issekutz B., Jr.** Role of beta-adrenergic receptors in mobilization of energy sources in exercising dogs. *Journal of Applied Physiology Respiratory Environmental and Exercise Physiology.* 1978;44(6):869–876.

47 **Richards J. C., Johnson T. K., Kuzma J. N., Lonac M. C.,** *et al.* (2010). Short-term sprint interval training increases insulin sensitivity in healthy adults but does not affect the thermogenic response to beta-adrenergic stimulation. J. Physiol. 588, 2961–2972.

48 **Tjønna, Arnt Erik** *et al.* "Aerobic interval training versus continuous moderate exercise as a treatment for the metabolic syndrome: a pilot study." *Circulation* vol. 118,4 (2008): 346-54.

49 **Prado WL, Lofrano-Prado MC, Oyama LM, Cardel M.**, Effect of a 12-Week Low vs. High Intensity Aerobic Exercise Training on Appetite-Regulating Hormones in Obese Adolescents: A Randomized Exercise Intervention Study. *Pediatr Exerc Sci.* 2015 Nov;27(4):510-7.

50 **Sim AY, Wallman KE, Fairchild TJ, Guelfi KJ.** High-intensity intermittent exercise attenuates ad-libitum energy intake. *Int J Obes* (Lond). 2014;38(3):417–22. 31.

PART 3: NUTRITION

CHAPTER 12: IF IT FITS MY WHAT...?

1 **Dr Eric Russel Helms**. The Muscle and Strength Pyramid. 24 March 2019.

2 **Hall KD, Heymsfield SB, Kemnitz JW, Klein S, Schoeller DA, Speakman JR.** Energy balance and its components: implications for body weight regulation. *Am J Clin Nutr.* 2012;95(4):989-994.

3 **Hill JO, Comerford R.** Exercise, fat balance and energy balance. *International Journal of Sports Nutrition.* 1996; 6:80–92.

4 **Horton TJ, Drougas H, Brachey A, Reed GW, Peters JC, Hill JO**. Fat and carbohydrate overfeeding in humans: different effects on energy storage. *Am J Clin Nutr. 1995 Jul; 62(1):19-29.*

5 **Leibel RL, Rosenbaum M, Hirsch J.** Changes in energy expenditure resulting from altered body weight. *N Engl J Med.* 1995 Mar 9; 332(10):621-8.

6 **Nelson KM, Weinsier RL, Long CL, Schutz Y.** Prediction of resting energy expenditure from fat-free mass and fat mass. *Am J Clin Nutr* (1992) 56(5):848–56.

7 **Speakman JR, Selman C.** Physical activity and resting metabolic rate. *Proc Nutr Soc (2003)* 62(3):621–3410.1079/PNS2003282

8 **Psota T, Chen KY.** Measuring energy expenditure in clinical populations: rewards and challenges. *Eur J Clin Nutr.* 67:436-442

9 **Levine J.** Non-exercise activity thermogenesis--liberating the life-force. *J Intern Med.* 2007;262(3):273–87.

10 **Helms E, Aragon A, Fitschen P.** Evidence-based recommendations for natural bodybuilding contest preparation: nutrition and supplementation. *J Int Soc Sports Nutr.* 2014; 11:20.

11 11.**Garthe I, Raastad T, Refsnes P, Koivisto A, Sundgot-Borgen J.** Effect of two different weight-loss rates on body composition and strength and power-related performance in elite athletes. *Int J Sport Nutr Exerc Metab.* 2011;21(2):97–104.

12 **Nackers L, Ross K, Perri M.** The association between rate of initial weight loss and long-term success in obesity treatment: does slow and steady win the race? *Int J Behav Med.* 2010;17(3):161–7.

13 **O'Rourke R.** Metabolic thrift and the genetic basis of human obesity. Ann Surg. 2014;259(4):642–8.

14 **Elwha K, Rössner S.** Who succeeds in maintaining weight loss? A conceptual review of factors associated with weight loss maintenance and weight regain. *Obes Rev.* 2005 Feb; 6(1):67-85.

15 **Wadden TA, Foster GD, Wang J, Pierson RN, Yang MU, et al;** Clinical correlates of short- and long-term weight loss. *Am J Clin Nutr.* 1992 Jul; 56(1 Suppl):271S-274S

16 **Jeffery RW, Wing RR, Mayer RR** Are smaller weight losses or more achievable weight loss goals better in the long term for obese patients? *J Consult Clin Psychol.* 1998 Aug; 66(4):641-5.

17 **Carels RA, Cacciapaglia HM, Douglass OM, Rydin S, O'Brien WH.** The early identification of poor treatment outcome in a women's weight loss program. *Eat Behav.* 2003 Sep; 4(3):265-82.

18 **Purcell K, Sumithran P, Prendergast LA, Bouniu CJ, Delbridge E, Proietto J.** The effect of rate of weight loss on long-term weight management: a randomised controlled trial. *Lancet Diabetes Endocrinol.* 2014;2(12):954–62.

19 **Kelly DM, Jones TH.** Testosterone and obesity. Obes Rev. 2015 Jul;16(7):581-606.

20 **Iraki J, Fitschen P, Espinar S, Helms E.** Nutrition Recommendations for Bodybuilders in the Off-Season: A Narrative Review. Sports (Basel). 2019 Jun 26;7(7):154

CHAPTER 13: THEN GOD CREATED PROTEIN

1 **Institute of Medicine of the National Academies:** Dietary reference intakes for energy, carbohydrate, fibre, fat, fatty acids, cholesterol, protein, and amino acids (macronutrients). 2002, Washington, DC, National Academies Pres

2 **Marcell TJ.** Sarcopenia: causes, consequences, and preventions. *J Gerontol A Biol Sci Med* 2003. 58: M911-6

3 **Keys A, Taylor HL, Grande F.** Basal metabolism and age of adult man. *Metabolism.* 1973 Apr; 22(4):579-87.

4 **Jäger R, Kerksick CM, Campbell BI, Cribb PJ, Wells SD, Skwiat TM, Purpura** M *et al.* International Society of Sports Nutrition Position Stand: protein and exercise. *Journal of the International Society of Sports Nutrition* volume 14, Article number: 20 (2017)

5 **Spendlove J., Mitchell L., Gifford J., Hackett D., Slater G., Cobley S., O'Connor H.** Dietary Intake of Competitive Bodybuilders. *Sports Med.* 2015; 45:1041–1063.

6 **Morton RW, Murphy KT, McKellar SR, *et al.*** A systematic review, meta-analysis and meta-regression of the effect of protein supplementation on resistance training-induced gains in muscle mass and strength in healthy adults. *British Journal of Sports Medicine* 2018; 52:376-384.

7 **Iraki J, Fitschen P, Espinar S, Helms E.** Nutrition Recommendations for Bodybuilders in the Off-Season: A Narrative Review. *Sports (Basel).* 2019;7(7):154. Published 2019 Jun 26.

8 **Schoenfeld, B.J., Aragon, A.A. & Krieger, J.W.** The effect of protein timing on muscle strength and hypertrophy: a meta-analysis. *J Int Soc Sports Nutr* **10,** 53 (2013)

9 **Phillips S.M. Van Loon L, JC.** Dietary protein for athletes: From requirements to optimum adaptation. *Journal of Sports Sciences.* 2011; 29; S29-S38

10 **Roubenoff R.** Catabolism of aging: is it an inflammatory process? *Curr Opin Clin Nutr Metab Care.* 2003 May;6(3):295-9

11 **Helms ER, Zinn C, Rowlands DS, Brown SR.** A systematic review of dietary protein during caloric restriction in resistance trained lean athletes: a case for higher intakes. *Int J Sport Nutr Exerc Metab.* 2014 Apr;24(2):127-38.

12 **Aragon A** http://72.21.17.51:15588/do_k_ument/The_Ark/Fitness_Books_Collection/Fitness_Programs/AARR/AARR_2013/aarr-aug-.2013.pdf

13 **Weigle DS, Breen PA, Matthys CC, Callahan HS, Meeuws KE, Burden VR, Purnell JQ.** A high-protein diet induces sustained reductions in appetite, ad libitum caloric intake, and body weight despite compensatory changes in diurnal plasma leptin and ghrelin concentrations. *Am J Clin Nutr.* 2005 Jul; 82(1):41-8

14 **Westerterp-Plantenga MS, Nieuwenhuizen A, Tomé D, Soenen S, Westerterp KR.** Dietary protein, weight loss, and weight maintenance. *Annu Rev Nutr.* 2009; 29():21-41.

15 **Truche AS, Bailly S, Fabre O, Legrand R, Zaoui P.** A Specific High-Protein Weight Loss Program Does Not Impair Renal Function in Patients Who Are Overweight/Obese. *Nutrients.* 2022;14(2):384. Published 2022 Jan 17.

16 **Devries MC, Sithamparapillai A, Brimble KS, Banfeld L, Morton RW, Philips SM.** Changes in kidney function do not differ between healthy adults consuming higher-compared with lower or normal-protein diets: a systematic review and meta-analysis. *J Nutr.* Nov 2018; 148 (11): 1760-75

17 **Antonio J. Ellerbroek A, Silver T, et al.** A high protein diet (3.4g/kg) combined with a heavy resistance training program improves body composition in healthy trained men and women – a follow up investigation. *J Int Soc Sports Nutr.* 2015; 12:39

18 **H Manninen, AH**. High-Protein Weight Loss Diets and Purported Adverse Effects: Where is the Evidence? *J Int Soc Sports Nutr.* 2004; 1(1): 45–51.

19 **Antonio, Jose et al**. "The Effects of a High-Protein Diet on Bone Mineral Density in Exercise-Trained Women: A 1-Year Investigation." *Journal of functional morphology and kinesiology* vol. 3,4 62. 5 Dec. 2018.

20 **Ten Have GA, Engelen MP, Luiking YC, Deutz NE**. Absorption kinetics of amino acids, peptides, and intact proteins. *Int J Sport Nutr Exerc Metab.* 2007 Aug;17 S23-36

21 **Atherton, P. J., Etheridge, T., Watt, P. W., Wilkinson, D., Selby, A., Rankin, D., et al.** (2010). Muscle full effect after oral protein: time-dependent concordance and discordance between human muscle protein synthesis and mTORC1 signalling. *Am. J. Clin. Nutr.* 92, 1080–1088.

22 **Moore D.R., Churchward-Venne T.A., Witard O., Breen L., Burd N.A., Tipton K.D., Phillips S.M**. Protein ingestion to stimulate myofibrillar protein synthesis requires greater relative protein intakes in healthy older *versus* younger men. *J. Gerontol. A.* 2015; 70:57–62.

23 **Rennie MJ, Bohe J, Wolfe RR.** Latency, duration and dose response relationships of amino acid effects on human muscle protein synthesis. *J Nutr* 2002; 132: 3225S–3227S, 2002.

24 **Garlick PJ.** The role of leucine in the regulation of protein metabolism. *J Nutr* 135: 1553S-1556S, 2005.

25 **25.J. Wilkinson, T. Hossain, D.S. Hill, B.E. Phillips, H. Crossland, J. Williams, *et al.*** Effects of leucine and its metabolite β-hydroxy-β-methylbutyrate on human skeletal muscle protein metabolism. *J Physiol.* 2013 Jun 1;591(11):2911-2

26 **Paddon-Jones D, Sheffield-Moore M, Zhang XJ, Volpi E, Wolf SE, Aarsland A, Ferrando AA, and Wolfe RR.** Amino acid ingestion improves muscle protein synthesis in the young and elderly. *Am J Physiol Endocrinol Metab 286*: E321–E328, 2004.

27 **Katsanos CS, Kobayashi H, Sheffield-Moore M, Aarsland A, and Wolfe RR.** Aging is associated with diminished accretion of muscle proteins after the ingestion of a small bolus of essential amino acids. *Am J Clin Nutr 82*: 1065–1073, 2005.

28 **Katsanos CS, Kobayashi H, Sheffield-Moore M, Aarsland A, Wolfe RR.** A high proportion of leucine is required for optimal stimulation of the rate of muscle protein synthesis by essential amino acids in the elderly. *Am J Physiol Endocrinol Metab.* 2006 Aug;291(2): E381-7. Epub 2006 Feb 28.

29 **Volpi E, Campbell WW, Dwyer JT, Johnson MA, Jensen GL, Morley JE, Wolfe RR**. Is the optimal level of protein intake for older adults greater than the recommended dietary allowance? *J Gerontol A Biol Sci Med Sci* 2013; 68:677–81

30 **Atherton PJ, Kumar V, Selby AL, Rankin D, Hildebrandt W, Phillips BE, Williams JP, Hiscock N, Smith K**. Enriching a protein drink with leucine augments muscle protein synthesis after resistance exercise in young and older men. Clin Nutr. 2017 Jun;36(3):888-895

31 **Norton, Layne**. https://www.slideshare.net/biolayne/optimal-protein-intake-and-meal-frequency-to-support-maximal-protein-synthesis-and-muscle-mass

32 **Bohe J, Low JF, Wolfe RR, Rennie MJ**. Latency and duration of stimulation of human muscle protein synthesis during continuous infusion of amino acids. *J Physiol. 2002; 532* (Pt 2):575–9.7.

33 **Schoenfeld, B.J., Aragon, A.A.** How much protein can the body use in a single meal for muscle-building? Implications for daily protein distribution. *J Int Soc Sports Nutr* 15, 10 (2018).

34 **Yasuda J, Tomita T, Arimitsu T, Fujita S**. Evenly Distributed Protein Intake over 3 Meals Augments Resistance Exercise-Induced Muscle Hypertrophy in Healthy Young Men. J Nutr. 2020 Jul 1;150(7):1845-1851

35 **Hayashi, A.P., de Capitani, M.D., Dias, S.F.** *et al.* Number of high proteins containing meals correlates with muscle mass in pre-frail and frail elderly. *Eur J Clin Nutr* **74,** 1047–1053 (2020).

36 **Dickinson J.M., Gundermann D.M., Walker D.K., Reidy P.T., Borack M.S., Drummond M.J.** Leucine-enriched amino acid ingestion after resistance exercise prolongs myofibrillar protein synthesis and amino acid transporter expression in older men. *J Nutr.* 2014; 144:1694–1702

37 **Anthony, J.C.; Anthony, T.G.; Kimball, S.R.; Jefferson, L.S.** Signalling pathways involved in translational control of protein synthesis in skeletal muscle by leucine. *J Nutr.* 2001, 131, 856S–860S.

38 **Escobar, J., Frank, J. W., Suryawan, A., Nguyen, H. V., & Davis, T. A. (2007).** Amino acid availability and age affect the leucine stimulation of protein synthesis and eIF4F formation in muscle. *American journal of physiology. Endocrinology and metabolism, 293*(6), E1615–E1621.

39 **Van Vliet S, Burd NA, Van Loon LJ.** The Skeletal Muscle Anabolic Response to Plant- versus Animal-Based Protein Consumption. *J Nutr. 2015 Sep; 145(9):1981-91.*

40 **Lord C, Chaput JP, Aubertin-Leheudre M, Labonte M, Dionne IJ.** Dietary animal protein intake: association with muscle mass index in older women. *J Nutr Health Aging* 2007; 11: 383–7

41 **Young VR, Pellett PL**. Plant proteins in relation to human protein and amino acid nutrition. *Am J Clin Nutr* 1994; 59 Suppl: 1203S–12S.

42 **Krajcovicova-Kudlackova M, Babinska K,Valachovicova M**. Health benefits and risks of plant proteins. *Bratisl Lek Listy.* 2005;106(6-7):231-4.

43 **Rutherfurd SM, Moughan PJ.** Available versus digestible dietary amino acids. *Br J Nutr* 2012; 108 Suppl 2: S298–305

44 **Moughan P, et al.** The assessment of amino acid digestibility in foods for humans and including a collation of published ileal amino acid digestibility data for human foods . *FAO.* (2011)

45 **Gran P, Larsen AE, Bonham M, Dordevic AL, Rupasinghe T, Silva C, Nahid A, *et al.*** Muscle p70S6K phosphorylation in response to soy and dairy rich meals in middle aged men with metabolic syndrome: a randomised crossover trial. Nutr Metab (Lond). 2014 Sep 30;11(1):46.

46 **Lim, M.T.; Pan, B.J.; Toh, D.W.K.; Sutanto, C.N.; Kim, J.E.** Animal Protein versus Plant Protein in Supporting Lean Mass and Muscle Strength: A Systematic Review and Meta-Analysis of Randomized Controlled Trials. *Nutrients* 2021, *13,* 661

47 **Boirie Y, Dangin M, Gachon P, Vasson MP, Maubois JL, Beaufrère BB.** Slow and fast dietary proteins differently modulate postprandial protein accretion. Proc Natl Acad Sci U S A. 1997 Dec 23; 94(26): 14930–14935.

48 **Cook, C.G. Andrews JM, Jones KL, Wittert GA, Chapman IM, Morely JE & Horowitz M** (1997) Effects of small intestinal nutrient infusion on appetite and pyloric motility are modified by age. The American journal of physiology 273(2 Pt 2): R755-61

49 **Dangin M, Boirie Y Garcia-Rodenas C, Gachony P et al;** The digestion rate of protein is an independent regulating factor of postprandial protein retention. *Am J Physiol Endocrinol Metab.* 2001 Feb; 280(2): E340-8.

50 **M, Guillet C, G Carcia-Rodenas, Gachon P, Bouteloup-Demange C, Reiffers-Magnani, Fauquant J, Ballèvre O, Beaufrère B.** The rate of protein digestion affects protein gain differently during aging in humans. *J Physiol*(2003), 549.2, pp. 635–644

CHAPTER 14: FAT, THE GOOD, THE BAD AND THE VERY UGLY

1 **Geyelin HR.** Fasting as a method for treating epilepsy. *Med Rec 1921; 99:1037–1039*

2 **Ashtary-Larky D., Bagheri R., Asbaghi O., Tinsley G., Kooti W.** Effects of resistance training combined with a ketogenic diet on body composition: A systematic review and meta-analysis. *Crit. Rev. Food Sci. Nutr.* 2021

3 **Gibson A.A., Seimon R.V., Lee C.M.Y., Ayre J., Franklin J., Markovic T.P., Caterson I.D., Sainsbury A**. Do ketogenic diets really suppress appetite? A systematic review and meta-analysis. *Obes. Rev.* 2015; 16:64–76.

4 **Anssi H Manninen** Very-low-carbohydrate diets and preservation of muscle mass Published online 2006 Jan 31. *Nutr Metab (Lond). 2006; 3: 9.*

5 **Cahill GF Jr.** Fuel metabolism in starvation. *Annu Rev Nutr. 2006; 26:1-22.*

6 **T.T. Aoki, C.J. Toews, A.A. Rossini, N.B. Ruderman, G.F. Cahill Jr.** Glucogenic substrate levels in fasting man *Advances in Enzyme Regulation. Vol. 13, 1975; 329-336*

7 **Wilson JM, Lowery RP, Roberts MD, Sharp MH, Joy JM, Shields KA, Partl JM, Volek JS, D'Agostino DP.** Effects of Ketogenic Dieting on Body Composition, Strength, Power, and Hormonal Profiles in Resistance Training Men. *J Strength Cond Res.* 2020 Dec;34(12):3463-3474

8 **Vargas S, Romance R, Petro JL, Bonilla DA, Galancho I, Espinar S, Kreider RB, Benitez-Porres J**. Efficacy of ketogenic diet on body composition during resistance training in trained men: a randomized controlled trial. J Int Soc Sports Nutr. 2020; 15:31

9 **Greene DA, Varley BJ, Hartwig TB, Chapman P, Rigney M.** A Low-Carbohydrate Ketogenic Diet Reduces Body Mass Without Compromising Performance in Powerlifting and Olympic Weightlifting Athletes. *J Strength Cond Res.* 2018; 32:3373–3382.

10 **Paoli A, Grimaldi K, D'Agostino D, Cenci L, Moro T, Bianco A, Palma A.** Ketogenic diet does not affect strength performance in elite artistic gymnasts. *J Int Soc Sports Nutr.* 2012; 9:34.

11 **Kysel P., Haluzíková D., Doležalová R.P., Laňková I. et al.** The influence of cyclical ketogenic reduction diet vs. Nutritionally balanced reduction diet on body composition, strength, and endurance performance in healthy young males: A randomized controlled trial. *Nutrients.* 2020; 12:2832

12 **Valenzuela, Pedro L et al.** "Effects of Combining a Ketogenic Diet with Resistance Training on Body Composition, Strength, and Mechanical Power in Trained Individuals: A Narrative Review." *Nutrients* vol. 13,9 3083. 1 Sep. 2021.

13 **Innes, JK, Calder PC.** Omega-6 fatty acids and inflammation. *Prostaglandins Leukot Essent Fatty Acids.* 2018 May; 132:41-48.

14 **Bloomer, R. J., Larson, D. E., Fisher-Wellman, K. H., Galpin, A. J., & Schilling, B. K.** (2009). Effect of eicosapentaenoic and docosahexaenoic acid on resting and exercise-induced inflammatory and oxidative stress biomarkers: a randomized, placebo controlled, cross-over study. *Lipids Health Dis. 2009 Aug 19; 8:36*

15 **Dunstan JA, Mitoulas LR, Dixon G, Doherty DA, Hartmann PE, Simmer K, Prescott SL.** The effects of fish oil supplementation in pregnancy on breast milk fatty acid composition over the course of lactation: a randomized controlled trial. *Pediatr Res. 2007 Dec; 62(6):689-94*

16 **Innis SM.** Dietary omega 3 fatty acids and the developing brain. *Brain Res. 2008 Oct 27; 1237:35-43*

17 17.**Mann NJ, O'Connell SL, Baldwin KM, Singh I, Meyer BJ.** Effects of seal oil and tuna-fish oil on platelet parameters and plasma lipid levels in healthy subjects. *Lipids. 2010; 45:669–81.*

18 **Simopoulos AP.** The importance of the ratio of omega-6/omega-3 essential fatty acids. *Biomed Pharmacother. 2002 Oct;56(8):365-79.*

19 **Kris-Etherton PM, Harris WS, Appel LJ.** Omega-3 Fatty Acids and Cardiovascular Disease. (2003). *Arteriosclerosis, Thrombosis, and Vascular Biology., 151-152*

20 **Couet, C., Delarue, J., Ritz, P., Antoine, J., & Lamisse, F.** (1997). Effect of dietary fish oil on body fat mass and basal fat oxidation in healthy adults. *International Journal of Obesity, 21(8), 637-643.*

21 **Noreen, E. E., Sass, M. J., Crowe, M. L., Pabon, V. A., Brandauer, J., & Averill, L. K.** (2010). Effects of supplemental fish oil on resting metabolic rate, body composition, and salivary cortisol in healthy adults. *Journal of the International Society of Sports Nutrition, 7(1), 31.*

22 **Gordon I. Smith.** The Effects of Dietary Omega-3s on Muscle Composition and Quality in Older Adults. *Curr Nutr Rep. 2016 Jun; 5(2): 99–105.*

23 **Swain, J., McCarron, P., Hamilton, E., Sacks, F. and Appel, L.** (2008). Characteristics of the Diet Patterns Tested in the Optimal Macronutrient Intake Trial to Prevent Heart Disease (Omni Heart): Options for a Heart-Healthy Diet. *Journal of the American Dietetic Association, 108(2), pp.257-265*

24 **Schwab U, Lauritzen L, Tholstrup T, Haldorsson T, Riserus U, Uusitupa M et al.** Effect of the amount and type of dietary fat on cardiometabolic risk factors and risk of developing type 2 diabetes, cardiovascular diseases, and cancer: a systematic review. *Food & Nutrition Research. 2014;58(1):25145.*

25 **Bautista MC, Engler MM.** The Mediterranean diet: is it cardioprotective? *Prog Cardiovasc. Nurs. 2005 Spring;20(2):70-6.*

26 **Keys, A.** (1970) coronary heart disease in seven countries. American Heart Association, New York, NY. *Nutrition. 1997 Mar;13(3):250-2.*

27 **Ference B, Ginsberg H, Graham I, Ray K, Packard C, Bruckert E et al.** Low-density lipoproteins cause atherosclerotic cardiovascular disease. 1. Evidence from genetic, epidemiologic, and clinical studies. A consensus statement from the European Atherosclerosis Society Consensus Panel. *European Heart Journal. 2017;38(32):2459-2472.*

28 **Kromhout D, Menotti A, Bloemberg B, Aravanis C, Blackburn H, Buzina R et al.** Dietary Saturated and trans Fatty Acids and Cholesterol and 25-Year Mortality from Coronary Heart Disease: The Seven Countries Study. Preventive Medicine. 1995;24(3):308-315.

29 **Oppenheimer GM, D.** McGovern's Senate Select Committee on Nutrition and Human Needs Versus the: Meat Industry on the Diet-Heart Question (1976–1977)

30 **The Feig JE, Feig JL, Dangas GD.** The role of HDL in plaque stabilization and regression: basic mechanisms and clinical implications. *Coron Artery Dis. (2016)*

31 **Millán J, et al.** Lipoprotein ratios: Physiological significance and clinical usefulness in cardiovascular prevention. *Vasc Health Risk Manag.* (2009)

32 **Hernáez Á, Martínez-González MÁ, de la Torre R, Fito M.** Mediterranean Diet Improves High-Density Lipoprotein Function in High-Cardiovascular-Risk Individuals: A Randomized Controlled Trial. Circulation. 2017 Feb 14;135(7):633-643

33 **Soliman, GA.** Dietary Cholesterol and the Lack of Evidence in Cardiovascular Disease. *Nutrients. 2018 Jun; 10(6): 780.*

34 **Harman NL, Leeds AR, Griffin B.** Increased dietary cholesterol does not increase plasma low density lipoprotein when accompanied by an energy-restricted diet and weight loss. *Eur J Nutr* 2008; 47: 287–93.

35 **Hu F.B., Manson J.E., Willett W.C.** Types of dietary fat and risk of coronary heart disease: A critical review. J. Am. Coll. Nutr. 2001; 20:5–19.

36 **Castelli W.** Lipids, risk factors and ischaemic heart disease. Atherosclerosis. 1996;124: S1-S9.

37 **Khot U, Khot M, Bajzer C.** Prevalence of conventional risk factors in patients with coronary heart disease. ACC Current Journal Review. 2003;12(6):2

38 **Clarke R, Frost C, Collins R, Appleby P, Peto R.** Dietary lipids and blood cholesterol: quantitative meta-analysis of metabolic ward studies. BMJ. 1997;314(7074):112-112.

39 **ACN.** Saturated fats and health: draft SACN report [Internet]. 2018 [cited 7/13/2018]. Available from: https://www.gov.uk/government/consultations/saturated-fats-and-health-draft-sacn-report

40 **O'Connor LE, Kim JE, Campbell WW.** Total red meat intake of ≥0.5 servings/d does not negatively influence cardiovascular disease risk factors: a systemically searched meta-analysis of randomized controlled trials. *Am J Clin Nutr.* 2017 Jan;105(1):57-69

41 **Shih CW, Hauser ME, Aronica L, Rigdon J, Gardner CD.** Changes in blood lipid concentrations associated with changes in intake of dietary saturated fat in the context of a healthy low-carbohydrate weight-loss diet: a secondary analysis of the Diet Intervention Examining the Factors Interacting with Treatment Success (DIETFITS) trial. *Am J Clin Nutr.* 2019 Feb 1;109(2):433-441.

42 **Martinez-Gonzalez MA, Bes-Rastrollo M.** Dietary patterns, Mediterranean diet, and cardiovascular disease. *Curr Opin Lipidol.* 2014; *25*:20–26

43 **Gotsis E., Anagnostis P., Mariolis A., Vlachou A., Katsiki N., Karagiannis A.** Health benefits of the Mediterranean Diet: An update of research over the last 5 years. *Angiology.* 2015; 66:304–318

44 **Mazzocchi A, Leone L, Agostoni C, Pali-Schöll I.** The Secrets of the Mediterranean Diet. Does [Only] Olive Oil Matter? *Nutrients.* 2019 Dec 3;11(12):2941.

45 **Hernaez A., Castañer O., Elosua R., Pinto X., Estruch R., et al.** Mediterranean Diet Improves High-Density Lipoprotein Function in High-Cardiovascular-Risk Individuals. *Circulation.* 2017; 135:633–643.

46 **Yuhanna IS, Zhu Y, Cox BE, Hahner LD, Osborne-Lawrence S, et al.** High-density lipoprotein binding to scavenger receptor-BI activates endothelial nitric oxide synthase. *Nat Med.* 2001; *7*: 853–857.

47 **Naseem KM.** The role of nitric oxide in cardiovascular diseases. Mol Aspects Med. 2005 Feb-Apr;26(1-2):33-65

48 **Foster R, Lunn J.** 40th Anniversary Briefing Paper: Food availability and our changing diet. Nutrition Bulletin. 2007;32(3):187-249

49 **Austin GL, Ogden LG, Hill JO.** Trends in carbohydrate, fat, and protein intakes and association with energy intake in normal-weight, overweight, and obese individuals: 1971-2006. Am J Clin Nutr. 2011 Apr; 93(4):836-43.

50 **Nielsen S, Siega-Riz A, Popkin B.** Trends in Energy Intake in U.S. between 1977 and 1996: Similar Shifts Seen across Age Groups. Obesity Research. 2002;10(5):370-378.

51 **Briggs MA, Petersen KS, Kris-Etherton PM.** Saturated Fatty Acids and Cardiovascular Disease: Replacements for Saturated Fat to Reduce Cardiovascular Risk . *Healthcare (Basel).* (2017)

52 **Pan A, Chen M, Chowdhury R, Wu J, Sun Q, Campos H et al.** α-Linolenic acid and risk of cardiovascular disease: a systematic review and meta-analysis. The American Journal of Clinical Nutrition. 2012;96(6):1262-1273

53 **Li Y, Hruby A, Bernstein A, Ley S, Wang D, Chiuve S et al.** Saturated Fats Compared with Unsaturated Fats and Sources of Carbohydrates in Relation to Risk of Coronary Heart Disease. Journal of the American College of Cardiology. 2015;66(14):1538-1548

54 2015 Food and Health Survey: consumer attitudes towards food safety, nutrition and health. 2015, International Food Information Council Foundation, conducted by **Greenwald & Associates of Washington, D.**

55 **Wallace SK, Mozaffarian D.** Trans-fatty acids and non-lipid risk factors. *Curr Atheroscler Rep.* Nov 2009; 11 (6): 423-33.

56 Fats and fatty acids in human nutrition Report of an expert consultation. **FAO Food Nutr Pap.** 2010; 91:1–166.

57 **Wang C, Catlin DH, Starcevic B, Heber D, Ambler C, Berman N, Lucas G, Leung A, Schramm K, Lee PW, Hull L, Swerdloff RS.** Low-fat high-fiber diet decreased serum and urine androgens in men . *J Clin Endocrinol Metab.* (2005)

58 **Dorgan JF, Judd JT, Longcope C, Brown C, Schatzkin A, Clevidence BA, et al.** Effects of dietary fat and fibre on plasma and urine androgens and oestrogens in men: a controlled feeding study. Am J Clin Nutr. 1996 Dec;64(6):850–5.

59 **Whittaker J, Wu K.** Low-fat diets and testosterone in men: Systematic review and meta-analysis of intervention studies. *J Steroid Biochem Mol Biol.* 2021 Jun; 210:105878

60 **Zamir A, Ben-Zeev T, Hoffman JR.** Manipulation of Dietary Intake on Changes in Circulating Testosterone Concentrations. *Nutrients.* 2021;13(10):3375. Published 2021 Sep 25.

CHAPTER 15: CARBOHYDRATES & MIDDLE AGE: FRENEMIES?

1 **Norton, L. 2012.** https://www.biolayne.com/articles/nutrition/anabolic-eating-for-your-age/

2 **Fujita S, Rasmussen BB, Cadenas JG, Grady JJ, Volpi E.** Effect of insulin on human skeletal muscle protein synthesis is modulated by insulin-induced

changes in muscle blood flow and amino acid availability. *Am J Physiol Endocrinol Metab.* 2006 Oct;291(4): E745-54.

3 **Gautsch TA, Anthony JC, Kimball SR, Paul GL, Layman DK, Jefferson LS.** Availability of eIF4E regulates skeletal muscle protein synthesis during recovery from exercise. *Am J Physiol.* 1998 Feb;274(2 Pt 1):C406-14.

4 4.**Szoke E, Shrayyef MZ, Messing S, Woerle HJ, van Haeften TW, *et al.*** Effect of Aging on Glucose Homeostasis. *Diabetes Care* 2008 Mar; 31(3): 539-543.

5 **Defronzo, Ralph A, and Devjit Tripathy.** "Skeletal muscle insulin resistance is the primary defect in type 2 diabetes." *Diabetes care* vol. 32 Suppl 2, Suppl 2 (2009): S157-63.

6 **Thurman, Jerome & Mooradian, A.D.** (2000). 31. Age—Related carbohydrate intolerance. *Facts, Research and Intervention in Geriatrics.* 2000. 409-417.

7 **Ralph A DeFronzo;** Glucose Intolerance and Aging. *Diabetes Care* 1 July 1981; 4 (4): 493–501.

8 **Ko GT, Wai HP, Tang JS.** Effects of age on plasma glucose levels in non-diabetic Hong Kong Chinese. *Croat Med J.* 2006;47(5):709-713.

9 **Rudrappa, SS, Wilkinson, DJ, Greenhaff, PL et al.** (2016) Human skeletal muscle disuse atrophy: effects on muscle protein synthesis, breakdown, and insulin resistance – a qualitative review. *Front Physiol* 7, 361.

10 **Goodpaster, BH, Park, SW, Harris, TB et al.** (2006) The loss of skeletal muscle strength, mass, and quality in older adults: the health, aging and body composition study. *J Gerontol Ser A, Biol Sci Med* 61, 1059–1064.

11 11.**De Fronzo RA, Sherwin RS, Kraemer N**. Effect of physical training on insulin action in obesity. Diabetes. 1987 Dec; 36(12):1379-85.

12 **Pesta, D.H., Goncalves, R.L.S.,** Madiraju, A.K. *et al.* Resistance training to improve type 2 diabetes: working toward a prescription for the future. *Nutr Metab (Lond)* 14, 24 (2017).

13 **Paquin J, Lagacé JC, Brochu M, Dionne IJ.** Exercising for Insulin Sensitivity—Is There a Mechanistic Relationship with Quantitative Changes in Skeletal Muscle Mass? *Front Physiol.* 2021; 12:656909. Published 2021 May 12.

14 14.https://www.gov.uk/government/publications/sacn-carbohydrates-and-health-report

15 https://www.nhs.uk/live-well/eat-well/the-eatwell-guide/

16 **Kaczmarczyk, M, Miller M, Freund G**. The health benefits of dietary fibre: beyond the usual suspects of type 2 diabetes, cardiovascular disease and colon cancer. Metabolism. 2012 Aug; 61(8): 1058–1066.

17 **Venn B, Mann J**. Cereal grains, legumes and diabetes. European Journal of Clinical Nutrition. 2004; 58 (11): 1443-1461

18 **Clark MJ, Slavin JL.** The effect of fiber on satiety and food intake: a systematic review. *J Am Coll Nutr.* 2013;32(3):200-11.

19 **McRae MP.** Dietary Fiber Is Beneficial for the Prevention of Cardiovascular Disease: An Umbrella Review of Meta-analyses. *J Chiropr Med.* 2017;16(4):289-299.

20 **Lee JK, Bettencourt R, Brenner D, Le TA, Barrett-Connor E, Loomba R.** Association between serum interleukin-6 concentrations and mortality in older adults: the Rancho Bernardo study. *PLoS ONE* 2012;7: e34218.

21 **Fardet A.** New hypotheses for the health-protective mechanisms of whole-grain cereals: what is beyond fibre? *Nutr Res Rev.* 2010 Jun;23(1):65-134

22 **Stephen A.M., Champ M.M., Cloran S.J., Fleith M., *et al.*** Dietary fibre in Europe: Current state of knowledge on definitions, sources, recommendations, intakes and relationships to health. *Nutr. Res. Rev.* 2017; 30:149–190.

23 **Schaumberg DA Liu S Seddon JM Willett WC Hankinson SE.** Dietary glycemic load and risk of age-related cataract. *Am J Clin Nutr.* 2004; 80: 489–495.

24 **Dickinson S, Hancock DP, Petocz P, Ceriello A, Brand-Miller J.** High-glycemic index carbohydrate increases nuclear factor-kappa B activation in mononuclear cells of young, lean healthy subjects. *Am J Clin Nutr* 2008; 87:1188–93.

25 **Jenkins, DJ, Wolever, TM, Taylor, RH, *et al.*** (1981) Glycemic index of foods: a physiological basis for carbohydrate exchange. *Am J Clin Nutr* 34, 362–366.

26 **Fiona S. Atkinson, Kaye Foster-Powell, Jennie C. Brand-Miller.** International tables of glycemic index and glycemic load values: Diabetes Care 2008; 31:12, 2281-2283.

27 **D.T., Erdman K.A., Burke L.M.** Position of the Academy of Nutrition and Dietetics, Dietitians of Canada, and the American College of Sports Medicine: Nutrition and Athletic Performance. *J. Acad. Nutr. Diet.* 2016;116:501–528.

28 **Knuiman, P.; Hopman, M.T.E.; Mensink, M.** Glycogen availability and skeletal muscle adaptations with endurance and resistance exercise. *Nutr. Metab.* **2015**, *12*, 59.

29 **Roach, PJ. Depaoli-Roach, A. Hurley, DT. Tagliabracci, VS.** Glycogen and its metabolism: some new developments and old themes. *Biochem J.* 2012 Feb 1; 441(3): 763–787.

30 **Coyle EF, Coggan AR, Hemmert MK, Lowe RC, Walters TJ.** Substrate Usage During Prolonged Exercise Following a Pre-exercise Meal. *J Appl Physiol.* 1985;59(2):429–33.

31 **Knuiman P, Hopman MT, Mensink M.** Glycogen availability and skeletal muscle adaptations with endurance and resistance exercise. *Nutr Metab (Lond).* 2015; 12:59

32 **Hepburn, D., R.J. Maughan.** Glycogen availability as a limiting factor in performance of isometric exercise. *J. Physiol.* 342:52P–53P. 1982

33 **Kerksick, C.M., Arent, S., Schoenfeld, B.J. *et al.*** International society of sports nutrition position stand: nutrient timing. *J Int Soc Sports Nutr* **14,** 33 (2017)

34 **Spendlove J., Mitchell L., Gifford J., Hackett D., Slater G., Cobley S., O'Connor H.** Dietary Intake of Competitive Bodybuilders. *Sports Med.* 2015; 45:1041–1063.

35 **Lambert C.P., Frank L.L., Evans W.J., Lambert D.C.P.** Macronutrient Considerations for the Sport of Bodybuilding. *Sports Med.* 2004; 34:317–327

36 **Henselmans M, Bjørnsen T, Hedderman R, Vårvik FT.** The Effect of Carbohydrate Intake on Strength and Resistance Training Performance: A Systematic Review. *Nutrients.* 2022 Feb 18;14(4):856

37 **MacDougall JD, Ray S, Sale DG, McCartney N, Lee P, Garner S.** Muscle substrate utilization and lactate production. *Can J Appl Physiol.* 1999; 24:209–215.

38 **Pascoe D.D., Costill D.L., Fink W.J., Robergs R.A., Zachwieja J.J.** Glycogen resynthesis in skeletal muscle following resistive exercise. *Med. Sci. Sports Exerc.* 1993; 25:349.

39 **Gautsch TA, Anthony JC, Kimball SR, Paul GL, Layman DK, Jefferson LS.** Availability of eIF4E regulates skeletal muscle protein synthesis during recovery from exercise. *Am J Physiol.* 1998 Feb;274(2 Pt 1):C406-14.

40 **Janzen, N.R, Whitfield, J, Hoffman N, J.** Interactive Roles for AMPK and Glycogen from Cellular Energy Sensing to Exercise Metabolism. *International journal of molecular sciences.* 2018

41 **Glynn EL, Fry CS, Drummond MJ, et al.** Muscle protein breakdown has a minor role in the protein anabolic response to essential amino acid and carbohydrate intake following resistance exercise. *Am J Physiol.* 2010;299: R533–R540.

42 **Borsheim E, Cree MG, Tipton KD, Elliott TA, Aarsland A, Wolfe RR.** Effect of carbohydrate intake on net muscle protein synthesis during recovery from resistance exercise. *J Appl Physiol.* (2004) 96:674–8.

43 **Chow L.S., Albright R.C., Bigelow M.L., Toffolo G., Cobelli C., Nair K.S.** Mechanism of insulin's anabolic effect on muscle: Measurements of muscle protein synthesis and breakdown using aminoacyl-tRNA and other surrogate measures. *Am. J. Physiol. Endocrinol. Metab.* 2006;291: E729–E736.

44 **Ivy J.L., Ferguson-Stegall L.M.** Nutrient Timing. *Am. J. Lifestyle Med.* 2014; 8:246–259.

45 **Fernández-Real JM, Ricart W, Casamitjana R.** Lower cortisol levels after oral glucose in subjects with insulin resistance and abdominal obesity. Clin Endocrinol (Oxf). 1997 Nov;47(5):583-8

46 **Lane AR, Duke JW, Hackney AC.** Influence of dietary carbohydrate intake on the free testosterone: cortisol ratio responses to short-term intensive exercise training. *Eur J Appl Physiol.* 2010 Apr;108(6):1125-31

47 **Glynn EL, Fry CS, Drummond MJ, Dreyer HC, Dhanani S, Volpi E, et al.** Muscle protein breakdown has a minor role in the protein anabolic response to essential amino acid and carbohydrate intake following resistance exercise. *Am J Physiol Regul Integr Comp Physiol.* (2010) 299: R533–40.

48 **Martí Juanola-Falgarona, Jordi Salas-Salvadó, Núria Ibarrola-Jurado, et al**; Effect of the glycemic index of the diet on weight loss, modulation of satiety, inflammation, and other metabolic risk factors: a randomized controlled trial, *The American Journal of Clinical Nutrition*, Volume 100, Issue 1, July 2014, Pages 27–35

49 **Barbara A Gower, Amy M Goss.** A Lower-Carbohydrate, Higher-Fat Diet Reduces Abdominal and Intermuscular Fat and Increases Insulin Sensitivity in Adults at Risk of Type 2 Diabetes, *The Journal of Nutrition*, Volume 145, Issue 1, January 2015, Pages 177S–183S

50 **Astrup A, Rössner S.** Lessons from obesity management programmes: greater initial weight loss improves long-term maintenance. *Obes Rev.* 2000; 1:17–9.

CHAPTER 16: MICRONUTRIENTS

1 **Bailey RL, Fulgoni VL 3rd, Keast DR, Dwyer JT.** Examination of vitamin intakes among US adults by dietary supplement use. *J Acad Nutr Diet. 2012 May; 112(5):657-663.e4.*

2 **Patrick J Stover** Vitamin B12 and older adults. *Curr Opin Clin Nutr Metab Care.* 2010 Jan; 13(1): 24–27.

3 **Pugach I, Pugach S.** Strong Correlation Between Prevalence of Severe Vitamin D Deficiency and Population Mortality Rate from COVID-19 in Europe. *medRxiv* 2020.

4 **National Research Council (US) Subcommittee** on the Tenth Edition of the Recommended Dietary Allowances. Recommended Dietary Allowances: 10th Edition. *National Academies Press (US);* 1989.

5 **Maughan RJ.** Role of micronutrients in sport and physical activity. *Br Med Bull.* 1999;55(3):683-90.

6 **Driskell J.** Summary: Vitamins and trace elements in sports nutrition. In: Driskell J, Wolinsky 1, editors. Sports Nutrition. Vitamins and Trace Elements. New York (NY): CRC/Taylor & Francis; 2006. P. 323-31

7 **Woolf K, Manore MM.** B-Vitamins and exercise: does exercise alter requirements? Int J Sport Nutr Exerc Metab. 2006; 16: 453-84

8 **Institute of Medicine.** Dietary Reference Intakes for Thiamine, Riboflavin, Niacin, Vitamin B6, Folate, Vitamin B12, Pantothenic Acid, Biotin, and Choline. Washington (DC) National Academies Press; 2000

9 **Lips P, Hosking D, Lippuner K, Norquist JM et al.** The prevalence of vitamin D inadequacy amongst women with osteoporosis: an international epidemiological investigation. *J Intern Med. 2006 Sep; 260(3):245-54.*

10 **Holick MF.** Vitamin D: Importance in the prevention of cancers, type 1 diabetes, heart disease, and osteoporosis. 2004. *Am J Clin Nutr **79**:362–371.*

11 **Wang, Lu, et al.** "Systematic review: Vitamin D and calcium supplementation in prevention of cardiovascular events." *Annals of Internal Medicine* 152.5 (2010): 315-323.

12 **Forney, Laura A., et al.** "Vitamin D Status, Body Composition, and Fitness Measures in College-Aged Students." *The Journal of Strength & Conditioning Research* 28.3 (2014): 814-824.

13 **Boland R.** Role of vitamin D in skeletal muscle function. *Endocr Rev. 1986 Nov; 7(4):434-48.*

14 **Wicherts IS, Van Schoor NM et al.** Vitamin D status predicts physical performance and its decline in older persons. *J Clin Endocrinol Metab.* 2007 Jun; 92(6):2058-65.

15 **Bischoff HA, Stahelin HB, Urscheler N et al.** Muscle strength in the elderly: its relation to vitamin D metabolites. *Arch Phys Med Rehabil. 1999 Jan; 80(1):54-8*

16 **Nair R, Maseeh A.** Vitamin D: The "sunshine" vitamin. *J Pharmacol Pharmacother.* 2012 Apr;3(2):118-26

17 **Institute of Medicine, Food and Nutrition Board.** Dietary Reference Intakes: Calcium, Phosphorus, Magnesium, Vitamin D, and Fluoride. Washington, DC: National Academy Press, 1997.

18 **Andersen R, Mølgaard C, et al.** *T*eenage girls and elderly women living in northern Europe have low winter vitamin D status. *Eur J Clin Nutr.* 2005 Apr; 59(4):533-41.

19 **Meehan M, Penckofer S.** The Role of Vitamin D in the Aging Adult. J Aging Gerontol. 2014 Dec; 2(2): 60–71.

20 **Brieger K, et al.** Reactive oxygen species: from health to disease. *Swiss Med Wkly (2012)*

21 **Eleuteri E, Magno F, Gnemmi I, Carbone M et al.** Role of oxidative and nitrosative stress biomarkers in chronic heart failure. *Front Biosci*, 2009 Jan 1;14:2230-7.

22 **Wei Y, Chen K, Whaley-Connell AT, Stump CS, Ibdah JA.** Skeletal muscle insulin resistance: role of inflammatory cytokines and reactive oxygen species. *Am J Physiol Regul Integr Comp Physiol*, 2008 Mar;294(3): R673-80.

23 **Fumihiro Sanada, Yoshiaki Taniyama, Jun Muratsu et al.** Source of Chronic Inflammation in Aging. *Front Cardiovasc Med.* 2018; 5: 12.

24 **Evans W.** Functional and metabolic consequences of sarcopenia. *J Nutr.* 1997; 127: S998–1003.

25 **Patel J, McLeod LE, Vries RG, Flynn A et al.** Cellular stresses profoundly inhibit protein synthesis and modulate the states of phosphorylation of multiple translation factors. *Eur J Biochem.* 2002 Jun;269(12):3076-85.

26 **Katsanos, C. S., Kobayashi, H., et al.** (2006). A high proportion of leucine is required for optimal stimulation of the rate of muscle protein synthesis by essential amino acids in the elderly. *American Journal of Physiology-Endocrinology and Metabolism, 291*(2), E381-E387.

27 **Marzani B, Balage M, Vénien A, et al.** Antioxidant supplementation restores defective leucine stimulation of protein synthesis in skeletal muscle from old rats. *J Nutr.* 2008 Nov;138(11):2205-11.

28 **World Cancer Research Fund/American Institute for Cancer Research** (1997) Food, Nutrition and the Prevention of Cancer: A Global Perspective. *American Institute for Cancer Research.* Washington, DC.

29 **Ames, B. N., Shigenaga, M. K. & Hagen, T. M.** (1993) Oxidants, antioxidants, and the degenerative diseases of aging. *Proc. Natl. Acad. Sci. U.S.A.* 90:7915–7922.

30 **Slavin, J.L., Lloyd, B.** Health Benefits of Fruits and Vegetables. *Adv Nutr.* 2012 Jul; 3(4): 506–516.

31 **Prior, R. L. & Cao, G.** (2000) Antioxidant phytochemicals in fruits and vegetables: dietary and health implications. *Hortic. Sci.* 35:588–592.

32 **Svilaas, A., Sakhi, A. K., Andersen, L. F. et al (2004).** Intakes of antioxidants in coffee, wine, and vegetables are correlated with plasma carotenoids in humans. The Journal of nutrition, 134(3), 562-567.

33 **Takanami Y, Iwane H, Kawai Y, Shimomitsu T.** Vitamin E supplementation and endurance exercise: are there benefits? *Sports Med.* 2000;29: 73-83.

34 **Institute of Medicine.** Dietary Reference Intakes for Vitamin C, Vitamin E, Selenium and Carotenoids. Washington (DC): The National Academies Press; 2000.

35 **Mielgo-Ayuso J, Zourdos MC, Calleja-González J et al.** Iron supplementation prevents a decline in iron stores and enhances strength performance in elite female volleyball players during the competitive season. *Appl Physiol Nutr Metab.* 2015 Jun;40(6):615-22.

36 **Lukaski HC.** Vitamin and mineral status: effects on physical performance. *Nutrition.* 2004;20: 632-44

37 **Ames BN, Atamna H, Killilea DW.** Mineral and vitamin deficiencies can accelerate the mitochondrial decay of aging. *Mol Aspects Med.* 2005 Aug-Oct;26(4-5):363-78.

38 **Helms, E.R., Aragon, A.A. & Fitschen, P.J.** Evidence-based recommendations for natural bodybuilding contest preparation: nutrition and supplementation. *J Int Soc Sports Nutr* 11, 20 (2014)

39 **A G Szent-Györgyi.** Calcium regulation of muscle contraction. Biophys J. 1975 Jul; 15(7): 707–723.

40 40.https://assets.publishing.service.gov.uk/government/uploads/system/uploads/attachment_data/file/618167/government_dietary_recommendations.pdf

41 41.**Roohani N, Hurrell R, Kelishadi R, Schulin R**. Zinc and its importance for human health: An integrative review. *J Res Med Sci.* 2013 Feb;18(2):144-57.

42 **Prasad AS**. Zinc: mechanism of host defence. *J Nutr.* 2007 May; 137(5):1345-9

43 **Hambidge KM, Miller LV, Krebs NF.** Physiological requirements for zinc. *Int J Vitam Nutr Res.* 2011 Jan; 81(1):72-8.

44 **Cabrera ÁJ.** Zinc, aging, and immunosenescence: an overview. *Pathobiol Aging Age Relat Dis.* 2015; 5:25592.

45 **García OP, Long KZ, Rosado JL.** Impact of micronutrient deficiencies on obesity. *Nutr Rev.* 2009 Oct; 67(10):559-72.

46 **Prasad AS, Mantzoros CS, Beck W, Hess JW, Brewer GJ.** Zinc status and serum testosterone levels of healthy adults. *Nutrition* 12, 5, May 1996, Pages 344-34.

47 **Netter A, Hartoma R, Nahoul K**. Effect of zinc administration on plasma testosterone, dihydrotestosterone, and sperm count. *Arch Androl.* 1981 Aug;7(1):69-73.

48 **Micheletti A, Rossi R, Rufini S**. Zinc status in athletes: relation to diet and exercise. *Sports Med.* 2001;31(8):577-82

49 **Kilic M, Baltaci AK, Gunay M, Gökbel H, Okudan N, Cicioglu I.** The effect of exhaustion exercise on thyroid hormones and testosterone levels of elite athletes receiving oral zinc. *Neuro Endocrinology.* Letters 01 Feb 2006, 27(1-2):247-252

50 **L.R. Brilla LR, Conte V**. Effects of a Novel Zinc-Magnesium Formulation on Hormones and Strength. *Journal of Exercise Physiology.* October 2000 3 (4)

51 **de Baaij JH Hoenderop JG Bindels RJ**. Magnesium in man: implications for health and disease. *Physiol Rev.* 2015 Jan;95(1):1-46

52 **Lukaski H. C.** (2001) Magnesium, zinc, and chromium nutrition and athletic performance. Can J. *Appl. Physiol.* 26 (suppl.) S13– S22

53 **Rosanoff A, Weaver CM, Rude RK**. Suboptimal magnesium status in the United States: are the health consequences underestimated? *Nutr Rev.* 2012 Mar;70(3):153-64.

54 **Y. Rayssiguier, J. Durlach, E. Gueux, E. Rock, A. Mazur**. "Magnesium and ageing—I. Experimental data: importance of oxidative damage," *Magnesium Research.* 1993 6 (4) 369–378

55 **L.R. Brilla LR, Conte V.** Effects of a Novel Zinc-Magnesium Formulation on Hormones and Strength. *Journal of Exercise Physiology.* October 2000 3 (4)

56 **Kaufman JM, Vermeulen A**. 1997 Declining gonadal function in elderly men. Baillieres Clin Endocrinol Metab. 11:289–309

57 **Maggio M, De Vita F, Lauretani F, et al**., "The Interplay between Magnesium and Testosterone in Modulating Physical Function in Men," *International Journal of Endocrinology*

CHAPTER 17: NUTRIENT TIMING

1 **Aragon, A.A., Schoenfeld, B.J.** Nutrient timing revisited: is there a post-exercise anabolic window? *J Int Soc Sports Nutr* 10, 5 (2013)

2 **Biolo G, Maggi SP, Williams BD, Tipton KD & Wolfe RR.** Increased rates of muscle protein turnover and amino acid transport after resistance exercise in humans. AM *J Physiol Endocrinol Metab* 268: E514-E520, 1995.

3 **Lemon, Berardi & Noreen (2002) Lemon PW, Berardi JM, Noreen EE.** The role of protein and amino acid supplements in the athlete's diet: does type or timing of ingestion matter? *Current Sports Medicine Reports.* 2002; 1:214–221

4 **Biolo G, Tipton KD, Klein S, Wolfe RR:** An abundant supply of amino acids enhances the metabolic effect of exercise on muscle protein. Am J Physiol. 1997, 273 (1 Pt 1): E122-9.

5 **Tipton KD, Ferrando AA, Phillips SM, Doyle D, Wolfe RR:** Postexercise net protein synthesis in human muscle from orally administered amino acids. Am J Physiol. 1999, 276 (4 Pt 1): E628-34.

6 **Moore DR, Tang JE, Burd NA, Rerecich T, Tarnopolsky MA, Phillips SM**. Differential stimulation of myofibrillar and sarcoplasmic protein synthesis with protein ingestion at rest and after resistance exercise. *J Physiol.* 2009;587(Pt 4):897–904.

7 **Yang Y, Breen L, Burd NA, Hector AJ, Churchward-Venne TA, Josse AR, et al.** Resistance exercise enhances myofibrillar protein synthesis with graded intakes of whey protein in older men. *Br J Nutr.* 2012;108(10):1780–1788.

8 **Phillips SM, Tipton KD, Aarsland A, Wolf SE, Wolfe RR**. Mixed muscle protein synthesis and breakdown after resistance exercise in humans. *Am J Physiol.* (1997) 273(1 Pt 1): E99–107

9 **Arent SM, Cintineo HP, McFadden BA, Chandler AJ, Arent MA.** Nutrient Timing: A Garage Door of Opportunity? Nutrients. 2020 Jun 30;12(7):1948.

10 **Bussau VA, Fairchild TJ, Rao A, Steele P Fournier PA.** Carbohydrate in human muscle: an improved 1-day protocol., *Eur J Appl Physiol.* 2002;87(3):290–5.

11 **Tarnopolsky MA, Gibala M, Jeukendrup AE, Phillips SM.** Nutritional Needs of Elite Endurance Athletes. Part I: Carbohydrate and Fluid Requirements. *Eur J Sport Sci.* 2005;5(1):3–14.

12 **Ivy JL:** Glycogen resynthesis after exercise: effect of carbohydrate intake. *Int J Sports Med.* 1998. 19 (Suppl 2): S142-5.

13 **Knuiman P, Hopman MT, Mensink M.** Glycogen availability and skeletal muscle adaptations with endurance and resistance exercise. *Nutr Metab (Lond).* 2015; 12:59

14 **Parkin JA, Carey MF, Martin IK, Stojanovska L, Febbraio MA**. Muscle glycogen storage following prolonged exercise: effect of timing of ingestion of high glycaemic index food. *Med Sci Sports Exerc.* 1997;29(2):220–4.

15 **Miller SL, Tipton KD, Chinkes DL, Wolf SE, Wolfe RR.** Independent and combined effects of amino acids and glucose after resistance exercise. *Med Sci Sports Exerc.* (2003) 35:449–55.

16 **Borsheim E, Cree MG, Tipton KD, Elliott TA, Aarsland A, Wolfe RR.** Effect of carbohydrate intake on net muscle protein synthesis during recovery from resistance exercise. *J Appl Physiol.* (2004) 96:674–8.

17 **Norton LE, Wilson GJ, Layman DK, Moulton CJ, Garlick PJ.** Leucine content of dietary proteins is a determinant of postprandial skeletal muscle protein synthesis in adult rats. Nutr Metab (Lond). 2012 Jul 20;9(1):67

18 **Witard OC, Wardle SL, Macnaughton LS, Hodgson AB, Tipton KD.** Protein Considerations for Optimising Skeletal Muscle Mass in Healthy Young and Older Adults. Nutrients. 2016 Mar 23;8(4):181.

19 **Power O, Hallihan A, Jakeman P.** Human insulinotropic response to oral ingestion of native and hydrolysed whey protein. *Amino Acids.* 2009;37(2):333–9.

20 **Stepien M, Gaudichon C, Azzout-Marniche D, Fromentin G, Tomé D, Even P.** Postprandial nutrient partitioning but not energy expenditure is modified in growing rats during adaptation to a high-protein diet. J Nutr. 2010 May;140(5):939-45.

21 **Richter E.A., Hargreaves M.** Exercise, GLUT4, and skeletal muscle glucose uptake. *Physiol. Rev.* 2013; 93:993–1017

22 **Mul JD, Stanford KI, Hirshman MF, Goodyear LJ.** Exercise and Regulation of Carbohydrate Metabolism. *Prog Mol Biol Transl Sci.* 2015; 135:17-37.

23 **Hansen PA, Nolte LA, Chen MM, Holloszy JO.** Increased GLUT-4 translocation mediates enhanced insulin sensitivity of muscle glucose transport after exercise. *J Appl Physiol* (1985). 1998 Oct;85(4):1218-22.

24 **Phillips, Bethan E et al.** "The effects of resistance exercise training on macro- and micro-circulatory responses to feeding and skeletal muscle protein anabolism in older men." *The Journal of physiology* vol. 593,12 (2015): 2721-34

25 **Steven S, Frenis K, Oelze M, et al.** Vascular Inflammation and Oxidative Stress: Major Triggers for Cardiovascular Disease. *Oxid Med Cell Longev.* 2019; 2019:7092151

26 **Pagan LU, Gomes MJ, Okoshi MP.** Endothelial Function and Physical Exercise. *Arq Bras Cardiol.* 2018;111(4):540-541.

27 **Timmerman K, L. Dhanani S. Glynn E, L. Fry, CS. Drummond M, J. et al;** A moderate acute increase in physical activity enhances nutritive flow and the muscle protein anabolic response to mixed nutrient intake in older adults, *The American Journal of Clinical Nutrition.* 2012 June; 95 (6): 1403–1412

28 **Soenen S, Rayner CK, Horowitz M, Jones KL.** Gastric Emptying in the Elderly. Clin Geriatr Med. 2015 Aug;31(3):339-53.

29 **Dangin M, Guillet C, Garcia-Rodenas C, et al.** The rate of protein digestion affects protein gain differently during aging in humans. *J Physiol.* 2003;549(Pt 2):635-644.

30 **Boirie Y, Dangin M, Gachon P, Vasson MP, Maubois JL, Beaufrère B.** Slow and fast dietary proteins differently modulate postprandial protein accretion. *Proc Natl Acad Sci USA.* 1997 Dec 23; 94(26):14930-5

31 **Pitkanen HT, Nykanen T, Knuutinen J, Lahti K, Keinanen O, Alen M, Komi PV, Mero AA:** Free amino acid pool and muscle protein balance after resistance exercise. Med Sci Sports Exerc. 2003, 35 (5): 784-92.

32 **Kumar V, Atherton P, Smith K, Rennie MJ:** Human muscle protein synthesis and breakdown during and after exercise. J Appl Physiol. 2009, 106 (6): 2026-39

33 **Bird SP, Tarpenning KM, Marino FE.** Liquid carbohydrate/essential amino acid ingestion during a short-term bout of resistance exercise suppresses myofibrillar protein degradation. Metabolism. 2006 May;55(5):570-7

34 **Tipton KD, Elliott TA, Cree MG, Aarsland AA, Sanford AP, Wolfe RR:** Stimulation of net muscle protein synthesis by whey protein ingestion before and after exercise. Am J Physiol Endocrinol Metab. 2007, 292 (1)

35 **Murray B, Rosenbloom C.** Fundamentals of glycogen metabolism for coaches and athletes. *Nutr Rev.* April 2018; 76 (4): 243-59

36 **Spriet LL, Watt MJ.** Regulatory mechanisms in the interaction between carbohydrate and lipid oxidation during exercise. *Acta Physiol Scand.* Aug 2003; 178 (4): 443-52.

37 **Krings B.M., Rountree J.A., McAllister M.J., Cummings P.M., et al;** Effects of acute carbohydrate ingestion on anaerobic exercise performance. *J. Int. Soc. Sports Nutr.* 2016; 13:40.

38 **Decimoni L.S., Curty V.M., Almeida L., Koch A.J., Willardson J.M., Machado M.** Carbohydrate mouth rinsing improves resistance training session performance. *Int. J. Sports Sci. Coach.* 2018; 13:804–809.

39 **Bohe J, Low JF, Wolfe RR, Rennie MJ.** Latency and duration of stimulation of human muscle protein synthesis during continuous infusion of amino acids. *J Physiol.* 2001; 532:575–579.

40 **Atherton, P. J., Etheridge, T., Watt, P. W., Wilkinson, D., et al.** (2010). Muscle full effect after oral protein: time-dependent concordance and

discordance between human muscle protein synthesis and mTORC1 signalling. *Am. J. Clin. Nutr.* 92, 1080–1088

41 **Areta JL, Burke LM, Ross ML, et al.** Timing and distribution of protein ingestion during prolonged recovery from resistance exercise alters myofibrillar protein synthesis. *J Physiol.* 2013;591(Pt 9): 2319–2331

42 **Moore DR, Churchward-Venne TA, Witard O, Breen L, Burd NA, Tipton KD, Phillips SM.** Protein ingestion to stimulate myofibrillar protein synthesis requires greater relative protein intakes in healthy older versus younger men. *J Gerontol A Biol Sci Med Sci.* 2015;70(1):57–62

43 **Kumar V, Selby A, Rankin D, Patel R, Atherton P, Hildebrandt W, et al.** Age-related differences in the dose-response relationship of muscle protein synthesis to resistance exercise in young and old men. *J Physiol.* 2009;587(1):211–17.

44 **Schoenfeld, B.J., Aragon, A.A.** How much protein can the body use in a single meal for muscle-building? Implications for daily protein distribution. *J Int Soc Sports Nutr* **15,** 10 (2018).

45 **Cameron JD, Cyr MJ, Doucet E.** Increased meal frequency does not promote greater weight loss in subjects who were prescribed an 8-week equi-energetic energy-restricted diet. Br J Nutr. 2010 Apr;103(8):1098-101.

46 **Ohkawara K, Cornier MA, Kohrt WM, Melanson EL.** Effects of increased meal frequency on fat oxidation and perceived hunger. *Obesity (Silver Spring).* 2013;21(2):336-343.

47 **Hayashi, A.P., de Capitani, M.D., Dias, S.F.** *et al.* Number of high protein containing meals correlates with muscle mass in pre-frail and frail elderly. *Eur J Clin Nutr* **74,** 1047–1053 (2020).

48 **Speechly DP Buffenstein R.** Greater appetite control associated with an increased frequency of eating in lean males. *Appetite.*1999;33:285–297.

49 **Bertelsen J Christiansen C Thomsen C et al.** Effect of meal frequency on blood glucose, insulin, and free fatty acids in NIDDM subjects. *Diabetes Care.*1993;16: 4–7

50 **H.R. Farshchi, I A Macdonald.** Regular meal frequency creates more appropriate insulin sensitivity and lipid profiles compared with irregular meal frequency in healthy lean women *European Journal of Clinical Nutrition* volume58, pages1071–1077 (2004)

51 **LeBlanc J' Mercier I, Nadeau A.** Components of postprandial thermogenesis in relation to meal frequency in humans. *Can J Physiol Pharmacol.* 1993 Dec;71(12):879-83.

CHAPTER 18: SUPPLEMENTS

1 **Thomas D.** The mineral depletion of foods available to us as a nation (1940-2002) a review of the 6th edition of McCance and Widdowson.

2 **USDA, USDHHS.** 2015-2020 Dietary Guidelines for Americans, 8th Edition. US Government Printing Office. https://health.gov/dietary guidelines/2015/resources/2015-2020_Dietary_Guidelines.pdf

3 **Misner B.** Food alone may not provide sufficient micronutrients for preventing deficiency. J Int Soc Sports Nut. June 2006; 3:51-5

4 **Kerksick, C.M., Wilborn, C.D., Roberts, M.D.** ***et al.*** ISSN exercise & sports nutrition review update: research & recommendations. *J Int Soc Sports Nutr* 15, 38 (2018).

5 **Travison, TG, Morley JE, Araujo AB, O'Donnell AB, McKinlay JB.** The Relationship between Libido and Testosterone Levels in Aging Men. (2006) *The Journal of Clinical Endocrinology & Metabolism.* 91 (7), 2509–2513.

6 **Nair R, Maseeh A.** Vitamin D: The "sunshine" vitamin. *J Pharmacol Pharmacother.* 2012 Apr;3(2):118-26

7 **Lips P, Hosking D, Lippuner K, Norquist JM et al.** The prevalence of vitamin D inadequacy amongst women with osteoporosis: an international epidemiological investigation. *J Intern Med.* 2006 Sep; 260(3):245-54.

8 **Holick MF.** Vitamin D: Importance in the prevention of cancers, type 1 diabetes, heart disease, and osteoporosis. 2004. *Am J Clin Nutr* 79:362–371.

9 **Wang, Lu, et al.** "Systematic review: Vitamin D and calcium supplementation in prevention of cardiovascular events." Annals of Internal Medicine 152.5 (2010): 315-323.

10 **Forney, Laura A., et al.** "Vitamin D Status, Body Composition, and Fitness Measures in College-Aged Students." *The Journal of Strength & Conditioning Research* 28.3 (2014): 814-824.

11 **Boland R.** Role of vitamin D in skeletal muscle function. *Endocr Rev.* 1986 Nov; 7(4):434-48.

12 **Suárez-Quian CA1, Martínez-García F, Nistal M, Regadera J.** Androgen receptor distribution in adult human testis. *J Clin Endocrinol Metab.* 1999 Jan;84(1):350-8.

13 **De Angelis C, Galdiero M, Pivonello C, Garifalos F et al.** The role of vitamin D in male fertility: A focus on the testis. *Rev Endocr Metab Disord.* 2017 Sep;18(3):285-305.

14 **Nimptsch, Katharina, et al.** "Association between plasma 25–OH Vitamin D and testosterone levels in men." *Clinical Endocrinology* 77.1 (2012): 106-112.

15 **Lee DM, Tajar A, Pye SR, Boonen S, et al.** Association of hypogonadism with vitamin D status: the European Male Ageing Study. *Eur J Endocrinol.* 2012 Jan; 166(1):77-85.

16 **Tak, Young Jin, et al.** Serum 25-hydroxy Vitamin D levels and testosterone deficiency in middle-aged Korean men: a cross-sectional study. *Asian Journal of Andrology* 17.2 (2015): 324.

17 **Lerchbaum E, Pilz S, Boehm BO, Grammar TB, Obermayer-Pietsch B, März W.** Combination of low free testosterone and low vitamin D predicts mortality in older men referred for coronary angiography. *Clin Endocrinol (Oxf).* 2012; 77 (3): 475–483.

18 **Holick MF, Binkley NC, Bischoff-Ferrari HA**. Evaluation, treatment, and prevention of vitamin D deficiency: an Endocrine Society clinical practice guideline. Endocrine Society. *J Clin Endocrinol Metab.* 2011 Jul; 96(7):1911-30.

19 **Matsuoka LY, Ide L, Wortsman J, MacLaughlin JA, Holick MF**. Sunscreens suppress cutaneous vitamin D3 synthesis. *J Clin Endocrinol Metab.* 1987 Jun; 64(6):1165-8.

20 **Clemens TL, Adams JS, Henderson SL, Holick MF.** Increased skin pigment reduces the capacity of skin to synthesise vitamin D3. *Lancet.* 1982 Jan 9; 1(8263):74-6.

21 **Pilz S., Frisch S., Koertke H., Kuhn J., Dreier J., Obermayer-Pietsch B., Wehr E., Zittermann A.** Effect of Vitamin D Supplementation on Testosterone Levels in Men. *Hormone and Metabolic Research.* 2011; 43:223.

22 **Lerchbaum E, Pilz S, Trummer C, Schwetz V, et al.** Vitamin D and Testosterone in Healthy Men: A Randomized Controlled Trial. *The Journal of Clinical Endocrinology & Metabolism*, Volume 102, Issue 11, 1 November 2017, Pages 4292–4302

23 23.**Roohani N, Hurrell R, Kelishadi R, Schulin R.** Zinc and its importance for human health: An integrative review. *J Res Med Sci.* 2013 Feb;18(2):144-57.

24 **Prasad AS**. Zinc: mechanism of host defence. *J Nutr.* 2007 May; 137(5):1345-9

25 **Hambidge KM, Miller LV, Krebs NF.** Physiological requirements for zinc. *Int J Vitam Nutr Res.* 2011 Jan; 81(1):72-8.

26 **Cabrera ÁJ.** Zinc, aging, and immunosenescence: an overview. *Pathobiol Aging Age Relat Dis.* 2015; 5:25592.

27 **García OP, Long KZ, Rosado JL.** Impact of micronutrient deficiencies on obesity. *Nutr Rev.* 2009 Oct; 67(10):559-72.

28 **Prasad AS, Mantzoros CS, Beck W, Hess JW, Brewer GJ.** Zinc status and serum testosterone levels of healthy adults. *Nutrition* 12, 5, May 1996, Pages 344-34.

29 **Netter A, Hartoma R, Nahoul K**. Effect of zinc administration on plasma testosterone, dihydrotestosterone, and sperm count. *Arch Androl.* 1981 Aug;7(1):69-73.

30 **Micheletti A, Rossi R, Rufini S**. Zinc status in athletes: relation to diet and exercise. *Sports Med.* 2001;31(8):577-82

31 **Kilic M, Baltaci AK, Gunay M, Gökbel H, Okudan N, Cicioglu I.** The effect of exhaustion exercise on thyroid hormones and testosterone levels of elite athletes receiving oral zinc. *Neuro Endocrinology.* Letters 01 Feb 2006, 27(1-2):247-252

32 **L.R. Brilla LR, Conte V.** Effects of a Novel Zinc-Magnesium Formulation on Hormones and Strength. *Journal of Exercise Physiology.* October 2000 3 (4)

33 **de Baaij JH Hoenderop JG Bindels RJ.** Magnesium in man: implications for health and disease. *Physiol Rev.* 2015 Jan;95(1):1-46

34 **Lukaski H. C.** (2001) Magnesium, zinc, and chromium nutrition and athletic performance. Can J. *Appl. Physiol.* 26 (suppl.) S13– S22

35 **Rosanoff A, Weaver CM, Rude RK.** Suboptimal magnesium status in the United States: are the health consequences underestimated? *Nutr Rev.* 2012 Mar;70(3):153-64.

36 **Y. Rayssiguier, J. Durlach, E. Gueux, E. Rock, A. Mazur.** "Magnesium and ageing—I. Experimental data: importance of oxidative damage," *Magnesium Research.* 1993 6 (4) 369–378

37 **L.R. Brilla LR, Conte V.** Effects of a Novel Zinc-Magnesium Formulation on Hormones and Strength. *Journal of Exercise Physiology.* October 2000 3 (4)

38 **Kaufman JM, Vermeulen A.** 1997 Declining gonadal function in elderly men. Baillieres Clin Endocrinol Metab. 11:289–309

39 **Maggio M, De Vita F, Lauretani F, et al.**, "The Interplay between Magnesium and Testosterone in Modulating Physical Function in Men," *International Journal of Endocrinology.* 2014 (9)

40 **Nielsen FH.** Is boron nutritionally relevant? *Nutr Rev.* 2008;66(4):183–191.

41 **Nielsen FH.** Boron—an overlooked element of potential nutritional importance. *Nutr Today.* 1988;23(1):4–7.

42 **Meacham S, Karakas S, Wallace A, Altun F.** Boron in human health: evidence for dietary recommendations and public policies. *Open Miner Process J.* 2010;3(1):36–53

43 **Naghii MR, Mofid M, Asgari AR, Hedayati M, Daneshpour MS.** Comparative effects of daily and weekly boron supplementation on plasma steroid hormones and pro-inflammatory cytokines. J *Trace Elem Med Biol.* 2011 Jan; 25(1):54-8.

44 **Nielsen FH, Hunt CD, Mullen LM, Hunt JR.** Effect of dietary boron on mineral, estrogen, and testosterone metabolism in postmenopausal women. *FASEB J.* 1987 Nov; 1(5):394-7.

45 **Naghii MR1, Samman S.** The effect of boron supplementation on its urinary excretion and selected cardiovascular risk factors in healthy male subjects. *Biol Trace Elem Res* (1997)

46 **Pizzorno L** Nothing Boring About Boron. *Integr Med (Encinitas).* 2015 Aug;14(4):35-48.

47 **N R Green NR, Ferrando AA**. Plasma boron and the effects of boron supplementation in males. Environ Health Perspect. 1994 Nov; 102 (Suppl 7): 73–77.

48 **Miljkovic D, Miljkovic N, McCarty MF**. Up-regulatory impact of boron on vitamin D function—does it reflect inhibition of 24-hydroxylase. Med Hypotheses (2004)

49 **Gorustovich AA, Steimetz T, Nielsen FH, Guglielmotti MB**. A histomorphometric study of alveolar bone modelling and remodeling in mice fed a boron-deficient diet. *Arch Oral Biol*. 2008;53(7):677–682.

50 **Ellulu MS, Patimah I, Khaza'ai H, Rahmat A, Abed Y.** Obesity and inflammation: the linking mechanism and the complications. *Arch Med Sci*. 2017;13(4):851-863.

51 **Khanna D, Khanna S, Khanna P, et al**. (February 28, 2022) Obesity: A Chronic Low-Grade Inflammation and Its Markers. *Cureus* 14(2): e22711.

52 **Dalle S, Rossmeislova L, Koppo K**. The Role of Inflammation in Age-Related Sarcopenia. *Front Physiol*. 2017 Dec 12;8:1045

53 **Gioxari A, Kaliora AC, Marantidou F, et al**. Intake of x-3 polyunsaturated fatty acids in patients with rheumatoid arthritis: a systematic review and meta-analysis. *Nutrition*. 2018; 45:114–124.e4.

54 **Natto ZS, Yaghmoor W, Alshaeri HK, et al**. Omega-3 fatty acids effects on inflammatory biomarkers and lipid profiles among diabetic and cardiovascular disease patients: a systematic review and meta-analysis. *Sci Rep*. 2019; 9:18867–18019.

55 **Goldberg RJ, Katz J.** A meta-analysis of the analgesic effects of omega-3 polyunsaturated fatty acid supplementation for inflammatory joint pain. *Pain*. 2007; 129:210–223.

56 **Gray P, Gabriel B, Thies F, Gray SR.** Fish oil supplementation augments post-exercise immune function in young males. *Brain Behav Immun*. 2012 Nov;26(8):1265-72

57 **Lemaitre R.N., King I.B., Mozaffarian D., Kuller L.H.** N-3 Polyunsaturated fatty acids, fatal ischemic heart disease, and non-fatal myocardial infarction in older adults: The Cardiovascular Health Study. *Am. J. Clin. Nutr.* 2003; 77:319–325

58 **Shearer GC, Savinova OV, Harris WS.** Fish oil—how does it reduce plasma triglycerides? *Biochim Biophys Acta*. 2012 May;1821(5):843-51

59 **Huang YH, Chiu WC, Hsu YP, et al.** Effects of omega-3 fatty acids on muscle mass, muscle strength and muscle performance among the elderly: a meta-analysis. *Nutrients*. 2020; 12:3739

60 **Morton RW, Murphy KT, McKellar SR, et al**. A systematic review, meta-analysis and meta-regression of the effect of protein supplementation on resistance training-induced gains in muscle mass and strength in healthy adults. *Br J Sport Med*. 2018;52(6):376–384.

61 **Battermann W**. Whey protein for athletes. *Dtsch Milchwirtschaft.* 1986;37(33):1010–1012.

62 **Naclerio F, Larumbe-Zabala E.** Effects of whey protein alone or as part of a multi-ingredient formulation on strength, fat-free mass, or lean body mass in resistance-trained individuals: a meta-analysis. *Sport Med.* 2016;46(1)

63 **Anthony JC, Anthony TG, Kimball SR, Jefferson LS**. Signalling pathways involved in translational control of protein synthesis in skeletal muscle by leucine. J Nutr. 2001;131(3):856S–8560S.

64 **Norton LE, Layman DK**. *J Nutr.* 2006 Feb;136(2):533S-537S. Leucine regulates translation initiation of protein synthesis in skeletal muscle after exercise.

65 **Areta et al**. Timing and distribution of protein ingestion during prolonged recovery from resistance exercise alters myofibrillar protein synthesis. *J Physiol.* 2013 May 1; 591(Pt 9): 2319–2331

66 **West et al**. Rapid aminoacidemia enhances myofibrillar protein synthesis and anabolic intramuscular signalling responses after resistance exercise. *Am J Clin Nutr.* 2011 Sep;94(3):795-803.

67 **Dangin M, Guillet C, Garcia-Rodenas C, Gachon P, et al**. The rate of protein digestion affects protein gain differently during aging in humans. J Physiol. 2003 Jun 1; 549(Pt 2):635-44.

68 **Pennings B, Boirie Y, Senden JM, Gijsen AP, Kuipers H, van Loon LJ.** Whey protein stimulates postprandial muscle protein accretion more effectively than do casein and casein hydrolysate in older men. Am J Clin Nutr. 2011 May; 93(5):997-1005.

69 **Mohanty DP, Mohapatra S, Misra S, Sahu PS**. Milk derived bioactive peptides and their impact on human health—A review. *Saudi J Biol Sci.* 2016 Sep;23(5):577-83.

70 **Bounous G**. Whey protein concentrate (WPC) and glutathione modulation in cancer treatment. *Anticancer Res.* 2000 Nov-Dec;20(6C):4785-92

71 **Morifuji M, Ishizaka M, Baba S, Fukuda K et al.** Comparison of different sources and degrees of hydrolysis of dietary protein: effect on plasma amino acids, dipeptides, and insulin responses in human subjects. *J Agric Food Chem.* 2010 Aug 11;58(15):8788-97.

72 **Jeewanthi RK, Kim MH, Lee NK, Yoon YC, Paik HD**. Peptide Analysis and the Bioactivity of Whey Protein Hydrolysates from Cheese Whey with Several Enzymes. *Korean J Food Sci Anim Resour.* 2017;37(1):62-70.

73 **Mobley CB et al**. Effects of Whey, Soy or Leucine Supplementation with 12 Weeks of Resistance Training on Strength, Body Composition, and Skeletal Muscle and Adipose Tissue Histological Attributes in College-Aged Males. *Nutrients.* 2017 Sep 4;9(9). pii: E972.

74 **McMorris T, et al.** Creatine supplementation and cognitive performance in elderly individuals. *Neuropsychol Cogn B.* 2007;14(5):517–28.

75 **Kreider RB, et al.** Effects of creatine supplementation on body composition, strength, and sprint performance. *Med Sci Sports Exerc.* 1998;30(1):73–82.

76 **Skare OC, Skadberg, Wisnes AR.** Creatine supplementation improves sprint performance in male sprinters. *Scand J Med Sci Sports.* 2001 Apr;11(2):96-102.

77 **Volek JS, Duncan ND, Mazzetti SA et al.** Performance and muscle fibre adaptations to creatine supplementation and heavy resistance training. *Med Sci Sports Exerc.* 1999 Aug; 31(8):1147-56.

78 **Cribb PJ, Williams AD, Hayes A**. A creatine-protein-carbohydrate supplement enhances responses to resistance training. Med Sci Sports Exerc. 2007 Nov; 39(11):1960-8.

79 **Cooke MB, et al.** Creatine supplementation enhances muscle force recovery after eccentrically induced muscle damage in healthy individuals. *J Int Soc Sports Nutr.* 2009; 6:13.

80 **Harris R**. Creatine in health, medicine and sport: an introduction to a meeting held at Downing College, University of Cambridge, July 2010. *Amino Acids.* 2011;40(5):1267–1270

81 **Hultman E, Sjoholm H.** Substrate availability. In: Knuttgen HG, Vogel JA, Poortmans J., eds. Biochemistry of exercise. 13. Champaign, IL: Human Kinetics Publishers, 1983:63–75

82 **Harris RC, Soderlund K, Hultman**. Elevation of creatine in resting and exercised muscle of normal subjects by creatine supplementation. *Clin Sci* 1992; 83:367–74

83 **Yquel R.J, L.M. Arsac, E. Thiaudiere, P. Canioni & G. Manier**. Effect of creatine supplementation on phosphocreatine resynthesis, inorganic phosphate accumulation and pH during intermittent maximal exercise. (2002) *Journal of Sports Sciences,* 20:5, 427-437

84 **Spillane M, Schoch R, Cooke M, et al.** The effects of creatine ethyl ester supplementation combined with heavy resistance training on body composition, muscle performance, and serum and muscle creatine levels. *J Int Soc Sports Nutr.* 2009 Feb 19; 6:6

85 **Poortmans JR, Francaux M.** Long-term oral creatine supplementation does not impair renal function in healthy athletes. Med Sci Sports Exerc. 1999;31(8):1108–10.

86 **Groeneveld GJ, Beijer C, Veldink JH, Kalmijn S, Wokke JH, van den Berg LH**. Few adverse effects of long-term creatine supplementation in a placebo-controlled trial. *Int J Sports Med.* 2005 May;26(4):307-13.

87 **Poortmans JR, Francaux M**. Adverse effects of creatine supplementation: fact or fiction? *Sports Med.* 2000 Sep;30(3):155-70.

88 **Buford TW, et al**. International Society of Sports Nutrition position stand: creatine supplementation and exercise. *J Int Soc Sports Nutr.* 2007; 4:6.

89 **Kreider RB.** Effects of creatine supplementation on performance and training adaptations. *Mol Cell Biochem.* 2003;244(1–2):89–9

90 **Toda, N.** Age-related changes in endothelial function and blood flow regulation. *Pharmacol Ther.* 2012 Feb; 133(2):159-76.

91 **Mozos I, Luca CT.** Crosstalk between Oxidative and Nitrosative Stress and Arterial Stiffness. *Curr Vasc Pharmacol.* 2017; 15(5):446-456

92 **J S Stamler, G Meissner.** Physiology of nitric oxide in skeletal muscle. *Physiol Rev* (2001)

93 **Schoenfeld, B, J., Contreras, B.** The Muscle Pump: Potential Mechanisms and Applications for Enhancing Hypertrophic Adaptations. *Strength and Conditioning Journal.* 2014. (36) 3: 21-25

94 **Guest, N.S., VanDusseldorp, T.A., Nelson, M.T. *et al.*** International society of sports nutrition position stand: caffeine and exercise performance. *J Int Soc Sports Nutr* **18**, 1 (2021)

PART 1V: PREPARATION

CHAPTER 19: "ALL IN THE MIND?"

1 **Korzybski, Alfred** (1933). *Science and Sanity. An Introduction to Non-Aristotelian Systems and General Semantics.* The International Non-Aristotelian Library Pub. Co. pp. 747–761. 2. Miller, G, A. The magical number seven plus or minus two: some limits on our capacity for processing information. *Psychol Rev. 1956 Mar; 63(2):81-97*

2 **Newberg, Andrew B.; Waldman, Mark Robert** (July 14, 2012). Words Can Change Your Brain: 12 Conversation Strategies to Build Trust, Resolve Conflict, and Increase Intimacy (hardcover). Hudson Street Press. ISBN 978-1-594 63090

3 **Connors, M. H., & Halligan, P. W.** (2015). A cognitive account of belief: A tentative road map. *Frontiers in Psychology,*

4 **Faries MD.** Why We Don't "Just Do It": Understanding the Intention-Behavior Gap in Lifestyle Medicine. *Am J Lifestyle Med.* 2016;10(5):322-329. Published 2016 Jun 22.

5 **Rhodes RE, de Bruijn GJ** How big is the physical activity intention-behaviour gap? A meta-analysis using the action control framework. *Br J Health Psychol.* 2013 May; 18(2):296-309

6 **Bigelow GE, Silverman K.** Theoretical and empirical foundations of contingency management treatments for drug abuse. In: Higgins ST, Silverman K, editors. Motivating Behavior Change Among Illicit-Drug Abusers: Research

on Contingency Management Interventions. Washington, DC: American Psychological Association; 1999.

7 **Schwartz J, Mochon D, Wyper L, Maroba J, Patel D, Ariely D.** Healthier by p recommitment. *Psychol Sci.* 2014 Feb; 25(2):538-46.

8 **Berkman ET**. The Neuroscience of Goals and Behavior Change. *Consult Psychol J.* 2018;70(1):28-44

CHAPTER 20: HACKING THE POWER OF HABIT

1 **Vohs KD, Baumeister RF, Schmeichel BJ, Twenge JM, Nelson NM, Tice DM**. Making choices impairs subsequent self-control: a limited-resource account of decision making, self-regulation, and active initiative. *J Pers Soc Psychol.* 2008 May;94(5):883-98.

2 **Hagger MS, Wood C, Stiff C, Chatzisarantis NL**. Ego depletion and the strength model of self-control: a meta-analysis. *Psychol Bull. 2010 Jul; 136(4):495-525.*

3 **Loth KA, Goldschmidt AB, Wonderlich SA, Lavender JM, Neumark-Sztainer D, Vohs KD**. Could the resource depletion model of self-control help the field to better understand momentary processes that lead to binge eating? *Int J Eat Disord.* 2016;49(11):998-1001.

4 **Gailliot MT, Baumeister RF, DeWall CN, Maner JK, Plant EA, Tice DM, Brewer LE, Schmeichel BJ**. Self-control relies on glucose as a limited energy source: willpower is more than a metaphor. *J Pers Soc Psychol.* 2007 Feb;92(2):325-36

5 **Mergenthaler P, Lindauer U, Dienel GA, Meisel A**. Sugar for the brain: the role of glucose in physiological and pathological brain function. *Trends Neurosci.* 2013; 36(10):587-597.

6 **Masicampo EJ, Baumeister RF.** Toward a physiology of dual-process reasoning and judgment: lemonade, willpower, and expensive rule-based analysis. *Psychol Sci. 2008 Mar; 19(3):255-60.*

7 **Muraven M**. Building Self-Control Strength: Practicing Self-Control Leads to Improved Self-Control Performance. *J Exp Soc Psychol.* 2010;46(2):465-468.

8 **Mateos-Aparicio P, Rodríguez-Moreno A**. The Impact of Studying Brain Plasticity. *Front Cell Neurosci.* 2019; 13:66

9 **Lally P, van Jaarsveld CHM, Potts HWW, Wardle J**. How are habits formed: modelling habit formation in the real world. *Eur J Soc Psychol.* 2010; 40:998-1009

10 **Fiese BH, Tomcho TJ, Douglas M, Josephs K, Poltrock S, Baker T.** A review of 50 years of research on naturally occurring family routines and rituals: cause for celebration? *J Fam Psychol.* 2002 Dec; 16(4):381-90

11 **Gardner, B, de Bruijn, G-J, & Lally, P.** (2011). A systematic review and meta-analysis of applications of the Self-Report Habit Index to nutrition and physical activity behaviours. *Annals of Behavioral Medicine, 42*(2), 174–187.

12 **Langeveld, M., & de Vries, J. (2013)**. The mediocre results of dieting. *Obesity Reviews,* 1(2), 113–119.

13 **Natvik E, Råheim M, Andersen JR, Moltu C**. Living a successful weight loss after severe obesity. *Int J Qual Stud Health Well-being.* 2018;13(1):1487762.

14 **Spreckley M, Seidell J, Halberstadt J.** Perspectives into the experience of successful, substantial long-term weight-loss maintenance: a systematic review. Int J Qual Stud Health Well-being. 2021 Dec;16(1):1862481

15 **Kristeller JL, Wolever RQ.** Mindfulness-based eating awareness training for treating binge eating disorder: the conceptual foundation. *Eat Disord.* 2011 Jan-Feb; 19(1):49-61

16 **Forman EM, Butryn ML**. A new look at the science of weight control: how acceptance and commitment strategies can address the challenge of self-regulation. *Appetite.* 2015 Jan; 84():171-80.

17 **Cassady BA, Hollis JH, Fulford AD, Considine RV, Mattes RD**. Mastication of almonds: effects of lipid bio accessibility, appetite, and hormone response. *The American journal of clinical nutrition.* 2009 Jan 14;89(3):794-800.

18 **Neyraud E, Palicki O, Schwartz C, Nicklaus S, Feron G.** Variability of human saliva composition: possible relationships with fat perception and liking. *Archives of Oral Biology.* 2012 May 1;57(5):556-66.

19 **Li J, Zhang N, Hu L, Li Z, Li R, Li C, Wang S.** Improvement in chewing activity reduces energy intake in one meal and modulates plasma gut hormone concentrations in obese and lean young Chinese men. *The American journal of clinical nutrition.* 2011 Jul 20;94(3):709-16.

20 **Makino K, Ihira H, Mizumoto A, Shimizu K, Ishida T, Furuna T.** Associations between the settings of exercise habits and health-related outcomes in community-dwelling older adults. *J Phys Ther Sci.* 2015;27(7):2207-2211.

21 **Akune T, Muraki S, Oka H, Tanaka S, Kawaguchi H, Nakamura K, Yoshimura N.** Exercise habits during middle age are associated with lower prevalence of sarcopenia: the ROAD study. *Osteoporos Int.* 2014 Mar; 25(3):1081-8.

22 **Aniansson A, Sperling L, Rundgren A, Lehnberg E.** Muscle function in 75-year-old men and women. A longitudinal study. *Scand J Rehabil Med Suppl.* 1983; 9():92-102.

23 **Tucker M, Reicks M.** Exercise as a gateway behavior for healthful eating among older adults: an exploratory study. *J Nutr Educ Behav. 2002 Mar-Apr; 34 Suppl 1(): S14-9.*

24 **Gardner B., Lally P.** (2018). "Modelling habit formation and its determinants," in *The Psychology of Habit: Theory, mechanisms, change, and contexts*, ed. Verplanken B. (Cham: Springer;), 207–229

25 **Yokoyama N, Nishijima T, Maeda S, et al.**: Effect of exercise program participation on personal factors of exercise adherence promotion in middle-aged and elderly subjects: comparison of group and individual exercise program. *Jpn J Phys Fit Sport Med*, 2003, 52: 249–258(in Japanese).

26 **Schumacher LM, Thomas JG, Raynor HA, Rhodes RE, O'Leary KC, Wing RR, Bond DS.** Relationship of Consistency in Timing of Exercise Performance and Exercise Levels Among Successful Weight Loss Maintainers. *Obesity* (Silver Spring). 2019 Aug;27(8):1285-1291.

27 **Hublin C, Partinen M, Koskenvuo M, Kaprio J**. Sleep and mortality: a population-based 22-year follow-up study. *Sleep*. 2007 Oct; 30(10):1245-53.

28 **Gottlieb DJ, Punjabi NM, Newman AB, Resnick HE, Redline S, Baldwin CM, Nieto FJ.** Association of sleep time with diabetes mellitus and impaired glucose tolerance. *Arch Intern Med*. 2005 Apr 25; 165(8):863-7

29 **Taheri S, Lin L, Austin D, Young T, Mignot E.** Short sleep duration is associated with reduced leptin, elevated ghrelin, and increased body mass index. *PLoS Med. 2004 Dec; 1(3): e62.*

30 **David M. Holtzman et al**. Slow wave sleep disruption increases cerebrospinal fluid amyloid-β levels. *Brain*. July 2017

31 **Urban, R. J., Bodenburg, Y. H., Gilkison, C., Foxworth, J., Coggan, A. R., Wolfe, R. R., & Ferrando, A**. (1995). Testosterone administration to elderly men increases skeletal muscle strength and protein synthesis. *American Journal of Physiology*, 269, E820–826.

32 **Wittert G.** The relationship between sleep disorders and testosterone in men. *Asian J Androl*. 2014;16(2):262-265.

33 **Cote KA, et al**. Sleep deprivation lowers reactive aggression and testosterone in men. *Biol Psychol*. (2013)

34 **Dattilo M, Antunes HK, Medeiros A; et al.** leep and muscle recovery: endocrinological and molecular basis for a new and promising hypothesis. *Med Hypotheses*. 2011 Aug; 77(2):220-2

35 **Everson CA, Crowley WR.** Reductions in circulating anabolic hormones induced by sustained sleep deprivation in rats. *Am J Physiol Endocrinol Metab*. 2004 Jun; 286(6): E1060-70.

36 **Leproult R, et al.** Sleep loss results in an elevation of cortisol levels the next evening. *Sleep*. (1997)

37 **Harding EC, Franks NP, Wisden W.** The Temperature Dependence of Sleep. *Front Neurosci*. 2019; 13:336. Published 2019 Apr 24.

38 **Institute of Medicine (US) Committee on Military Nutrition Research**. Caffeine for the Sustainment of Mental Task Performance: Formulations

for Military Operations. Washington (DC): National Academies Press (US); 2001. 2, Pharmacology of Caffeine.

39 **Matthew Walker.** Why We Sleep: The New Science of Sleep and Dreams. Penguin Books, 2018

CHAPTER 21: THE BIG VISION

1 **Bryan, J. F., & Locke, E. A.** (1967). Goal setting as a means of increasing motivation. *Journal of Applied Psychology, 51*(3), 274–277

2 **The Essential Drucker.** The Best of Sixty Years of Peter Drucker's Essential Writings on Management. HarperCollins, 13 Oct 2009

3 **Simon Sinek.** Start with Why: How Great Leaders Inspire Everyone to Take Action". 2009. www.ted.com/talks/simon_sinek_how_great_leaders_inspire_action

4 **M. Prefontaine.** The Greatest: The Quotes of Muhammed Ali. CreateSpace Independent Publishing Platform, 7 Jun 2016

5 **Cohen R, Bavishi C, Rozanski A.** Purpose in Life and Its Relationship to All-Cause Mortality an: Cardiovascular Events: A Meta-Analysis. *Psychosom Med.* 2016 Feb-Mar;78(2):122-33

6 **Ryff CD** (2014) Psychological well-being revisited: Advances in the science and practice of eudaimonia. *Psychother Psychosom* 83(1):10–28

7 **Mcknight, P. Kashdan T, B.** Purpose in Life as a System That Creates and Sustains Health and Well-Being: An Integrative, Testable Theory. September 2009. *Review of General Psychology* 13(3)

8 **Sheldon K. M. (2002).** "The self-concordance model of healthy goal striving: when personal goals correctly represent the person" in *Handbook of self-determination research.* eds. Deci E. L., Ryan R. M. (Rochester, NY: The University of Rochester Press;), 65–86.

9 **Schippers MC, Ziegler N.** Life Crafting as a Way to Find Purpose and Meaning in Life. *Front Psychol.* 2019; 10 :2778. Published 2019 Dec 13.

10 **McGregor I, Little BR.** Personal projects, happiness, and meaning on doing well and being yourself. *J Pers Soc Psychol. 1998 Feb; 74(2):494-512.*

11 **Locke, A, E. Latham, G, P.** A Theory of Goal Setting & Task Performance. 1991. The Academy of Management Review 16(2)

12 **Matthews, G.** http:// scholar.dominican.edu/cgi/viewcontent.cgi?article=1265&context=news-releases

13 **Rosner ZA, Elman JA, Shimamura AP.** The generation effect: activating broad neural circuits during memory encoding. *Cortex.* 2013;49(7):1901-1909.

14 **Locke, A, E.** Toward a theory of task motivation and incentives. Organizational Behavior and Human Performance. 3 (2)

15 **Collins, J. Porras J, I.** Built to Last. Harper Business. October 26, 1994

Printed in Great Britain
by Amazon

29868855R00176